Having a go at the
KAISER

Having a go at the
KAISER

A Welsh Family at War

GETHIN
MATTHEWS

UNIVERSITY OF WALES PRESS

2018

www.uwp.co.uk

British Library Cataloguing-in-Publication Data
A catalogue record for this book is available from the British Library.

ISBN   978-1-78683-347-1
eISBN   978-1-78683-348-8

The right of Gethin Matthews to be identified as author of this work has been asserted by him in accordance with sections 77 and 79 of the Copyright, Designs and Patents Act 1988.

Typeset by Marie Doherty
Printed by CPI Antony Rowe, Melksham.

*For a chess player, an optimist
and a cricketer*

Contents

Acknowledgements

The first I heard of the story of the Eustis brothers at war was in 2010–11, when I was running the 'Welsh Voices of the Great War Online' project at Cardiff University. Marianne Eustis told me the outline of the story, though she had few concrete details of the war service of her uncles Richard and Ivor Eustis. She shared photographs of her father, Gabriel, in his Royal Navy uniform, but had no written matter by him. I was interested, because these were my grandfather's cousins, but in truth I did not pursue the research because I had many other collections to study, where there was a wealth of written material.

In 2013–14 I co-ordinated a HLF-funded project at Treboeth, centred upon the Roll of Honour at Caersalem Newydd Baptist Chapel. With a lot of help from the community, it was possible to piece together not just the story of the eighty-one men listed on that memorial, but also of the impact of the war upon their families and the whole community. The sources unearthed by the project gave me much information about the activities of Richard Eustis's unit, the 3rd Welsh Field Ambulance, as a dozen Caersalem men served alongside him. It became clear that this was a 'local' story with a very broad sweep: many of these men, like Richard, were members of the Treboeth Temperance Brass Band who enlisted as Territorials in July 1913, and then served together in England, Gallipoli, Egypt and Palestine from the very beginning of the war through to 1919.

Then in 2015, quite by chance, I got to know Ian Eustis, son of Daniel, the younger brother of Richard, Gabriel and Ivor. One day he said to me, 'I have something that I think will interest you', which has turned out to be something of an understatement. He entrusted to me a small box full of the family's treasures. I did not expect the quantity of letters that had been preserved thanks to the parents, and then the sisters Bess Ann and Lottie Eustis: only one other family collection that I had encountered while running the 'Welsh Voices' project had more than a dozen letters in total. It took me some time to appreciate the quality of these hundred-plus letters, and the window they provide into the family conversation, in particular of 1916–18. After I realised the value of the material, I am grateful that Dr Llion Wigley and the staff of the University of Wales Press were so willing to listen to my proposal, and that they concurred that this was a story that deserved to be told, and material that demanded a book-length analysis.

I am very grateful to Swansea University for providing financial backing for the publication of the book and to the Coleg Cymraeg Cenedlaethol, who sponsor my post, for their support and encouragement. The book has also benefited from the insights I have gained while running the 'Welsh Memorials to the Great War' project, which was generously funded by the Living Legacies WW1 Engagement Centre from 2015 to 2017.

Specialist help regarding military matters has come from the Rev. Clive Hughes and Hywyn Williams, and from some of the contributors to the Great War Forum, most notably Horatio2 who assisted greatly in deciphering Gabriel's war record. Ivor Williams of the Treboeth History Group passed on a copy of the programme for the unveiling of the Treboeth War Memorial and Peter Williams shared a photograph of the Mynyddbach rugby team from 1913–14. I am grateful to the staff at the Richard Burton Archives, Swansea University; West Glamorgan Archives; the National Library of Wales and my colleagues at the Department of History at Swansea for their interest and support. Prof. Paul O'Leary at Aberystwyth University provided very valuable feedback and encouragement at different stages of the project. My father has been supportive throughout and my wife has been very patient.

The most substantial support for this project has come from three grandchildren of John and Mary Eustis and one great-granddaughter. I am particularly indebted to Ian Eustis for opening up the family's treasures to me, and to Marianne Eustis for her support and encouragement. Pamela John (daughter of Grace, and thus a niece of the Eustis brothers) has also been generous in sharing some of the material safeguarded by her side of the family with me. Rhian McGivan (granddaughter of Richard, the eldest brother) lent me his diaries from 1916 and 1917. Other family members have shared pieces of information: Christine Collins, Dave Gordon, Julie Eustace and the late Rose Davies. *Diolch yn fawr* to all for every piece of assistance.

Illustrations

Abbreviations

Newspapers
CDL   *Cambria Daily Leader*
HoW   *Herald of Wales*
SWWP *South Wales Weekly Post*

Military terms
ADS   Advanced Dressing Station
CB   Confined to Barracks
CO   Depending on the context, either Conscientious Objector
         or Commanding Officer
DCM   Distinguished Conduct Medal
MM   Military Medal
MO   Medical Officer
OC   Officer Commanding
OR   Other Ranks
NCO   Non Commissioned Officer (typically corporal or sergeant)
SBR   Small Box Respirator

Units
BEF   British Expeditionary Force
EEF   Egyptian Expeditionary Force
KOSB   King's Own Scottish Borderers
RAMC   Royal Army Medical Corps
RFA   Royal Field Artillery
RWF   Royal Welsh Fusiliers
RNVR   Royal Naval Volunteer Reserve
SWB   South Wales Borderers
WFA   Welsh Field Ambulance

Other abbreviations
CWGC   Commonwealth War Graves Commission
WGAS   West Glamorgan Archive Services

1

Introduction – the Eustis family; the local community; the letters

TABLE 1: **The Eustis family of Pengwern Road, Mynyddbach**

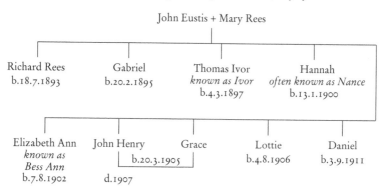

John Eustis + Mary Rees

Richard Rees	Gabriel	Thomas Ivor	Hannah
b.18.7.1893	b.20.2.1895	*known as Ivor*	*often known as Nance*
		b.4.3.1897	b.13.1.1900

Elizabeth Ann	John Henry	Grace	Lottie	Daniel
known as	b.20.3.1905		b.4.8.1906	b.3.9.1911
Bess Ann	d.1907			
b.7.8.1902				

Three days before the Armistice brought the fighting on the Western Front to a close, Ivor Eustis wrote a letter home to his mother from the Wrexham barracks of the Royal Welsh Fusiliers, where he was convalescing after being wounded a month earlier. He was in high spirits as he pondered the fate of 'poor old Kaiser Bill', and in the letter he dreams of inflicting a series of indignities upon the Kaiser which correlate with the pain and discomfort he has been through in his two and a half years of active service. Like almost all of the letters sent home by the Eustis brothers, it was written in English, but with a smattering of Welsh words. When he wrote that '"Boys Jack Eustis" have each had a "go" at him, somewhere or other', Ivor used the Welsh word order but the English spelling to refer to himself and his elder brothers Richard and Gabriel.

This letter is possibly the most joyful of all the letters written by the brothers that can be found in a family collection. There are over a hundred letters written by the brothers as they served: Richard in the 1/3rd Welsh Field Ambulance (WFA), a unit of the Royal Army Medical Corps (RAMC); Gabriel in the Royal Navy; and Ivor in the Royal Welsh Fusiliers (RWF). These letters, considered as a whole, tell us not only of the men's actions and movements in the war years, but also of their hopes, fears, expectations, beliefs and state of mind – and allow us to analyse how these feelings evolved as they experienced years of discomfort, danger and conflict in unfamiliar surroundings.

These hundred-plus letters, and several postcards sent home by the brothers, form the backbone of this volume. This material comes to just under 57,000 words: only a thousand or so have been excised. A range of other material is deployed to add the necessary context to assist the reader to understand the references to people and places, and to appreciate the nuances of this intricate resource. Thus this book has drawn upon the local newspapers of Swansea, a variety of official sources such as the census and military records, material from the local chapels and some items that have come from other family collections. Other relatives of the Eustis brothers have kept photographs and a few postcards written by them, and two diaries have come to light that were written by Richard Eustis in 1916 and 1917 which are valuable in filling out many of the details of his activities in Egypt and Palestine.

The brothers travelled to many places and witnessed many events between 1914 and 1919: from Archangel in the north to Cairo in the south; from Limerick in the west to Jerusalem in the east. Ivor fought on the Western Front, the battlefront of the First World War that is most familiar and which steers the public's understanding of the war, while the others served in less well-known theatres. Richard's letters take us to Egypt and Palestine with the Egyptian Expeditionary Force (EEF); Gabriel served on an armed trawler in the inhospitable waters of the North Atlantic. However, wherever the brothers went and whatever their conditions, the letters reveal that they remained rooted – indeed, the letters were a means of confirming and preserving that rootedness, and keeping alive their civilian identity. To put it another way, '368053 Pte R.Eustis, R.A.M.C' was Richard or Dick to his family: his military identity did not expunge his role as son or brother. 'Telegraphist Eustis' remained Gabriel (or Gib or Gab), and whether Ivor was a private, a lance-corporal, a corporal or a sergeant, to his family he was still the shining scholar, brimming with promise.

This question of identity resonates through the text, mostly implicitly rather than explicitly. The letters give the perspective of three young Welshmen caught up in the Great War. This Welsh dimension is one of the facets that sets this collection apart for while there is a long-established historiography of the common soldier in the First World War, very few have given the point-of-view of the Welsh servicemen.[1] In essence, this book provides a fillip towards a 'four nations' approach to the social history of British involvement in the war.[2] The amount of colour and emotion shared within these letters gives a captivating micro-history of the war, which reflects elements of a wider 'national' experience at a personal level.

To understand these letters it is therefore necessary to appreciate where the brothers came from. Thus this introductory chapter sketches out the family and the community that the three brothers were born into, and which nourished their development and also describes the physical collection of evidence that is set out in the succeeding chapters.

Roots

The surname Eustis is Cornish. Several generations of ancestors of the three brothers can be found in the parish records of Crowan, near the south-western tip of Britain, in the eighteenth and early nineteenth centuries.[3] The connection with the Swansea area comes from the beginning of the 1840s when the experienced tin miner John Eustis was recruited to work for the Swansea Coal Company, sinking the shaft of the Mynydd Newydd colliery. At the time of the 1841 Census (taken in June), John was living in lodgings in Morriston; his wife Elizabeth and the rest of the family were still in the parish of Crowan. It is clear that they joined him not long afterwards because John and Elizabeth's son Richard was born in Morriston on 2 June 1843. John died in 1850 aged forty-three, following an accident in the mine. In the 1851 Census, the family resided at Mynydd Newydd Colliery Cottage.

TABLE 2: The Eustises of Crowan and north Swansea

John Eustis (1807–50) m. Elizabeth Gundry, at Crowan, Cornwall, 1829

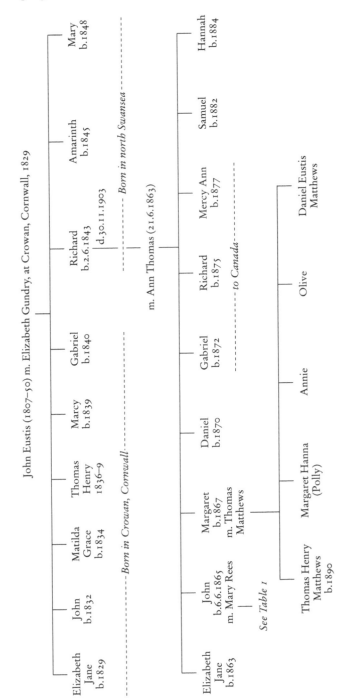

m. Ann Thomas (21.6.1863)

Elizabeth Jane b.1829 | John b.1832 | Matilda Grace b.1834 | Thomas Henry 1836–9 | Marcy b.1839 | Gabriel b.1840 | Richard b.2.6.1843 d.30.11.1903 | Amarinth b.1845 | Mary b.1848

------ Born in Crowan, Cornwall ------

------ Born in north Swansea ------

Elizabeth Jane b.1863 | John b.6.6.1865 m. Mary Rees | Margaret b.1867 m. Thomas Matthews | Daniel b.1870 | Gabriel b.1872 | Richard b.1875 | Mercy Ann b.1877 | Samuel b.1882 | Hannah b.1884

See Table 1

------ to Canada ------

Thomas Henry Matthews b.1890 | Margaret Hanna (Polly) | Annie | Olive | Daniel Eustis Matthews

The Mynydd Newydd colliery was located between Treboeth and Fforestfach, in an area known by locals as Pen-lan; now Ysgol Bryn Tawe occupies the site. This area of northern Swansea was thoroughly Welsh-speaking throughout the nineteenth century and it is clear that the children very soon became immersed in the prevailing Welsh culture. Aged twenty, Richard married 18-year-old Ann Thomas: his occupation was noted as 'engineer'. Richard chose to be baptised in Caersalem Newydd Baptist chapel in September 1866 – one of forty-five who were received into the chapel's membership that day. This chapel had been formed in 1841 following a rancorous disagreement between two factions in Mynyddbach chapel. Ann's family had been heavily involved in this event: her grandfather Samuel Samuel was the leader of those who walked out of Mynyddbach, and was listed as the first member of Caersalem Newydd.[4]

Richard and Ann had nine children over a period of twenty years, the first being born in the same year as their marriage. At the time of the 1891 Census, the first to record the knowledge of language, Ann (by then 46 years old) was marked as bilingual, but all of her children were listed as speaking Welsh only. However, the family was recorded as speaking both languages in 1901.

Richard Eustis was not present at the time of the 1891 Census because he was working in Nipissing, Ontario, as a mine foreman. There was at this period a strong current of emigration by skilled workers from Wales, which often (either by design or due to changing circumstances) turned out to be temporary. This was certainly the case with Richard, because at some point over the next few years he returned to Wales before setting out again to work overseas, this time in South Africa, in the company of his son Daniel. Details are sketchy, but there is a newspaper report from 1899 reporting how both had to flee back home on the outbreak of hostilities with the Boers.[5]

The connection with Canada remained strong. Richard's son, Richard (b.1875), apparently joined his father in Ontario: he married there before venturing west to British Columbia. Amongst the collection of First World War letters, the family has preserved the first page of a letter written from the province by Richard (junior) in 1897, in which he gives advice to a brother on how and whether to emigrate to Canada. It is not certain to whom this was addressed, but it might well have been Gabriel (b.1872). He emigrated soon after his marriage in 1901 to Elizabeth Rees (whose sister Mary was married to John Eustis).

The significance of this letter from the perspective of this volume is that it shows that the family did have some kind of letter-writing culture, and that in the English language. Another letter from 1903 has survived which reinforces this point. In this, Elizabeth (Gabriel's wife) writes to her nephew Richard (then aged 9, the son of John and Mary and one of the subjects of this book), in reply to a letter in which he had stated that he would like to go to British Columbia.[6]

In the 1901 Census, John and Mary Eustis and their four children were living in Park Hill Terrace, Treboeth, on the same street as his parents and his sister Margaret (Matthews). He was recorded as a coal miner (hewer) and the three eldest children (Richard, 7, Gabriel, 6, and Ivor, 4) were recorded as scholars. All were noted as bilingual. By the time of the 1911 Census, the family had moved to Pengwern Road, Mynyddbach, which was to stay in the family's possession for several decades. John (45) was still a coal miner, hewer, while Richard (17) was a colliery labourer (below ground), Gabriel (16) was a tinworker (cold-roller) and Ivor (14) was a student at secondary school. There were three daughters present in the home: Hannah (11) and Elizabeth Ann (8), both at school, and Lottie (4). The family were noted as bilingual except for Lottie who was recorded as speaking only Welsh.

Another daughter, Grace (6, at school), was living in Laurel Cottage (about 250 yards away from John and Mary's home) with her grandparents (Elizabeth and Rees Rees) and aunt Charlotte Rees (39, single, certificated assistant teacher). They were all recorded as being bilingual, as was the Rees family next door, headed by Mary's brother Thomas Rees: his son Uriel (11) was also noted as being at school.

Table 3: The Rees family of Mynyddbach

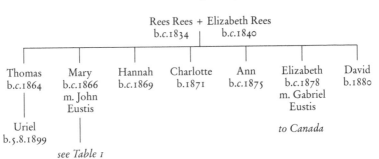

| Rees Rees + Elizabeth Rees |
| b.c.1834   b.c.1840 |

Thomas	Mary	Hannah	Charlotte	Ann	Elizabeth	David
b.c.1864	b.c.1866	b.c.1869	b.1871	b.c.1875	b.c.1878	b.1880
	m. John				m. Gabriel	
	Eustis				Eustis	
Uriel					*to Canada*	
b.5.8.1899						
	see Table 1					

Thus although at a century's distance we do not have the evidence to prove to what extent everyone in the wider family got along, all the indications are that this was a close-knit family. Not only were the homes in close proximity, but John and Mary sent a daughter to live with her maternal grandparents. There are numerous references in the collection of letters to 'Granny', meaning Elizabeth Rees (though only one to 'Mamgu', meaning Ann Eustis). As will be seen, there are also several references to the cousins Thomas Henry Matthews and Uriel Rees.

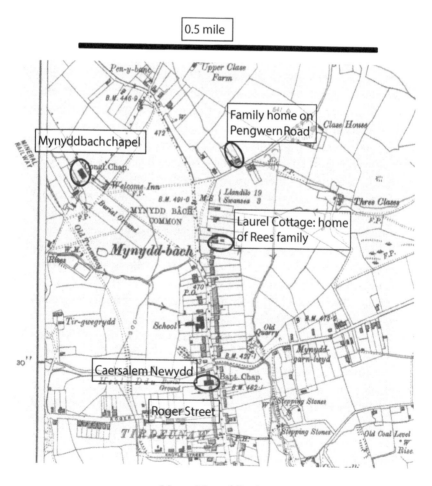

MAP 1: Mynyddbach

Community and locality

When the brothers posted letters home, they addressed the envelopes 'Pengwern Road, Mynyddbach, Landore, Swansea'. Where exactly the settlement of Mynyddbach ends and Tirdeunaw begins is a moot point that not even a local of several decades' residence would be able to define. 'Treboeth' is the term generally preferred by residents today, although Treboeth 'proper' has its centre a few hundred yards south, towards Swansea. In 1914 administrative boundaries cut across this locality: whereas Treboeth was within the county borough of Swansea, Mynyddbach lay outside, in the Swansea rural district.

Richard Eustis referred to 'the village boys' in numerous letters, but there is no indication of how he defined this term. His best friend in the 1/3rd WFA, David Rees Thomas (known as 'Dai') lived on Roger Street, just to the south of Caersalem Newydd. At least another five men who served with them lived on the same street.

It is clear from the letters that there was a lively and efficient information network, of which the Eustis brothers were an integral part, which transmitted news of local people to those who were physically far removed from Mynyddbach and Tirdeunaw. In Richard's letters there are multiple mentions of a core group, of those who went out with him in the 1/3rd WFA, and then a string of references to other men from the area whose paths crossed with his. One can be sure that the Eustis family passed on news of these local men to their friends and relatives, and also that they received information from other sources of the brothers' movements. Many of these men were members of either Mynyddbach or Caersalem Newydd chapels, and so it is likely that the latest news was exchanged after the services on Sundays.

The community gave its support to the men who served in a variety of ways. There was the formal initiative of the local support fund: this went by various names, the most long-winded of which was the 'Mynyddbach, Treboeth and District Soldiers' and Sailors' Succour Fund'. This organised events to raise money and to honour soldiers and sailors who were home on leave from late 1915 onwards. Most of the servicemen mentioned in the brothers' letters are reported as having received medals and gifts from this group.[7] Other initiatives to support the servicemen who were away from home (mentioned in the letters) came from the brothers' chapel

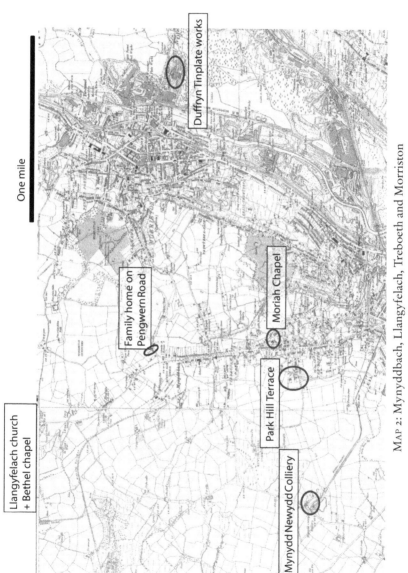

One mile

Duffryn Tinplate works

Family home on Pengwern Road

Moriah Chapel

Park Hill Terrace

Mynydd Newydd Colliery

Llangyfelach church + Bethel chapel

MAP 2: Mynyddbach, Llangyfelach, Treboeth and Morriston

and the Treboeth Ladies' Comforts Guild. It is also clear, both from references in the letters and from entries in Richard's diaries for 1916 and 1917, that a wide variety of local people corresponded with the brothers – some of them occasionally, some repeatedly.

Thus, although the term 'close-knit' can be overused to the point of cliché, it does describe the community of Mynyddbach/Tirdeunaw/Treboeth in the early twentieth century. The population was relatively homogenous, being overwhelmingly working class and mainly Welsh in culture and ethnic background. This is not, of course, to paint a picture of an idyllic community in a tranquil environment. A small colliery, Cefngyfelach, had operated just to the west of Mynyddbach chapel for about three decades from 1880: the old tramway that cut across the landscape to the south is marked upon the contemporary maps. A visitor in 1918 who sought to find the well-known local poet Gwyrosydd in the Mynyddbach area was taken aback by the unpleasantness of the surroundings in Treboeth and Tirdeunaw, declaring 'Mae athrylith a diwylliant yr hen Gymro yn medru bwrlymu drwy y bryntni a'r mwg' ('The genius and culture of the Welshmen of old is capable of thriving despite the dirt and the smoke').[8] This area on the edge of the Swansea conurbation was physically on the border between industrial and rural Wales, but in terms of male employment it was tipped towards the industrial. The census returns for the area show a large number of colliery workers, principally at Mynydd Newydd and Tirdonkin. Many (including Gabriel) also worked in the tinplate works of Morriston.

Language and culture

This area was on another borderline too: that between Welsh-speaking and English-speaking Wales. By the second decade of the twentieth century, the Welsh language was in retreat in most parts of Wales: the proportion of Welsh speakers in the population had fallen from 49.9 per cent in 1901 to 43.5 per cent in 1911, while the proportion of those noted as monoglot Welsh almost halved in this decade from 15.1 per cent to 8.5 per cent. In Glamorgan the decline was from 44 per cent to 39 per cent for Welsh speakers, 6.7 per cent to 3.2 per cent for monoglot Welsh. Boundary changes in the Swansea area in this decade complicate the picture, but for the county borough of Swansea, the proportion of Welsh speakers decreased from 33 per cent to 28 per cent between 1901 and 1911, and in Swansea rural district, the figure went from 83 per cent to 73 per cent.

Within this wider picture of language retreat it is possible to focus on specific localities to gauge how the situation developed in particular communities. A detailed study of Fforestfach (1.5 miles to the south-east and, like Treboeth, 3 or 4 miles away from Swansea's centre) demonstrates that at the turn of the twentieth century the Welsh language was strong in the outer fringes of the Swansea district. Robert Bevan states that

> In 1891, it is doubtless that the Fforestfach collier lived in a thoroughly Welsh community and that Welsh was the language of the coalface and the rest of the coalfield, as well as the dominant language of the hearth, chapel, street, fairground and public house ...[9]

and one could substitute 'Mynyddbach' or 'Tirdeunaw' for 'Fforestfach' in that sentence. The English language was making inroads, and Bevan's research shows that bilingualism, as opposed to families speaking only Welsh, made significant gains in Fforestfach in the ten years to 1901: the same pattern can be seen in the Treboeth area. As noted, the children of Richard and Ann Eustis were registered as speaking only Welsh in 1891, but were bilingual in 1901, and the same is true of many other local families.

Yet the 1911 Census shows clearly that the vast majority of the residents of Mynyddbach/Tirdeunaw/Treboeth were able to speak Welsh. Every single one of the men listed in Appendix 2, of local servicemen mentioned in the letters, was bilingual. There were pockets of English and anglophone Welsh individuals, but also cases (as had occurred with the first generation of Eustises born in Wales) where the Welsh-born children of English-speaking incomers were fluent in both languages. Thus the area was, and had been for some time, on a border between two cultures, and able to develop a particular hybrid culture that profited from its ability to take from both.[10]

As noted below, community life here was strongly influenced by the chapels, which were centres not only of religious life but also for cultural and social events. The local chapels were Mynyddbach for the Independents, Moriah and Bethel for the Calvinistic Methodists and Caersalem Newydd for the Baptists.[11] All of these were thoroughly Welsh in all their internal dealings in 1914. Mynyddbach chapel bred a number of poets, the most prominent of whom has left a legacy that is still popular today. Daniel James (1848–1920), universally known under his pen-name of Gwyrosydd, was born in Treboeth into a family that worshipped at Mynyddbach, and it was following a service here that he wrote one of his best-known poems, 'Ble'r aeth yr Amen'. He moved away with his work in 1890, only returning to live in the Morriston area towards the end of his life, but Treboeth still lays claim to his best-loved work, the hymn 'Calon Lân'.

Further evidence of the vibrant Welsh-language culture of the area comes in the reports of local and regional eisteddfodau. A famous local choirmaster, William Jenkins, conducted both the Treboeth and district choir and the Mynyddbach Chapel Choir to success in many an eisteddfod until his death in 1913.[12] The chapels hosted public lectures on a variety of topics, two subjects in 1913 being the Welsh Liberal politician Tom Ellis and Abraham Lincoln.[13] There were also concerts and organ recitals held in the chapels.[14]

It is possible to find some concrete evidence of how the circumstances of the war affected the cultural practices of the area. A concert was held in Mynyddbach chapel at the end of 1917 to raise money for the chapel's Soldiers' and Sailors' Fund. The presentation evenings of the district's Soldiers' and Sailors' Support Fund were regular occasions in the latter part of the war. As well as the ceremonies to honour the servicemen there were musical contributions and speeches by local dignitaries. From 1916 the organisation held an annual eisteddfod to raise funds.[15] No information has come to light regarding the poetry composed for these events, but many local eisteddfodau around Swansea set war-related titles for their poetry competitions, such as Fforestfach's 'Trannoeth y Frwydr' (The Day after the Battle) or Pentre Estyll's 'Milwr Cymraeg y Noson Cyn y Frwydr' (A Welsh Soldier the night before battle).[16]

There were, of course, plenty of other poems in the public sphere that presented participation in the war as a noble undertaking, characterised by Gerard DeGroot as '"bad" patriotic poetry'.[17] The pages of Welsh newspapers are replete with examples of poetry which would never win any prizes for style or composition, but which gain full marks for blinkered patriotism. This is true in both languages and in fact the Welsh-language denominational press probably contains more war-related poetry per page than the English-language newspapers. Much of this poetry portrays the fight as one between good and evil. The Kaiser is regularly compared to the devil. In Welsh, the fact that the word for enemy, 'gelyn', rhymes with the word for harp, 'telyn', makes for some convoluted allusions.[18]

Mynyddbach's most famous son, the poet Gwyrosydd, was one of those who penned a poem, 'Cadfloedd Rhyddid' (Freedom's war cry) that reads like a call to arms, urging the young men of Wales to volunteer in the cause of right.

> Clywch yr udgorn-floedd i'r rhyfel
> Yn dyrwygo bron yr awel;
> Duwies Rhyddid eilw'n uchel
>   Ar ei phlant i'r gad:
> Gormes gyda'i lu arglwyddi
> Sydd yn chwifio eu baneri:
> Nawr neu byth, wroniaid Cymru,
>   Awn i'r gad, i'r gad;
> Dewrder ein cyndeidiau
> Enyn ein mynwesau,
> Megys tân, i'n gyru'n mlaen
> Nes mynu ein hiawnderau:
> Os gorchfygir ni gan ormes.
> Na foed neb i ddweyd yr hanes;
> Marw'n wrol wnawn ar fynwes
>   Rhyddid yn y gad[19]

> [Hear the trumpet call to war,
> tearing the bosom of the breeze;
> the Goddess of Freedom loudly calling
> her children to the battle.
> Oppression with its multitude of lords
> is waving its banners;
> now or never, brave men of Wales,
> let us go to the battle, to the battle;
> [may] the bravery of our forefathers
> kindle our bosom
> like a fire, to drive us on,

> until we claim our rights;
> if we are defeated by oppression
> let no one tell the tale;
> we will die bravely in the war
> on the bosom of Freedom.]

Another local poet, Joseph Jones of Treboeth (who would later become Gabriel Eustis's father-in-law) wrote 'Milwr mewn Ffos' (A soldier in a trench) in 1916. Over seven verses it glorifies the soldiers who are fighting for king and country, and also for God.

> Caru'r cartre wna'r bechgyn yn ddiwad,
> Carwn ninau wneud ein goreu trwy y wlad;
> Cydymdeimlwn ymhob ardal; i'r bechgyn gael eu cynal
> Am eu bod yn ymladd drosom ni ar wlad.[20]

> [It cannot be denied that the lads love their homes,
> we would like to do our best throughout the land;
> in every district we sympathise; the boys should be supported
> because they fight on our behalf and for the country.]

Whether or not the Eustis family were familiar with these particular poems, they are representative of the way that those in the public sphere across Wales presented the war to their audience. The point that the local soldiers were fighting for Wales, for Welsh honour and the survival of Welsh culture, and to protect their families against a vicious foe is drummed home in a swathe of Welsh war poems, songs and artistic works.

Religion

This part of Wales, on the border between the industrial and the rural, had a strong tradition of Protestant Nonconformity. The Eustis family were members of the Independent chapel at Mynyddbach. This place of worship proudly traced its lineage back to the earliest days of Nonconformity, and indeed it was boasted that the chapel 'was the outcome of the birth of Welsh Nonconformity in the Swansea district in 1640'.[21] In 1914 its membership stood at 400, with 486 attending the Sunday school.

Measuring the religious sentiment of a family from the distance of a century later – and in an age when ideas about religion have been transformed in Wales – is fraught with difficulty. Twenty-first-century Wales has very different ideas about religious thought and practice than the Christian orthodoxy prevalent in early twentieth-century Wales. However, all the indications are that John and Mary Eustis were faithful members at Mynyddbach and sought to transmit their beliefs to their children. Mary's sister Charlotte was a Sunday school teacher: a position of status and influence within the chapel. One can be sure that from an early age, the Eustis children were immersed into Welsh chapel culture, which expected the Sabbath to be strictly observed with attendance at three services the norm.

It was not just in chapel on Sunday that religious ceremonies were observed in this locality. The colliery at Mynydd Newydd had a degree of fame in Wales and beyond because of the religious services that took place every Monday morning, prior to the start of the week's work. There were two 'chapels' underground, one in the 'five foot seam', the other in the 'six foot seam', where these services were held. The tradition stretched back to the 1840s: other collieries had underground chapels that were established at times of religious revival, but no other colliery in Wales had such a long and continuous tradition of prayer meetings. Dozens of newspaper articles had remarked upon the special nature of these services.[22] John Eustis worked here, as his father Richard and grandfather John had done, and his son Richard was employed here until he joined up in 1914.

Other family members attended the nearby Baptist chapel of Caersalem Newydd, including John's sister Margaret. This had the largest membership of any Welsh Baptist church in west Glamorgan in 1914, with 543 full members and 510 attending the Sunday school.

There were two Calvinistic Methodist chapels nearby. The nearest was Moriah, Treboeth: its membership stood at 119 in 1914, with 60 young attendees. A mile to the north was Bethel, Llangyfelach, with 131 members and 112 youngsters. Unfortunately no records can be found regarding the contribution of Moriah's congregation to the war, but for the other three chapels the Rolls of Honour listing all those who served are still extant, and provide a valuable insight both into how the chapels contributed to the war effort and how they understood the war at the time, and in its immediate aftermath.

There are twenty-two names on Bethel's Roll of Honour, of whom two appear in the Eustis brothers' letters.[23] There are eighty-one names on Caersalem Newydd's Roll of Honour, of whom ten appear in the letters.[24] There are two Rolls of Honour in Mynyddbach chapel. The first was created in February 1916: the design has pillars either side of the list of names of those who have joined and their regiments. At the bottom it says in capital letters 'Gweddiwch Drostynt' (Pray for them). There are nineteen names here, listed more or less by the date of volunteering: Richard is the fifth name on the list; Gabriel is twelfth. It seems that the list was discontinued as it became clear that there would be insufficient room for all the recruits. The second Roll of Honour was created in June 1921. The design has pillars either side of the names, with laurel wreaths of victory at their top, and above the names a crown and the flags of the United Kingdom, Belgium, France and the United States. There are fifty-nine men listed (including the three Eustis brothers) and at the end one woman, Eunice Thomas, who served with the Women's Auxiliary Army Corps.[25] Fourteen men on this list are named in the letters.

The question of how the Welsh Nonconformist denominations managed to reconcile their Christian teaching with support for the war effort is vexing. Prior to 1914, the dominant attitude of the chapels of Wales had been anti-militaristic, with a strong tendency towards pacifism and the rejection of all wars. When the situation in Europe in the summer of 1914 suddenly deteriorated and the Continent slid towards an all-out war there was a brief period of uncertainty when people (in Wales as all over the United Kingdom) had to adjust their beliefs to the new reality. However, once the fighting began, the tide of opinion raced so strongly towards supporting Britain's war effort that only a very few resisters were able and willing to stand their ground. Those ministers who did question the argument that Britain's cause was just were subject to scorn and, in the highly polarised atmosphere of 1914, were abused as unpatriotic and disloyal, or even denounced as pro-German traitors.[26] A study of the attitudes of Swansea chapels towards the war demonstrates that they became willing accomplices in the recruitment campaign, with some ministers actively exhorting the young men of their congregations to join up.[27] There is no evidence that the ministers of Mynyddbach nor Caersalem Newydd were themselves direct agents of recruitment but the chapels did count and publicise the number of volunteers they had provided for the army and navy. Both chapels raised money for war-related charities, such as the Welsh Hospital at Nettley and destitute Belgian refugees.[28] Mynyddbach chapel organised its own Soldiers' and Sailors' Fund, and sent gifts to its members who were serving overseas. The minister, the Rev. James Davies, corresponded with servicemen and when one of his flock, Thomas J. Cole, was killed in action late in the war a service was devoted to his memory, with an 'eloquent sermon … dwelling on his pure character and self-sacrifice'.[29]

One mile north of the family home was the nearest Anglican place of worship to the Eustis home, the ancient church at Llangyfelach. Although John Eustis's Cornish grandfather John is buried here, there is no evidence that the Church of England had much relevance to the Eustis family. For decades, the Nonconformist denominations had been in the ascendancy in Wales, in an alliance with the Liberal Party. Indeed, it is generally the case that relations between the different Nonconformist denominations were warm because they made common cause to work together for the abolition of the privileges of the Established Church. There is no evidence in the letters of the three brothers that these political manoeuvrings were a concern to them, yet it is clear that when they had a choice both Ivor and Richard chose to attend Nonconformist services on Sundays rather than join the Church of England parade. When he enlisted, Gabriel gave his religion as 'Nonconformist'.

Another of Welsh Nonconformity's particular obsessions in the decades leading up to the First World War was temperance. Excessive consumption of alcohol was decried as an evil that not only led to sinful behaviour by the imbibers and lured them away from the path of righteousness, but also disrupted family life and led to poverty and misery for the drunkard's wife and children. This was not (necessarily) a campaign by killjoys, as one of the tactics of the temperance campaign and the chapels was to organise alternative, improving, recreational activities to keep the populace away from the pubs. The chapels of Treboeth and Mynyddbach scheduled their choral festivals (*cymanfa ganu*) to coincide with the (famously rowdy) Llangyfelach Fair. In the 1890s there was a Treboeth Temperance Drum and Fife Band; in the period leading up to the war Richard Eustis played his cornet in the Treboeth Temperance Brass Band. Both Gabriel and Ivor mention their distaste for drunkards in their letters, although one should be aware of the possibility that this was being said to please their correspondents back home. The only detailed evidence we have of a brother's relationship with alcohol shows that there were times in 1916–17 when Richard was drinking too much.

The collection of letters

Over a hundred letters sent by the three brothers, Richard, Gabriel and Ivor Eustis, as they served in the First World War have been kept by the family. There are also a number of postcards, photographs and other ephemera, which together provide a detailed (though incomplete) narrative of the brothers' actions in the war years, shedding light upon their beliefs, hopes and expectations. The collection allows us to build a picture of the impact of the war upon the family and the local community, and gives us an indication of how the ideas of people who lived through these momentous events changed, and how they responded to the course of events that was unexpected and unprecedented.

Most of the letters are addressed to 'Mother', but a substantial minority were sent to Aunt Charlotte at Laurel Cottage.[30] It is clear that letters sent to one family home were passed on to be read by others. It may well have been Aunt Charlotte who was primarily responsible for safeguarding the letters during the war years. Then the letters were kept as a collection in a small box in the cottage in Pengwern Road. After the parents' deaths they were kept safe (in the same cottage) by Bess Anne and Lottie, and they were subsequently passed down to Ian, son of the youngest brother, Daniel. Martyn Lyons has noted that 'Nothing is quite as destructive of family archives as moving house', and in this case it is fortunate that this branch of the Eustis family were so rooted to the spot.[31]

These letters are referenced in this book using the format GE, IE or RE for Gabriel, Ivor or Richard Eustis, then YYYY-MM-DD for those letters where the year, month and date of the letter is known. Thus the first letter in the collection, RE1914-09-19, was written by Richard Eustis on 19 September 1914. Over half of the letters were dated by their authors and in most other cases the date of writing of undated letters can be pin-pointed. For some letters, only the month can be inferred, such as a letter from Ivor which appears to be from October 1916, and so this has the reference IE1916-10-a.

The letters as physical artefacts

It appears that the brothers wrote their letters using whatever material was to hand. Most are written in pencil, though many that Ivor wrote from the training camp at Kinmel Park are in ink. Several of these (and some of Richard's) have been written on YMCA paper, but others were written on pages taken from exercise books or other scraps of loose paper.

Given their age, the letters and postcards are in a very good condition. Although the pages have been folded, there are very few tears and in the vast majority of letters almost every word is legible. Only one letter has substantial passages where the words cannot be made out. Around half of the original envelopes have survived and sometimes it is clear that the letters are in the original envelopes, and so the date stamp is a way to confirm the date of writing. Many of the envelopes posted by Gabriel from Scotland in 1918 have the message 'Buy National War Bonds' stamped upon them, demonstrating how reminders of the war were ubiquitous at the time.

For long, long periods of the war, the elder boys were absent from the family home: their letters and any ephemera sent home (photographs and other souvenirs) were the only tangible link the parents and younger siblings had with their boys' present lives. As Martha Hanna has put it, 'the letter itself was a physical artifact that could cultivate intimacy by making the absent correspondent seem almost palpably present'.[32] The brothers' letters were eagerly anticipated, and the rough opening of some of the envelopes indicates that the recipients literally could not wait to read the contents. They would have been read multiple times: their creases are testimony to that. One wonders whether among the thumbprints there are other traces left by the readers – that of their tears.

Censorship and self-censorship

Only one of these letters has been explicitly censored by the authorities, but we know that a great number of these letters passed through the hands of the censors.[33] Many of the envelopes have the censor's stamp upon them. However, a number of the surviving envelopes are what were known as 'green' or 'honour' envelopes. These were distributed to soldiers on active service, usually one per month, and they could write in the knowledge that their letters would not be read by a regimental censor, although the envelope warned them that 'the contents are liable to examination at the Base'. The writer had to sign a declaration on his honour 'that the contents of this envelope refer to nothing but private and family affairs', and they knew that to be caught breaking the rules and passing on sensitive information could lead to a serious punishment.[34]

There is also the question of self-censorship. The knowledge that the censors would not allow details of their current location to be passed on directly affected the way the brothers wrote. Many of Ivor's letters in 1918 were simply addressed 'France'; one to a sister in February is from '"Somewhere", France'. Another letter sent that month to his mother states 'We came out of the line to a town called ———— about 6 miles from the trenches.'[35] One of Gabriel's letters states that he had sent packets to Richard 'from ———— just before coming to sea'.[36] It is a moot point whether this self-censorship explains the general lack of descriptions of military activities in the brothers' letters, or whether they chose not to give details of this side of their lives to the family back home because they did not want to cause further anxiety by dwelling on issues of blood and killing.

Lacunae

It is not fruitful to spend too much time regretting what has been lost, but there are substantial gaps in what has been preserved, particularly from the first twenty-two months of the war. Richard Eustis was in uniform from the very beginning of the war, but the only examples of Richard's early letters to have survived are three that he sent to Ivor. Gabriel volunteered in November 1914, but only one letter he sent that month has survived and the next one in the collection dates from two years later. Clearly no one had any idea at the start of the war of its length and severity, and so perhaps the impulse to preserve the letters received in the family home was not strong. On the other hand it is possible that these letters were kept in a different box that has been mislaid or lost over the intervening decades. Thus there are many questions from the beginning of the family's involvement with the Great War that must remain unanswered.

Some letters written to the family clearly never made it to this archive. There are only a few letters here to sisters Hannah and Lottie, even though we know that the brothers wrote regularly to them. No letters addressed to Elizabeth Ann nor Grace have come to light. Nor have letters written to people outside the immediate family circle been found. It appears that the letters which Gabriel sent to his sweetheart (and future wife) Theodosia Jones were kept by her, but were lost when she passed away. Of all the letters and postcards sent by Richard to his sweetheart (and future wife) Mary Lizzie Morgan, only two postcards have survived.

One major gap which must be borne in mind is that we do not have any of the letters which the brothers received from their family at home. Although we can recreate much of the content of these, as so many parts of the brothers' letters respond directly to news from home, we can but guess at the details that were not replied to, and the particulars and the minutiae that needed no acknowledgement. Nor can we say whether these lost letters were written solely in English or whether sections (or even entire letters) were in Welsh.

We know that many photographs of the brothers were sent home, but there was also, undoubtedly, a traffic of pictures from home to the servicemen. The only one to have survived is an image of Mary, the mother, sent to Gabriel in October 1916. The reverse of this contains the only writing we have by the family to the brothers: 'Dear Gib, With Mother's love to her little angel'.

1.1: Photograph of Mary Eustis

The fact that most of these letters were addressed to the mother is not unusual. A study by Michael Roper of the Imperial War Museum's extensive collection found that there were six times as many letters to mothers as there were to fathers.[37] There are two references made in Gabriel's letters of parcels sent to the father but otherwise it is clear that it was mainly through the females that the brothers communicated with the family.

We only have access to one of the letters written from one serviceman brother to another while the war was on (along with one written after the Armistice), although the letters home show that they frequently corresponded with one another – sometimes using those at home to forward the message to the correct address. From the example we have (RE1917-11-20: a letter from Richard in Egypt sent to Ivor in the training camp), it is clear that the tone the brothers adopted to one another was different to that in their letters to female family members at home. This letter is noticeably more brash in its style than the ones Richard wrote to his mother, aunt and sisters, and contains language that would have been considered coarse at home, such as 'God only knows'. Also the word 'hell' appears twice in this letter but in none of the others, although it is a very common occurrence in Richard's diaries from 1916 and 1917 (as in 'hell of a gale'; 'shelled like hell'; 'hell of a sensation'; 'hell of a journey', etc.). However, the evidence does not exist to take this analysis further.

Additional material and other evidence

The collection, as it has been preserved by the family, contains some items in addition to the letters from the brothers. The two letters written by relatives from Canada (referred to earlier) have been kept here, and some other material from 1914–18 has found its way into this collection, such as a receipt for seed potatoes (February 1918), a postcard congratulating Lottie on passing her exam (July 1918) and an invitation to Gowerton School's prize-giving in 1918. There is also a letter from Hannah to her mother (August 1917, briefly referred to in chapter 7) and two letters sent by servicemen to one of the brothers. The letter to Gabriel from his shipmate Bunty (April 1916) is briefly referred to in chapter 5, and the letter to Richard from his friend Dai Harris (December 1918) is included in chapter 13.

There are a few 'field service postcards' sent by Ivor and Richard in the collection. These were pre-printed postcards with standard messages on them that soldiers could send home – they crossed out any unwanted messages but were not allowed to write anything on them besides their signature and the date. All of these postcards have the message 'I am quite well' and 'Letter follows at first opportunity'. It is highly likely that many more of these postcards were sent in 1915–18, but not kept.

In addition to the main collection, some material kept by other branches of the family has been used in this volume. One of Richard's granddaughters has two of the postcards that he sent to his sweetheart, Mary Lizzie Morgan, and also the diaries he kept while he served in Egypt and Palestine in 1916 and 1917. A number of photographs have been kept in a collection inherited by Grace's daughter, and some of Gabriel in uniform have been kept by his daughter.

The letters provide a window into how the family understood and talked about the war at the time. Of course this family conversation was guided and constrained by discussions they encountered about the war in other spheres. The folk at Mynyddbach would have been influenced by the way the local newspapers presented and described the war. We do not have direct evidence of which newspaper they read, though of the two Swansea dailies, one would hazard a guess that the Liberal *Cambria Daily Leader* would be more likely than the Conservative-inclined *South Wales Daily Post*.[38] Various letters from the three brothers refer to newspapers being sent out with their letters, including snippets of local news, and so we can be sure that some of these local newspapers were read by the family, and helped to shape their view of the war. Thus at various points in the book extracts from the local papers are used to flesh out what is in the text of the letters. Chapter 4, which considers Ivor's movements in the early part of the war, considers in some detail the way that his school magazine presented the war between 1914 and 1916.

Spelling, grammar and emphases

In general, the spelling (in English) of the three brothers was very good. However, Richard did make some consistent mistakes: he spelled 'receive', 'receiving', etc. with the 'i' before the 'e', he wrote 'exept' instead of 'except' and he always spelled 'daresay' as 'darsay'. Ivor spelt 'opinion' with a double 'p', 'inoculated' with a double 'n' and often finished his letters 'yours affectionatly'. These and some other trivial spelling mistakes have been corrected in the text.[39]

The brothers' use of apostrophes was not always conventional. Richard mostly omitted to use an apostrophe when writing 'don't' or 'doesn't'. Ivor and Gabriel also did not always use apostrophes properly, but all these slips have been regularised in the text.

Some of the letters are laid out well, but others have a lot crammed onto the page, meaning that there are no paragraph breaks. Thus some have been added to make the letters easier to read.

The words of Welsh included in the letters were often written in a colloquial style, and frequently spelt phonetically. These are included in the text as they appear, with an English translation in italics in square brackets to follow.

Often, the author uses a technique to emphasise certain words or phrases. When words are underlined in the original, this has been replicated in the book's text, but on other occasions segments are written in a larger font and in these cases bold text is used to indicate the parts that are thus emphasised.

Slang and idioms

All three brothers use (English-language) slang words that had a particular meaning in 1914–18. Gabriel refers disparagingly to 'knuts' at home: the term meant 'a fashionable or showy young man' with overtones of one who shirked his duty.[40] He referred to items that someone had received for nothing as 'Harry Free's'.[41] Ivor, in a passage that belittles the masculinity of one of his fellow soldiers, compares him to a 'flapper'. Some novel military terms make their way into the letters, particularly in Gabriel's. He describes the armed trawlers as 'Jellicoe's Rocking Horses'. He also describes his ship ironically as 'H.M.Super-Super-Dreadnought Saxon', and as 'the old raft', 'the old lifeboat' and 'the Old North Atlantic Lifeboat'.

Although we cannot say how much military slang was current in the brothers' vocabulary prior to August 1914, such terms were sprinkled liberally through the letters of 1918. All three refer to Britain as 'Blighty'. Gabriel uses the term 'burgoo' for the Royal Navy's porridge, and 'crusher' for the naval police.[42] Ivor uses the term 'buckshee', meaning free of charge: this corruption of

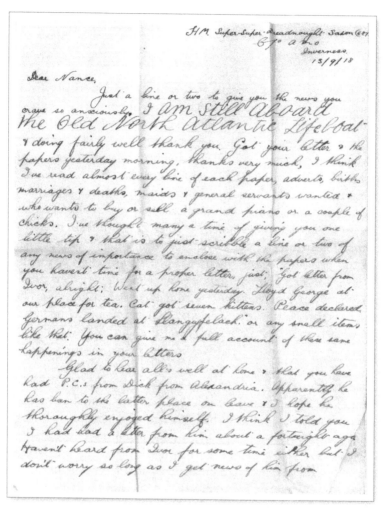

1.2: Gabriel Eustis's letter to his sister Hannah (GE1918-09-13)

'baksheesh' became popular in soldiers' slang during the war.[43] Once in France, he took to referring to the Germans as 'Jerry'.[44] Even references to family matters could be couched in military terms: little brother Daniel was jocularly referred to as 'O.C.' (officer commanding) of his class at school; the home at Pengwern Road was called 'Headquarters'.[45]

Another way in which the brothers' vocabulary evolved during the war was through the borrowing of local words from places they passed through. Gabriel, who was stationed in Scotland for most of the war, uses some Scottish terms in his letters, such as 'a wee nap' and 'the "wee yins"'.[46] Richard's diary from 1917 refers to a 'cacolet', a seat or bed fitted to a camel.

However, other aspects of the brothers' letters are firmly anchored in their home patch. The letters are full of references to family and friends, and even though a century has passed it is possible to make sense of many of these. The 1911 Census has been useful in identifying most of the individuals referred to, along with some of the local memorials and information from local families. Thus it is possible to understand, for example, Ivor's reference in a letter to 'someone the size of Herbert Evans': a photograph of Mr Evans shows a large, portly individual.[47] Other references are impossible to interpret fully a century on, but despite this they have mostly been included in the transcripts as they reinforce the idea that the brothers were constantly seeking to compare their current circumstances with familiar ideas from home. Sometimes these idiosyncrasies are clearly local sayings with an injection of humour, such as when Ivor adapts the saying 'After the Lord Mayor comes the dust-cart' to 'After the Lord Mayor comes Twm Evan Y Clâs'.[48]

Visualisation

One of the aims of many of the letters is to convey to the recipients at home what it was like to be in the author's location, be that an army camp, a foreign land, the front line or a distant harbour. Ivor Eustis's letters describe the YMCA hut in which he was writing his letters, his hospital ward in Chatham and the appearance of the barracks in Wrexham. Ivor sent a sketch home of his living space at Kinmel Park and another sketch (now lost) showed his parents the extent of the wound on his forehead. He also gives a flavour of the sounds around him, such as the bugler blowing out a call or his comrades roaring with laughter while looking at an amusing photograph.

Richard, being the one who travelled to the most distant destination, gave descriptions of the 'exotic' sights that he witnessed – from the 'fine old' colleges at Cambridge to the wonders of Ancient Egypt. These written descriptions were backed up by photographs: the image of Richard on a camel alongside two comrades, with the Sphinx and the Great Pyramid in the background is indeed worth a thousand words. Richard makes reference to having sent 'a few snapshots of Jerusalem, Bethlehem, Hebron, etc.': we do not know for sure how many of these arrived in Mynyddbach and were shared around the family.[49] One collection that has been preserved is a series of photographs of Egypt and Palestine sent home by Evan Samuel Rees, one of Richard's comrades (mentioned in a number of his letters) and it is possible that these and others were seen by the Eustis family at the time.[50]

Gabriel's descriptions of his surroundings are more limited. At the time of writing most of the letters he was stationed on an armed trawler, *HMT Saxon*, but in none of the surviving letters does he describe the ship nor give any descriptions of their voyages. However, he (like the other brothers) does give multiple descriptions of the food that was available.

Format of the book

Letters written by servicemen have been used by historians to get close to the thoughts of those who experienced the challenges of battle in a variety of wars. For conflicts prior to the mid-nineteenth century only a small fraction of the 'other ranks' were literate enough to leave such evidence, but from the time of the American Civil War onwards, the range of contemporary material generated by soldiers at war is enormous.[51]

Depending on the quantity of the material and the inclination of the researcher it is possible to carry out studies that trace the career of an individual soldier, to look at the responses of a particular unit or men from a certain locality, or to examine a range of different testimonies to discover the prevalent attitudes on a specific issue. When the researcher is fortunate enough to have access to an extensive run of letters from one serviceman, it is possible to build up an intricate picture of his 'emotions and ideas', his 'ambition and sense of accomplishment', his 'expressing and understanding the absurdity of war', his military identity and 'sentiments towards civilians' and his understanding of concepts such as 'manhood' and 'courage'.[52] The most sophisticated of these studies consider the things left unsaid as well as what is explicit in the sources, an approach that is productive when considering concepts such as masculinity, where the soldier-authors would be unlikely to broach the issue directly.[53]

There are a number of factors that make the Eustis collection of letters so rich and so productive to study. Even though we know that there are substantial gaps in the archive, there are extensive periods where much has survived, allowing us to gauge the mood of the correspondents and how that develops with time. The fact that this is a family collection, in a case where we know so much about that family, allows us to view the intra-familial dynamics, and how the roles of particular family members are defined, and how that changes with time. Furthermore, the fact that the three brothers were part of a local community that was largely homogenous and tightly knit, and that the brothers were so linked to the community despite being physically away from it, means that the letters give us an insight into how the life of that community was affected by the war. The brothers also belonged to a national community, within the broader framework of the United Kingdom. There are obviously great similarities between the 'Welsh' experience of the First World War and the 'English', 'Scottish' or indeed 'Irish' experience, but equally there is no doubt that studying the details in cases such as this one finds a range of differences which demonstrate the distinctiveness of how the Welsh lived through and understood the war.

The next chapter deals with the limited amount of evidence that exists regarding the actions, movement and responses of the two elder brothers from 1913 to 1915. Then the following ten chapters deal in turn with the letters sent by one brother from a period of the war. The lengths of these chapters vary greatly according to the quantity of letters that have survived, so that chapter 4 dealing with Ivor's period in the training camp in north Wales in 1916 (nineteen letters and a postcard) is much longer than chapter 12 dealing with his convalescence in England and Wales in late 1918 (three letters and two postcards). Chapter 13 deals with the letters sent home by three brothers after the Armistice up to the final postcards they sent whilst in uniform. Both chapter 3 and chapter 6 make extensive use of Richard's diaries for 1916 and 1917, which are extremely valuable both in terms of telling us much about his day-to-day activities that is missing in the letters and as they allow us to compare what he wrote in his own private record with the information he shared with his family.

Chapter 14 deals with the aftermath of the war and its impact upon the family. There is then an analysis in chapter 15 of what the corpus as a whole can tell us about the impact of the war upon the brothers, their family and the wider community. Taking a step back allows us to consider the changing perspectives of the Eustis family at war, and questions of masculinity, belonging and identity.

This book is a partial biography of the three brothers. It is partial first because it is limited to a particular time – especially the years from 1916 to 1918. It is partial also because it draws overwhelmingly from a specific set of sources. It does not attempt to capture the complete arc of the three brothers' lives. It is also partial in another sense, in that the editor – and perhaps the reader also – cannot help but be emotionally involved in the subject matter. I doubt it is possible for anyone to immerse themselves in this source material and not get to like the three brothers.

Notes

1. One volume which gives a detailed account of a Welsh soldier's campaign on the Egypt/Palestine front, quoting from over fifty letters, is Rhys David, *Tell Mum Not to Worry: A Welsh Soldier's World War One in the Near East* (Cardiff: Deffro, 2014). Another, which includes almost eighty letters written by three serving brothers is G. D. Roberts, *Witness these letters: Letters from the Western Front 1915–18* (Denbigh: Gee, 1983).

2. Key works which explore the 'Welsh' dimension to the First World War are Robin Barlow, *Wales and World War One* (Llandysul: Gomer, 2014) and Matthew Cragoe and Chris Williams (eds), *Wales and War: Society, Politics and Religion in the Nineteenth and Twentieth Centuries* (Cardiff: University of Wales Press, 2007).

3. For much of the information about Eustis genealogy I am indebted to the late Eurwen Mascall, who engaged in very detailed work in the 1970s and 1980s.

4. D. Hugh Matthews, '"Eithr Duw…" – Dechreuadau Caersalem Newydd, 1839–1841', *Trafodion Cymdeithas Hanes y Bedyddwyr* (1991), 43–52.

5. The newspaper report, 'Transvaal Refugees', *South Wales Daily Post*, 28 November 1899, 4, confuses the names.

6. Further correspondence has survived in another family archive between the family in Wales and Mercy Ann, another of the Eustis siblings who emigrated to Canada early in the twentieth century.

7. See Appendix 2.

8. O. T. Hopkins, 'Awr gyda Gwyrosydd', *Y Darian*, 18 July 1918, 3.

9. Robert Bevan, 'The Welsh Language in Fforestfach (Glamorgan), 1891–1901', *Studia Celtica*, XLVI (2012), 165–90.

10. See Brynley F. Roberts, 'Diwylliant y Ffin', in Hywel Teifi Edwards (ed.), *Cwm Tawe* (Llandysul: Gomer, 1993), pp. 45–80.

11. The Independent denomination in Wales ('Annibynwyr' in Welsh) is analogous to the Congregationalists in England.

12. 'Famous Choir Leader', *Cambria Daily Leader* (hereafter *CDL*), 24 November 1913, 6. See also 'The success of the Treboeth choir', *The Cambrian*, 30 December 1904, 6.

13. 'Moriah, Treboeth', *CDL*, 17 October 1913, 4; 'Treboeth Lecture', *CDL*, 1 December 1913, 5.

14. 'Treboeth Concert', *CDL*, 8 December 1913, 5; 'Mynyddbach', *CDL*, 17 March 1913, 2.

15. 'Treboeth', *Herald of Wales* (hereafter *HoW*), 23 September 1916, 2.

16. 'Beirniadaethau', *Y Darian*, 17 June 1915, 7; 'Beirniadaethau', *Y Darian*, 20 July 1916, 6.

17. Gerard J. DeGroot, *Blighty: British Society in the era of the Great War* (London and New York: Longman, 1996), p. 10. Cf. the poetry considered in the *Gowertonian* in chapter 4.

18. Even talented poets could include this awkward rhyme: see the poem by Gwyrosydd quoted in Alan Llwyd, *Colli'r Hogiau: Cymru a'r Rhyfel Mawr 1914–1918* (Llandysul: Gomer, 2018), p. 264.

19. Gwyrosydd, 'Cadfloedd Rhyddid', *Y Genhinen* 2, XXXIII (April 1915), 76.

20. Typescript poem in the collection of Marianne Eustis.

21. 'The Welsh Congress', *CDL*, 8 July 1913, 3. See also the report of a public lecture on this topic: 'Mynyddbach, ger Abertawe', *Y Tyst*, 10 October 1917, 4.

22. At least nine articles about the underground chapel were published in *Llais Llafur* in 1900; there were six articles published in *Cymru* between 1900 and 1903, and an article in the *Sunday Magazine* in 1899 was reprinted in a number of American newspapers.

23. For an image of this memorial see *http://walesatwar.org/en/memorial/detail/1416* (accessed January 2018). See Appendix 2 for details of which servicemen on these local memorials are named in the letters.

24. For a detailed analysis of this memorial and the men named on it, see Gethin Matthews, *Gwrol Ryfelwyr Caersalem Newydd* (Treboeth: Treboeth History Society, 2014). For an image, see *http://walesatwar.org/en/memorial/detail/1400* (accessed January 2018).

25. Both these memorials were created by Ivor S. Rees of Plasmarl. The frame for the first cost 7s. 6d; the second Roll of Honour cost £7 (information from the accounts books of the chapel: WGAS, D/D Ind 24, 6 and 9). For images of these memorials, see *http://www.walesatwar.org/en/memorial/detail/1414* (accessed January 2018).

26. Dewi Eirug Davies, *Byddin y Brenin* (Abertawe: Tŷ John Penry, 1988), pp. 131–43.

27. Gethin Matthews, '"For Freedom and Justice": The Responses of Chapels in the Swansea Area to the First World War', *Welsh History Review*, 28.4 (December 2017), 676–710.

28. For Caersalem Newydd see *Gwrol Ryfelwyr*, pp. 3–4. The accounts books of Mynyddbach (WGAS, D/D Ind 24 6; 9) show a variety of payments and special collections from 1915 onwards.

29. 'Mynyddbach', *CDL*, 28 October 1918, 4.

30. Charlotte Rees can be seen in a 1923 photograph of the staff of Tirdeunaw School, included in *Treboeth Historical & Pictorial Record* (Treboeth: Treboeth History Society, 2013), p. 87.

31. Martyn Lyons, *The writing culture of ordinary people in Europe, 1860–1920* (Cambridge and New York: Cambridge University Press, 2013), p. 55.

32. Martha Hanna, 'A Republic of Letters: The Epistolary Tradition in World War I France', *American Historical Review*, 108.5 (December 2003), 1338–61, 1348.

33. For details of the censorship, see RE1917-02-26 in ch. 3.

34. For more details see Ifor ap Glyn, '"Dear Mother, I am very sorry I cannot write to you in Welsh …": Censorship and the Welsh Language in the First World War', in Julian Walker and Christophe Declercq (eds), *Languages and the First World War: Communicating in a Transnational War* (London: Palgrave Macmillan, 2016), pp. 128–41, 133–5.

35. IE1918-02-12 (ch. 9).

36. GE1918-07-27 (ch. 10).

37. Michael Roper, *The secret battle: emotional survival in the Great War* (Manchester and New York: Manchester University Press, 2009), p. 6.

38. In addition to the daily edition, both of these newspapers produced a weekly digest: the *Herald of Wales* and the *South Wales Weekly Post*, respectively.

39. Words whose spelling have been corrected include memento, souvenir and disillusioned.

40. GE1918-04-24 (ch. 10). See Lynda Mugglestone, 'How to be "knuts" for war: refashioning male identity in WW1', available via *http://torch.ox.ac. uk/how-be-%E2%80%9Cknuts%E2%80%9D-war-refashioning-male-identity-ww1* (accessed July 2017).

41. GE1918-10-30 (ch. 10). 'Harry Freeman' is noted as naval slang from *c*.1870, with 'Harry Frees' dating from the twentieth century. See Eric Partridge, *A Dictionary of Slang and Unconventional English*, 5th edn (London: Routledge and Kegan Paul, 1961), pp. 377 and 300.

42. GE1918-02-01 (ch. 10); GE1918-12-28 (ch. 13).

43. IE1918-09-19 (ch. 9).
44. IE1918-06-02 (ch. 9); GE1918-07-27 (ch. 10).
45. IE1918-06-02 (ch. 9); GE1918-09-13 (ch. 10).
46. GE1918-04-24 (ch. 10); GE1917-02-02a (ch. 5).
47. IE1916-10-a (ch. 4).
48. IE1918-12-15 (ch. 13).
49. RE1918-05-12 (ch. 8).
50. See ch. 6, and the details in n. 23.
51. For the American Civil War the works of Bell Irvin Wiley, *The life of Johnny Reb: the common soldier of the Confederacy* (Baton Rouge: LSU Press, 1943) and *The life of Billy Yank: the common soldier of the Union* (Baton Rouge: LSU Press, 1952) are seminal.
52. David W. Blight (ed.), *When this cruel war is over: The Civil War letters of Charles Harvey Brewster* (Amherst: University of Massachusetts Press, 1992): introduction reproduced as 'A Union Soldier's Experience' in Michael Perman (ed.), *Major problems in the Civil War and Reconstruction: documents and essays*, 2nd edn (Boston: Wadsworth, 1998), pp. 134–44.
53. A key work on masculinity, which focuses upon the men's relationships with their mothers, is Roper, *The secret battle*.

2

Richard and Gabriel, 1913–1915

Tracing the activities of Richard and Gabriel Eustis, the two brothers who signed up in 1914, is difficult for the early stages of the war. The only material to have survived in the family collections from 1914 and 1915 are three letters from Richard to Ivor whilst he was training in England, one letter from Gabriel to his mother six days after he volunteered, and a few photographs that are undated but which most probably date from 1915. As Richard joined a local unit, there are a variety of snippets of information in the Swansea newspapers which help to indicate his movements, but for Gabriel we only have the brief outline offered by his naval record.

Although it is impossible to give full details of the brothers' motivation for joining up, there are both local factors and a broader picture to be considered. The public discourse stressed that it was the patriotic duty of young men to fight for Britain's cause. Once the war began the local newspapers of Swansea, just like the vast majority of newspapers from Wales and all over the United Kingdom, strongly emphasised that Britain's cause was just (and that the war was entirely the fault of Germany's evil warmongering).[1] After the initial rapid advance of the German army towards the Channel, much of the rhetoric emphasised that this was a war in defence of the homeland and its culture (and sometimes that homeland was explicitly characterised as Wales). Other factors that influenced young men to join up in the first weeks of the war were economic considerations, youthful bravado, the possibility of adventure and notions of masculinity.

For Richard, it is possible that his involvement in the war was inevitable from the moment of Britain's entry, for he was already in uniform. In July 1913, a large number of young Treboeth men joined the 3rd Welsh Field Ambulance, a Territorial force. One group that joined up en bloc was the Treboeth Temperance Brass Band: Richard, who played the cornet, was among them. It is possible to speculate about the motivation for this movement. Most of these men were colliers, working either at the Tirdonkin Colliery or (like Richard) at Mynydd Newydd. It is not known whether their employers encouraged the men to volunteer: perhaps, in addition to any patriotic motives on their part, there was the incentive that the men would receive some first aid and medical training which might come of use in the workplace. It might well have been an inducement for the volunteers that they would then go on a two-week training camp in Glanrheidiol, near Aberystwyth, in July 1913. Given that so many of them joined up together, there must have been a strong element of peer pressure. The fact that most, if not all, of the band members joined the unit led to a brief notice in the local newspaper that 'The Treboeth Temperance Brass Band will in future be attached to the 3rd Welsh Field Ambulance R.A.M.C.'[2]

The band was involved in local parades by the unit, such as that held in November 1913, and the Palm Sunday Drumhead Service in April 1914.[3] They also took part in training events such as the manoeuvres held at Mumbles in June 1914.[4] It is highly likely that on his twenty-first birthday, 18 July 1914, Richard played with the band at the annual tea of the Caersalem Newydd Sunday school.[5] A week later, the men of the 3rd WFA (8 officers and 177 other ranks) departed for Glanrheidiol.[6] Thus, when the war broke out in Europe, Richard was at a training camp at Aberystwyth together with several thousand other Territorial soldiers.

These men were not necessarily committed to becoming full-time soldiers, as they had only sworn to perform defensive duties at home. However, a host of factors made their embodiment (the term for Territorials joining the ranks) inevitable. Given the prevailing mood of support for Britain's war effort (which could, in some cases develop into war enthusiasm), there was an expectation that these men would volunteer for service overseas.[7] It is surely also pertinent that at the moment of the outbreak of war the men were serving together, away from home. Once some of their number had declared their intention to serve, the peer pressure to join would have been difficult to resist. It seems likely that Richard and the others became embodied before they spoke or corresponded to anyone at home about their decision.

As the Swansea newspapers adopted an utterly supportive attitude towards Britain's cause, within days of the outbreak of the war these publications gave prominence to examples of local men volunteering ('Joining the Colours' was the epithet of choice) and praised those individuals and organisations that were promoting recruitment. The fact that they were local men was emphasised time and again: this responded to (and fostered) a spirit of rivalry and local pride. It allowed the suburbs of Swansea to take pride that they were 'doing their bit', for those employers who could show a long 'Roll of Honour' to congratulate themselves for their patriotism, and for those chapels and churches whose young men volunteered to claim that their denomination was just as loyal as any other.[8] The sense of rivalry also operated at a wider level, with Swansea jostling with other towns to boast of its contribution, the better to prove that it was doing more than any other part of Wales. There was excitement on 21 August 1914 that the 3rd Welsh Field Ambulance, 'a Swansea unit', would be 'selected for active service abroad', though it was understood that this would not mean immediate deployment overseas.[9] Given the traditional rivalry with Cardiff, it comes as no surprise to see reports comparing Swansea's contribution with that of its eastern neighbour.[10]

Richard Eustis's diary from 1916 notes the places where he was stationed on active service: 'Aberystwyth to Shrewsbury, to Church Stretton, then to Northampton, to Ipswich, to Northampton, to Cambridge, B Section, to Northampton, to Royston, to Bedford.' Details are sketchy as to when he arrived at many of these places, but the Swansea newspapers noted that the Welsh Territorial Division was stationed at Northampton at the beginning of September, and a report on 10 September noted that 'the Swansea boys' of the 3rd WFA were being 'splendidly treated' by the people of the town.[11]

None of the letters written by Richard to his mother, aunt and sisters have survived from this period, so we only have three letters sent by him to Ivor. The first extant letter was written by Richard on 19 September 1914 from Northampton, and is reproduced here in full:

Dear Kid,

I had your epistle & was glad to hear that you'd had
a medal. Yes, I suppose there'll be no end of your telling the
tale now. I'd like to see it, but don't send it on, for fear it
should go astray, take care of it till I come & then I'll relieve
you of it. I had already seen the mugs with Johnnie Phillips.[12]
It has come out great, the only blot on the page being
W.J.Lewis. I fancy Dai John stands out even there above the
others. Why didn't you cover Bill Hayden's bladder of lard, it
looks very prominent on the P.C. [postcard]. I am enclosing
a few P.C's which are only in the way up here, but might help
to fill that album. But I suppose that Dan is tearing them
out faster than they go in. You're quite right kid you needn't
write often, but you can ask mother to send me 2 or 3 tablets
of Pynka.[13] They don't know what it is up here. I suppose
Mam sees every letter that comes around there, but I'll write
to her of course. I daresay you've heard of the chicken that
granny sent me. We had it for dinner today and those who
tasted it said they never had such a feed in their lives. I read a
letter with a Cheshire Terrier last night which he'd had from
a pal in Shorncliffe, Kent, saying that 84 of the regiment had
deserted. That is where Thos Henry is. I wonder whether
he's one of the deserters. I had a P.C. from Auntie Hannah,
saying that he'd sent home begging for fags. You'll find the
P.C. among the others. I am just going to have a bath, so I had
better close now with my best wishes to all from

Dick

I'm having such small money now that I'm sorry I can't oblige
you with a few bob, it would be different if I were at home.

We lack the knowledge to make sense of all of the references here
– we do not know what medal Ivor had been awarded, though we
might guess that it was for a sporting achievement. W. J. Lewis
was captain of the Mynyddbach rugby team in 1913–14, for
which Ivor played.[14] We do not have a copy of the photograph on
the postcard, and we cannot be sure who all the lads named are,
although Bill Hayden must be the Willie Haydn who is included on

Mynyddbach's WWI Rolls of Honour. However, we can see even in this early letter how the family's information network was taking shape. The letters that are received at home are read by all (with the mother apparently at the centre of the information network) and news of family members is disseminated. 'Auntie Hannah' is the youngest sister (b.1884) of the father. 'Thos Henry' is a cousin, Thomas Henry Matthews, son of John Eustis's sister, Margaret (b.1867). He (like Richard) had been a collier at Mynydd Newydd before the war, but had joined the Hussars on 2 September. 'Dan' is of course the youngest brother, who had just celebrated his third birthday.[15] The reference to the album indicates that the family was already collecting material about their war experiences.

The second brother to volunteer for the war was Gabriel. As with Richard, we do not have any direct evidence as to the reasons why he joined up, but it is worth considering his economic circumstances and what was going on at his workplace. He was employed at Duffryn Tinplate works when the war broke out. This industry was heavily dependent upon exports, including to some countries, such as Belgium and Austria, where the export trade came to an abrupt end on 3 August. The *Cambria Daily Leader* had an alarming front-page report three days later of the effect upon local employment, with fears that hundreds, if not thousands, would be out of work within a week. Duffryn Tinplate works, with its 1,350 employees, was listed as one that had closed, or was about to close.[16] However, the lay-offs were short-lived, and on 17 August six of the mills at the works recommenced, although the men were only on four-hour shifts.[17] It is reasonable to assume that the uncertainty of work at Duffryn and the other tinplate works was one spur for men employed there to consider volunteering.

From early September onwards, the *Cambria Daily Leader* published a series of 'Rolls of Honour', which listed the names of those who had volunteered by workplace. Richard's name is included on 11 September, among the fourteen who had joined the colours from Mynydd Newydd Colliery.[18] The list for Duffryn Steel and Tinplate Works, published the following day, contains sixty names, though not yet Gabriel's.[19] In other tinplate works (notably those in Pontardawe owned by F. W. Gilbertson), the management actively encouraged their employees to volunteer, offering inducements such as pay to their dependents and guaranteeing their jobs back at the war's end.[20] It is not clear whether such measures were used at Duffryn, but it is worth noting one report from October 1914 in which the chief of the office staff at the works was commended for having three of his four sons serving with the Colours.[21] By this stage both the Swansea daily newspapers had fully adopted a style of referring to volunteering in terms that praised the loyalty and masculinity of those who had taken the king's shilling. Words like 'honour' and 'duty' were used with a purpose, to idealise those who were in uniform and to raise questions about those who were not seen to be doing their bit. There is no doubt that Gabriel would have known most of the twenty-one men who had volunteered from Mynydd Newydd colliery by late October 1914, or the thirteen from Tirdonkin colliery, as well as dozens of those who had worked with him at Duffryn.[22] The local chapels (as happened all over Wales) put aside their moral objections to war as they accepted the assertion that Britain's cause was just. By late September, twenty-two men from Caersalem Newydd had volunteered (a figure that included up to fourteen men with the 3rd WFA). Gabriel's is the twelfth name on the Mynyddbach chapel Roll of Honour (which is ordered, more or less, by the date of volunteering).

Gabriel joined the Royal Navy on 7 November 1914, RNVR number Bristol Z282, with the rank 'ordinary telegraphist'. His enrolment form says his chest measured 33 in., he was 5' 6¾" tall, with fair complexion, dark brown eyes and brown hair.

The only letter from this period to have survived dates from 13 November 1914, and was sent from 'Hepburn Rd, Stokes Croft, Bristol'.

GE1914-11-13

Dear mother,

I am writing to let you know how things are going here. As I said before I have a nice landlady & a nice place. We get good food & plenty of variety & there is no stinting it. Today we had a bit of a novelty (for me at any rate) at dinner we had boiled leeks instead of cabbage & they were all right too. We had about 20 minutes squad drill to-day, right turn, left turn, form fours etc., preparatory to going on a route march to-morrow Saturday. We are to be sent to the

Crystal Palace, London on Monday by the 12 o'clock train but if there are any letters for me they'll be sent on after me. I am told that within a week or two we'll be given our kits, bell bottoms, pneumonia blouse etc. won't I look a fright in them? We are also to be given 2 suits of under-clothing so everything's allright. I've had a letter from Ivor Humphries to-day to say he's going to join to-morrow if he'll pass.[23] About [*60 per cent crossed out*] ½ of them are sent back daily from here, some very big chaps being sent back yesterday through defective eyesight or teeth. How are things going down there just now? Have you had any letters from Dick lately & what does he say, has he shifted from Coddenham? Is father working every day now? Is Danny still going to school? How often does he have a scrap with Arthur now?

We are to march to the station on Monday, starting out about 11-0 with the scouts band, a squad of bluejackets, and a small cannon. Gipsy Smith is here in Bristol. I hope to go & hear him Sunday night.[24] Did Willie Evans bring my pay & how much was it?[25] Ask him how is the Duffryn going now. I'm writing this in the messroom now & as I expect the order to 'fall in' any minute, I will now close, with best love to all at home,
Gab

Again, we do not have sufficient knowledge to make sense of every single piece of information here – we do not know who Arthur was – but the letter as a whole fits the pattern of a family conversation about friends and neighbours. Willie Evans was also a Mynyddbach man working at Duffryn tinplate who volunteered for the navy at much the same time as Gabriel. It appears that Ivor Humphreys (as his name was usually spelt) did not join the navy until 1917. Both of these men appear in subsequent letters by the Eustis brothers. The reference to the evangelist Gipsy Smith could be taken as an indication that Gabriel took his Christian faith seriously: one can surmise that his mother would have been glad to hear that he was keeping up his attendance at religious services.

Gabriel's naval record confirms that he was at the Signal School in Crystal Palace until March 1915. The next extant letter from Gabriel was written in November 1916: information regarding his progress from 1915 onwards is outlined in chapter 5.

The reference to Coddenham, which is 8 miles north of Ipswich, fits in with Richard's list of places he had served: he was based here between two stints at Northampton. Many Welsh newspapers have detailed reports of the activities of the Welsh Territorials at Northampton, including a glowing report of a Welsh service held on 20 September in a chapel with room for a thousand that was full to capacity.[26] Three months later it was reported that the division had left Northampton for Cambridge, with Richard's unit (described in the local paper as the 'Swansea Ambulance') departing at 2 a.m. on 22 December.[27]

The next letter to have survived was written by Richard to Ivor from Portugal Place, Cambridge on 13 January 1915. It was clearly sent with a package attached, the contents of which are unknown.

RE1915-01-13

Dear Kid,

Just a line in answer to yours. You needn't send me any writing material, for I have just dropped on a cosy little spot where I can have plenty, free of charge. As for coming home, well, there are so many rumours about. I don't think that we'll be able to come till the match is over. I heard from Gib that Dai Cockett had joined something or other and that he had been speaking with him in London. By the way, Gib is coming down here to spend a week end. It seems to me that he is having the cream of this affair. Never mind, let's hope that it will soon be over, & that we'll soon be home again together. Yes the colleges will be open but from what I hear, there won't be many in them while this affair is on.

I haven't seen any boating yet as the river on which they row has been flooded ever since we've been here, but I've been through most of the colleges, & fine old buildings they are too, especially King's Coll & Church. It is the finest Church I've ever been in, being illuminated by candles, & they say that it has the second best choir in the world, only Westminster being considered better.

The letter finishes with an apology that he was unable to send Ivor anything for Christmas, but that he hopes that the contents of this package will make up for it.

The only other letter from 1915 to have survived was written to Ivor by Richard from Portugal Place, Cambridge on 13 March. Richard had clearly just returned from a visit home, as the letter begins with an apology that due to a misunderstanding and a rushed exit they had not had the opportunity to say 'goodbye'. The letter continues:

RE1915-03-13

I'm very sorry to hear that you've been laid up Ivor, but never mind, I hope it won't last very long. How is Danny? Did he kick up a fuss after I'd gone. I'll send him an engine as soon as I spot one …

Well we played the Cheshires today, & were photographed again before starting, but I don't think they'll make postcards so it doesn't matter. It was a regular Mynyddbach team today, with Harry Lewis, Johny Phillips, in the forwards, I was inside half, & Dai Rees Thomas played centre.[28] We beat them by 17 pts to 3, & the Mynydd boys gave a very good account of themselves allround. I shall send you a P.C. of the team as soon as I can get hold of one. As for that postage for the kitbag I have no change tonight, but I shan't forget it. No more this time hoping that you have quite recovered from the Flu.

Dick

There are no further letters in the family archive from either brother for the period of over a year. There are, however, some photographs amongst the Eustis family treasures that certainly come from the first year of the war. It is unclear how much home leave Richard and his comrades in the 3rd WFA had, but there are photographs of Richard Eustis together with Dai Rees Thomas and others in a garden, probably that of Dai's home in Roger Street.

Apparently there was once in existence another photograph, which must have been taken prior to July 1915, featuring Ivor in his cricket whites alongside his elder brothers in their uniforms. It is more than likely that this was the final time the brothers were together until after the end of the war.

2.1: Richard Eustis (on the right); Dai R. Thomas (centre), plus an
unknown comrade and boy

2.2: Richard Eustis

Richard Eustis's unit, the 1/3rd Welsh Field Ambulance was attached to the 53rd (Welsh) Division. This was made up of a number of Territorial units, most of which were from the different Welsh regiments and the Cheshire Regiment. The division moved from Cambridge to Bedford in May 1915, where training continued until early July when they were ordered to prepare for service in the Mediterranean. The 1/3rd WFA (comprising ten officers and 197 ORs) embarked upon the *SS Wiltshire* at Devonport on 14 July, sailing a couple of days later.[29] Thus Richard celebrated his twenty-second birthday on 18 July 1915 at sea. After passing Gibraltar and briefly stopping at Malta the ship arrived at Alexandria on 26 July. Letters were written home to Swansea by the soldiers: extracts from a letter by Lieut. Quick, attached to the unit, noted that he had 'just finished censoring a bundle of letters of the men, who are ALL IN EXCELLENT SPIRITS and delighted with the voyage and the food. They have a concert every night.'[30]

From Alexandria, the unit sailed to the Greek island of Lemnos, arriving on 6 August. This was a base for the Gallipoli campaign, which was about to undergo a new initiative to break the deadlock. British and Dominion troops began the attack upon Suvla Bay late on 6 August; two days later soldiers from the 53rd Division began to land, with Richard's unit disembarking on 11 August, by which time the entire venture was in confusion. There were tremendous losses as the troops battled against the conditions as well as the Turkish soldiers who were in well-defended positions. The bases set up by the field ambulance units were hit by shells, and a number of men from the 1/3rd WFA were killed.[31] One who was wounded on 22 August was Walter Evans, one of the Treboeth contingent.[32]

Having arrived in the blazing summer, the soldiers remained through the autumn and into the winter. Very little first-hand information is available for this period from Richard. In his diaries for 1916 and 1917 he gives a list of places he has served in, noting that he was at A Beach, B Beach and C Beach. He recalls in a subsequent letter that he suffered a blizzard while at Suvla Bay.[33] The hopelessness of the campaign soon became apparent to all, and the troops at Suvla were pulled out in the second week of December. The 1/3rd WFA travelled via Imbros and Lemnos to Alexandria, arriving on 19 December. Thus Richard spent his second Christmas away from home on Egyptian soil.

Despite the absence of any first-hand information from Richard, it is possible to build a picture of how the actions of his unit were understood by the people of Swansea by reading the contemporary reports in the local newspapers. Whatever the reality on the ground, the campaign at Suvla Bay was presented by the *Cambria Daily Leader* as it happened as a success, with reports of 'fresh progress' and 'an appreciable gain of ground'.[34] Then, when the forces were pulled out, the *South Wales Weekly Post* deemed it a 'brilliant operation', with an explanation of 'how the Turks were hoodwinked'.[35] In 1916 Swansea men serving in the 1/3rd WFA were singled out for praise for their actions in the 'tragic but glorious story of the Suvla Bay expedition'. Lance-Cpl Clifford Jones recounted the story of how he was mentioned in dispatches for saving a comrade.[36] When Sgt Harold F. Phillips was awarded the Distinguished Conduct Medal, the *Cambria Daily Leader* boasted that 'Another of Swansea's sons has earned honour by his heroic conduct on the field of battle'.[37] Extensive extracts from Pte George Rogers's diary gave a 'vivid record of Swansea boy's work'.[38] Thus we can be confident that the Eustis family at Mynyddbach were presented with a narrative of courageous actions and heroic sacrifice by Richard's unit. We do not have any evidence to judge what they made of this tale, nor how they coped with the anxiety of being separated from two of their sons. Up to this point, there had only been a limited number of local casualties, with only one death of a serviceman from the Treboeth/Tirdeunaw/Mynyddbach area.[39] However, more young men from the area were joining up every month, and given that conscription was on the horizon and Ivor was eighteen years old, John and Mary Eustis surely knew that a third son was soon to be in uniform.

Notes

1. Meilyr Powel, 'The Welsh press and the July Crisis of 1914', *First World War Studies*, 8 (2017), *http://doi.org/10.1080/19475020.2017.1385408* (accessed December 2017).
2. 'Treboeth Brass Band', *CDL*, 30 July 1913, 3.
3. 'The Citizen Army', *CDL*, 1 December 1913, 5; 'Drumhead Service', *CDL*, 4 April 1914, 1.
4. 'The "Battle" of Mumbles Hill', *CDL*, 22 June 1914, 8.
5. 'Public Notices', *CDL*, 16 July 1914, 4.
6. 'Territorial Camp', *Cambrian News*, 31 July 1914, 8.

7. One needs to be careful before using words like 'jingoism', given that Britain's efforts were widely understood as defensive: see Catriona Pennell, *A Kingdom United: Popular Responses to the Outbreak of the First World War in Britain and Ireland* (Oxford: Oxford University Press, 2012), especially chapters 1 and 2.

8. For more on the latter issue, see Gethin Matthews, '"For Freedom and Justice": The Responses of Chapels in the Swansea Area to the First World War', *Welsh History Review*, 28.4 (December 2017), 685–94.

9. 'Active Service', *CDL*, 24 August 1914, 3.

10. See 'Service Abroad', *CDL*, 24 August 1914, 1, and Matthews, 'For Freedom and Justice', 685.

11. 'Welsh Territorials', *CDL*, 5 September 1914, 6; 'A Poem from Northampton', *CDL*, 10 September 1914, 4.

12. See Appendix 2.

13. Pyn-ka was a polish for metal, glass and silver goods, sold in tablets.

14. A photograph of this team can be seen in *Treboeth Historical & Pictorial Record* (Treboeth: Treboeth History Society, 2013), p. 61.

15. A photograph of Thomas Henry Matthews in uniform, alongside his little brother Daniel, is on the cover of Gethin Matthews (ed.) *Creithiau*.

16. 'Many men idle', *CDL*, 6 August 1914, 1.

17. 'Duffryn to restart', *CDL*, 14 August 1914, 1.

18. 'Roll of Honour', *CDL*, 11 September 1914, 3.

19. 'Roll of Honour', *CDL*, 12 September 1914, 6.

20. 'Pontardawe Steel, Tinplate and Galvanizing Works', *Llais Llafur*, 5 September 1914, 8.

21. 'Three sons with the Colours', *CDL*, 24 October 1914, 6.

22. Roll of Honour supplement, special souvenir edition of the *CDL*, 23 October 1914, 1 and 2.

23. See Appendix 2.

24. Rodney 'Gipsy' Smith was 'probably the best-known and most successful international evangelist of his day': John A. Vickers, 'Smith, Rodney (1860–1947)', *Oxford Dictionary of National Biography* (Oxford: Oxford University Press, 2004); online edn, October 2013 *https://doi.org/10.1093/ref:odnb/36155* (accessed July 2017).

25. See Appendix 2.

26. Rev. Robert Lewis, 'Yn Northampton', *Y Goleuad*, 9 October 1914, 4.

27. 'Farwell Northampton', *CDL*, 23 December 1914, 10.

28. For David Rees Thomas see Appendix 2.

29. C. H. Dudley Ward, *History of the 53rd (Welsh) Division (T.F.) 1914–1918* (Cardiff: Western Mail, 1927), p. 250.

30. 'Swansea Field Ambulance out in the Mediterranean', *SWWP*, 7 August 1915, 2.

31. For more on this, see the diary entries of Lieut. Charles Nyhan of the RAMC, available online via *http://www.mywelshancestry.co.uk/ Arthur%20Jones/Diary%20of%20an%20RAMC%20Lt%20-%20 Suvla%20Bay.html* (accessed July 2017).

32. See 'Treboeth Boy Wounded', *CDL*, 13 September 1915, 3.

33. RE1917-11-14 (ch. 6): the blizzard of November 1915 froze 280 men to death.

34. 'Hard fighting at Suvla', *CDL*, 9 September 1915, 5; 'Gallipoli gains', *CDL*, 8 October 1915, 1.

35. 'Brilliant operation', *SWWP*, 25 December 1915, 6; 'The Suvla withdrawal', *SWWP*, 8 January 1916, 7.

36. 'At Suvla Bay', *CDL*, 1 February 1916, 3.

37. 'Gallant action wins D.C.M.', *CDL*, 4 February 1916, 3.

38. 'At Suvla Bay', *CDL*, 12 May 1916, 2.

39. David Williams of the Rifle Brigade died at an army camp in Aldershot in March 1915: see 'Brynhyfryd soldier's death', *CDL*, 5 March 1915, 6.

3

Richard Eustis in Egypt, 1916–February 1917

By the beginning of 1916, Richard had been a full-time soldier for sixteen months and had experienced the traumatic conditions at Gallipoli for four months. After arriving in Egypt, the 1/3rd Welsh Field Ambulance was posted with the rest of the 53rd (Welsh) Division to Wardan, a base about 25 miles north of Cairo.[1] No letters have survived from the first nine months of the year, and only four for the period October 1916 to February 1917, but Richard's diaries from 1916 and 1917 have survived. They are Boots pocket editions, 4 inches by 3 inches. None of the entries are lengthy, and some are very difficult to read, but on the whole they give a good sense of his mood and preoccupations at the time.

In the very first entry, for New Year's Day, Richard notes 'Writing to M.L.' This is Mary Lizzie Morgan, his sweetheart. Throughout the diary there are many mentions of letters being sent to her (at least twenty-seven), or received from her (at least twenty letters and two parcels). It is not clear how advanced their relationship was when the war started, but they were certainly not engaged. She was a year younger than Richard, being seventeen years old at the time of the 1911 Census. She was then recorded as a domestic servant, living with her grandmother and two uncles in Morriston: the family was bilingual save for the grandmother who declared that she spoke only Welsh.

On this issue of language, it is worth noting that the diaries are exclusively in English. As will be seen, almost all of Richard's surviving letters are almost entirely in English: some have a smattering of Welsh words, and half of one letter was written in Welsh. There is evidence in the 1917 diary that he did write in the language to one other correspondent: he notes on two occasions that he wrote to William Davies in Welsh.[2]

Other parcels were received from a variety of friends and relatives, including at least six from 'home'. Occasionally the contents of the parcels and letters are noted: some included photographs; one included cigarettes; one from home included a watch and a mouthorgan (eliciting the comment 'Great'); but mostly they contained food. Unfortunately, one that arrived from home on 7 January was spoilt, but others were much appreciated: Richard notes that the parcel received from home on 1 October was 'Beautiful'. The contents of parcels were shared amongst the peer group, and so helped to cement the bonds between comrades.[3] Very often the diary notes that Richard wrote to relatives and friends a day or so after receiving something from them.

Other themes that are common throughout the diary are present in this first entry, for 1 January 1916. He notes that he was paid the equivalent of £3 in Egyptian money: some of this was later spent on a bottle of beer. Food is a persistent issue, sometimes to the point of obsession. On 1 January he had a tin of salmon ('Fine') and some tea. He notes 'Ivor Lewis came into our tent' and they went to the canteen together (for the beer) and later to the YMCA. This is (Edward) Ivor Lewis, who, like Richard, was employed at Mynydd Newydd and joined the 3rd WFA in July 1913.[4] The diary is full of references to friends and comrades, many of whom are referred to in the surviving letters. His best friend, referred to as 'Dai', was Dai Rees Thomas.

There are also some disquieting events reported in the diary. On 1 January 1916 he notes 'Sgt Holmberg let off a gun in tent. Still ringing in my ears dinner time.' There are many reports of fights in the early months of the year. On 7 January Richard gave a man called Bates a hiding. On 16 January there was a 'Deuce of a row in tent.' It appears that some of the bad feeling was caused by playing cards for money: there are many mentions of playing pontoon, sometimes under the influence of alcohol. There are other outlets for the men's aggression: for most weeks of the time at Wardan there are reports of rugby matches played (and usually won) by Richard's unit, and a number of soccer matches (where victories were less common).

Being close to Cairo, it wasn't long before the troops had the opportunity to visit and enjoy the sights of the city. Richard's chance came on 15 January, when he travelled to the city with Dai and a comrade he names only as 'Hutchings':

> Left Wardan for Cairo 8.a.m. Arr. Cairo. Breakfast. Train to Pyramids. Mounted a camel each. Went into Shadow of the Sphinx. Photos taken. Into Gheiza Pyramid. No boots. Wonderful. Like glass, all Marble Granite & Alabaster. Met Letherland in there.

3.1: Richard Eustis (centre) and Dai R. Thomas (left) in front of the Great Pyramid and Sphinx

A photograph of Richard, Dai and another (presumably Hutchings) was made into a postcard and sent to Aunt Charlotte:

> Do you see the little black Arab standing between Dai & myself? Only his hat can be seen plainly. The one kneeling in front was the guide we had for the day. His name is Ali Maghoub Elgabri, & he treated us fairly well. The Pyramid is about 3/4 mile behind us
>
> > Dick

In the early months of 1916 the unit was recovering its strength and retraining. Recorded in the diary are multiple route marches, physical drills and stretcher drills, and a variety of lectures. Richard had plenty of guard duty, responsibilities at the hospital and a few trips to Cairo with patients. There were also times of inactivity: 'Nothing doing' is a familiar refrain. The men became accustomed to the desert conditions – Richard notes a variety of instances of unfamiliar weather, such as on 2 March: 'Extraordinary sight. Could see a sandstorm coming. Hell of a gale.'

On 24 April Richard's unit moved north-west to Wadi Natrun (a six-hour journey). The first death noted in the diary occurred four days later:

> [28 April] Alf Lloyd, one of our number, died with dysentery. I gave a hand to lay him out ... Very sad affair

> [29 April] We bury him about half hour's walk from the camp. An European resident in a native village here made him a beautiful wreath. A very impressive service. Full military funeral. Volleys and 'Last Post'.[5]

The routine at Wadi Natrun was similar to that at Wardan, except that the heat precluded the opportunity to play much rugby. Instead, there are many reports of going for a swim. Richard also took up giving haircuts to his comrades.

He briefly returned to Wardan at the end of May before moving on to Heliopolis on 29 May. Now a suburb of eastern Cairo, this was an upmarket area with some of the grandest facilities in Egypt, including the Heliopolis Palace Hotel which had been turned into the 1st Australian General Hospital by 1916. Richard noted that Heliopolis was 'Far prettier than Cairo. Some beautiful buildings. Open air cinemas.' However he and his friends still enjoyed their many visits to Cairo, and one entry that stands out in his diary is that of 1 June: 'Met Australian who knew my Granddad & uncles in Sth Africa.' The diary continues to note letters to and from home, but the only one to survive from this period is a postcard to Mary Lizzie of Kasr-El-Nil Bridge, written on 5 June:

> A view of the prettiest bridge in Cairo, spanning the Nile. It has a pair of lions on each end, carved out of marble, which are worth seeing. I spent the day in Cairo yesterday, & enjoyed myself. I will write a letter as soon as I have a chance
>
> > Dick

The entry for 19 June notes 'Went to Cairo for the last time': his unit moved out from Heliopolis on 20 June to Moascar. This camp was about six miles east of Ismailia, which is on the west bank of the strategically vital Suez Canal. Turkish forces had been advancing across the Sinai Peninsula and were seeking the opportunity to attack the canal, so the 53rd (Welsh) Division were moved to defensive positions along the waterway. The weather was extremely hot, but swimming was possible most days in Lake Timsah: the comment 'beautiful' is common.

On 3 July he was given the duty of looking after the Pack Store (the room in the hospital where the patients' belongings and kit were kept). This was his job for much of the following months, though there were plenty of other activities such as route marches. On his twenty-third birthday, 18 July, he wrote letters to Mary Lizzie, Gabriel, Ivor and his mother, and then: 'Went to Dai Lougher's funeral. Very sad.'[6]

After one route march and a swim on 3 August, the diary entry notes 'Two enemy planes came over, dropped twelve bombs. No damage.' Later that day the Battle of Romani began some 40 miles to the north-east, when Turkish forces sought to attack British positions guarding the northern approaches to the Suez Canal. Their attacks were repulsed and this would mark the end of Turkish attempts to threaten the canal. Indeed, the retreating Ottoman forces were pushed all the way back to their base at El Arish, and the next phase of the war in this theatre was an Allied advance across the Sinai Peninsula.

However, although elements of the 53rd (Welsh) Division were involved at Romani, Richard's unit was for the time being well away from the battlefield action. From 12 August onwards there are entries recording practices of the male voice choir and a number of concerts, including one at the 1st Australian General Hospital on 15 August. After further practices, the choir performed their biggest concert, noted both in the entry for 23 August and in a separate note at the end of the diary:

> Concert aboard the H.M.S. Euryalis Cruiser. Admiral Weamis enjoyed it.[7] Came to speak with us. Greatest reception I ever had. 850 crew. Never heard such applause. Took us round to see the guns 6 in, & 9.2. Electric, Hydraulic & Manual. Wonderful. Hospital[ity?] Great. Welsh Chaplain delighted with Welsh singing. Motor pinnace took us back, motor van took us from Quay to the camp.

The next day the unit left Moascar for El Fardan (on the Suez Canal three miles north of Ismailia). Richard noted 'Nice spot but will miss my swim', but a few days later he was on the move again. The location of Richard's next camp is uncertain: the list of Richard's postings at the beginning of the diary states 'Rail Head'.

The diary for this period is full of non-military activities. Soccer returned on 24 September (Richard's unit lost 2–1 to the Cheshire Royal Field Artillery). Within three weeks he would note that they 'Have a game of football after tea every night', and presumably it is the round-ball game as on 17 October he notes 'Soccer all the rage.' The iced beer available in the canteen was much appreciated, and there were games of pontoon and musical evenings. On 11 October Richard had his first cornet practice for a long while: he noted 'Would soon pick it up.'

The next day he sent a letter home, the first from Egypt to have survived in the collection.

RE1916-10-12

Dear Mother,

Just a few lines to say that I received your letter dated
Sept 25th also one of your parcels containing fags & tinned
stuff. I am very glad to learn that Granny is better hoping
that by the time you receive this, she will be quite alright
again. I cannot blame Dan for not going to school, for I well
remember my school days. It's not bad of Miss Williams to
send him a ball. How is Nance getting on down there? I think
she must be giving satisfaction or she wouldn't be made such
a fuss of by her mistress.[8] Let her stick to it, & I don't think
she will be worse off for it. I cannot help laughing about Dan
and his dug-out on the tip of Pwll Jones. I had a letter from
Gabe last night saying that he was alright & had been having
his teeth out. Well I'm expecting to be sent to have my teeth
out too. Well Mam, I cannot believe that the Band have gone
to Mesopotamia or I would have heard from Jack Phillips,
for he writes to me now & again, and I'm sure that if he had
gone he would have written to tell me. Well things are going
on just the same here with me, nothing to grumble about. The
same old thing day after day, & it is getting very monotonous.
We get an occasional swim in the Suez Canal, which is about
5 or 6 miles away. Oh well it cannot go on for ever, & I
sincerely hope that it will all be over before Ivor will have
to go out to France, for that climate is not very healthy at
present. I don't expect Harry Watkins to go, for I don't think
they would take a boss-eyed Johnnie like him.[9] Anyhow, they
wouldn't give him a gun, or he might do more harm than
good. It is not quite as hot here now as it has been these last
couple of months, but it is still too hot to be comfortable, &
it's very little work we do during the hot hours of the day.
I have heard that Jack John has been wounded.[10] Is it right?
And what has he had? He was home, if you remember, the
same time as I was on my last leave from Bedford. How is
Uncle Dai getting on in Glasgow?[11] Gabe says he doesn't
stand a chance of seeing him. Well I think I have told you all
this time again, so I close with love to you all from
      Dick

He failed to post the letter that day, and so he wrote a postscript on 16 October: 'I have received the tin of biscuits. Will write again in a day or two.'

His diary shows that it was on 23 October when he next wrote to his mother, when he also wrote letters to Ivor and Uriel Rees. However, once again there is a gap in the collection, and none of his letters from the next two months have survived. This was clearly a relaxed period for Richard: his entry for 24 October reads 'Having the time of my life. Doing nothing all day. Dinner. Swim. Tea. Grub in the mess.' The unit's military activities during this period appear to have been minimal: 'Lying about' is a very common refrain. Many of the entries mention listening to the gramophone, and there is plenty of football and rugby. On 7 November Richard played rugby for the base against the Australian Light Horse but lost a fast game by nine points. The next day he was 'Stiff as a broom. Effects of the match.'

The unit returned to El Ferdan on 18 November, and on that day they won a rugby match against the Royal Engineers by nineteen points. Richard scored in this game and the post-match celebrations must have been vigorous: the diary notes that Richard 'swam across the canal after lights out'. However, from this point on there are many more reports in the diary of drills, fatigues, kit inspections and training. On 28 and 29 November Richard had 'Camel instruction' – he noted that the animals were 'Stinking like skunks'. The entry for 7 December reads 'Drills again. Camels. Am sick of the smell of them. Tea. Swim. Canteen.'

There was still time for rugby (despite a twisted knee Richard suffered while doing drills), and for musical activities. The entry for Saturday 16 December reads:

> Choir practice. Concert at 2 p.m. Miss Lena Ashwell party. Beautiful. Miss Francon Davies singing Welsh. Fine. Most beautiful concert I've heard in Egypt. Thoroughly enjoyed it. Tea. We gave the first half of the Concert. Fine, about 800 present.[12]

After over a month without any reports of incoming mail, on 20 December Richard received numerous letters including one from Ivor and a parcel from his mother. This prompted a letter home, which has survived:

RE1916-12-20

Dear Mother,

Just a few lines to thank you for the parcel of biscuits and pudding, which I received today. The biscuits are going great, but as yet, I haven't sampled the pudding, but I daresay it will be famous for it looks beautiful. I received a parcel from Rev. J. Davies the other day on behalf of the members of Mynyddbach Chapel, and he included a little case of ink tablets, which I took as a hint to use the pen. I acknowledged it last Sunday, and I daresay you'll hear even if you don't see it. Well, its gone so I hope it will arrive home there safely, and I had a letter today, too, from Ivor, enclosing one of your letters saying that you had not heard from me for something like two ['*years*' *crossed out*] months. I cannot make that out, for I write more often to you than anywhere else. Also before I had this parcel from you today I had not had a letter from you for about six weeks or two months. Not only from you but I don't get letters from anywhere, except the Penny Pictorial which I receive pretty regular from Ivor.[13]

As for Gib, I haven't heard from him for months, but of course we cannot blame him, for he spends so much time out at sea. I see Ivor has been a fine time at Altcar. Well, I hope he won't be too eager to go abroad. No doubt there is a great deal to be seen in foreign countries, but he will find that he would have to pay dearly for what he saw, the same as I've had to. Well we have spent a solid year on the sands of Egypt now, and I don't care how soon they'll take us from here again. We have been joined recently by one of our Officers who used to be with us in England. The one who gave us the dinner in Cambridge and he has arranged to give us a real turkey dinner this Xmas again. So I think we shall be alright, that is if we don't move before then, for we are expecting to go again, but God only knows where to, and what's more I don't care as long as my health remains as it is at present.

I had a day in Port Said one day last week, in fact. I only had about 4 hours there, and it is the dirtiest town I've seen in Egypt. The only notable thing about it was the entrance of the Suez Canal and the monument which they

have erected to the memory of Ferdinand de Lesseps, the
engineer of the Canal. Of course we are glad to have a day
off, if only to sit down to a really distant meal. After being
so long without such luxuries as butter and cake and such
things, you can imagine how we appreciate a good meal like
that. Well I have no more to say this time, but I am expecting
a letter from you every day. Will write again in a day or two
Love to all from
Dick

On Christmas Day there were a variety of sporting activities: a boat
race, a relay race and a rugby match against 158 Brigade which was
won by seven tries. Then: 'Canteen. Supper Officers. Drunk', so no
details as to whether the promise of turkey was fulfilled. Despite
a day of 'Lying about' on 26 December, Richard was still 'Very
stiff and sore' as they did a route march on 27 December, and his
knee was so sore that he had to sit out the rugby on 30 December.
On New Year's Eve Richard's tent shared two bottles of port wine
between them, after which he declared in his diary 'My last burst.
I'm finished with it all', which appears to be a New Year's resolution
to give up alcohol.

The year 1917 began with a week of wind and rain, despite
which the unit had to move:

[4 January] Packed up and marched to Kantara (15 miles).
Raining like blazes. Put up with the Scottish Horse. Played
them soccer & beat them. Turned in early dogtired.

[5 January] Up at 6. Packed up and marched off at 10 a.m.
another fifteen miles to a place called Gilburn. Slept in the
open. Enough dew on our sheet to wash & shave 4 men.

[6 January] Up at 5.30. Packed up and marched away at
9 a.m. Another 15 miles. We have an hour rest for mid-day
meal. Bread, cheese & water. There is not even a bush to be
seen during these marches, except sand for miles all around.
Arrived at a place called Pelusium. Not a sparrow to be
seen here again, except two or three graves of fallen heroes.
Turned in early.

[7 January] Up at 5.30. Marched off at 8. This time about
18 or 20 miles. Through Romani on to the dead city of
Mohamdiya, on the coast of the Mediterranean. Dogtired and
sore owing to septic sores on hand & leg.

For the rest of the week Richard was in pain and confined to his
tent: 'I haven't felt so bad for 15 years.' However, by 17 January he
was well enough to be back on the rugby field, where his team beat
the Australians and Richard scored the first try. They were on the
move again on 20 January, with Richard being in charge of some
camels, who gave him a 'Hell of a game.' The movement continued over the next few days: Richard's diary notes Rhaba, Khirba
and El Abd, where a very welcome mail caught up with them. As
was the case in 1916, the diary notes when letters and parcels are
received from a variety of friends and family members: this bumper
mail on 24 January contained letters from 'M.L., Gib, Ivor, Nance,
Aunt Charl[otte], Carrie, Mam' and a 'beautiful' parcel from Mary
Lizzie.

It was not just Richard's unit that was on the move during this
period, for by the end of December the EEF had secured the Sinai
Peninsula. Engineers were at work to construct a railway and water
pipeline to support the advance, and once the Allied forces were
within striking distance of the base at El Arish on the Mediterranean
coast, the Turkish forces abandoned it.

On 15 February there was 'News of a shift' and the unit
packed up their camp: two days later Richard noted that they had a
'Beautiful view of El Arish from our new camp.' He had duties in
the packstore and on the rugby field (his team won a match against
the 1st Welsh on 19 February), but throughout this period there are
also sightings of enemy planes, referred to as 'Taubes' (a monoplane
of pre-war German design). One was shot down on 14 February,
and when another Taube flew over on 21 February Richard noted
that they 'shelled like hell'. That day the mail arrived including a
letter from Aunt Charlotte, and he began his reply the following
day. This letter contains the only explicit act of censorship in the
entire collection of letters, although it is not effective. Two words,
which might have helped the reader to work out the location, have
been obliterated. However, the place given at the top of the letter,
above 'Egypt' is 'El A', which has been lazily crossed out but is still

clearly legible, so that it is possible that the family could deduce that Richard was at El Arish.[14]

RE1917-02-26

Dear Aunt,

Just a few lines to let you know that I received your letter dated Jan 29th today. You must please excuse me for not having written to you sooner, & no doubt you were wondering what had become of me. Well, we have been rather busy lately, what with moving & one thing & another, so I haven't had a chance to write anywhere. No sooner do we get settled in a camp than we are off again. I have no idea where our final destination will be for we are marching on to the **XXXX** all the time, a little further & we shall be clear of the **XXXXX** altogether, and I may say we shall not be sorry either, for we are sick & tired of this sand having been over a twelvemonth on it. I'm very sorry to hear that mother's health is not up to scratch, hoping that by the time you get this, she will be alright again. I cannot understand why mother worries about me, for surely things are not half as bad with me here as they are in France. I explained in one of my last letters that I should not be able to write so often because of this stunt, but they should not worry because of that, I can assure you that I write either to you or mother as often as I possibly can, but I know that lately letters have been slow owing to our being busy. I am very glad to hear that little Danny's health is improving & that he is such a regular attendant at school. I must say he likes it better than I used to …

Well Auntie Charlotte, perhaps you don't remember that my time is up next July, that is, the four years I signed for, so I shall apply for leave to England. Others have had it, being time-expired, & bar accidents I may have the same. Anyhow I mean to make a bid for it, but don't build you hopes on it for fear that all leave may be stopped before my time. Have you received my letter saying that I have met Trev. James Pen-y-bank out here?[15] Well. I fancy he is looking better now than ever I saw him. He was as pleased as

Punch to see the village boys, for I brought him to our camp
to see Sam Rees, D.R.Thomas, etc, etc.[16] Well we have a little
excitement here now & again, for we have hostile aeroplanes
coming over. So far, I haven't seen them dropping bombs,
for our gunners don't give them much time, and no sooner
do they come near, than they have to clear away again. Well,
all is well with me at present hoping that all at home are the
same, so I close with love to all

> from Dick

P.S. I will write as often as I possibly can.

On the same day as he began this letter, Richard wrote a declaration
towards the end of his diary, in which he and his comrades made
some plans for the future:

> Feb 22nd 1917 El Arish
>> I have to meet G.M. Ted Evans & Will James on the
> 22nd Feb. 1919 at the Load of Hay, Praed St, London, with
> the 1/4 piastre at 12 or 1 mid-day,
>> Dick Eustis

'G.M.' is George Morris Williams, one of his principal friends in
the 1/3rd WFA; it is not clear who Ted Evans is, but Will James is
undoubtedly William (Charles) James of Port Tennant, Swansea,
who also served in the 1/3rd WFA. Thus some fourteen months
after landing in Egypt, these Swansea men were envisaging meeting
in a Paddington pub two years thereafter: implicit in these plans
is that by then they will have completed their duty in the war
and defeated the enemy. However, one of them would never leave
Egypt.

Notes

1. For the experiences of soldiers who served with the EEF, the most use-
    ful works are Edward C. Woodfin, *Camp and combat on the Sinai and
    Palestine front: the experience of the British Empire soldier, 1916–18*
    (Houndmills: Palgrave Macmillan, 2012) and David R. Woodward,
    *Forgotten Soldiers of the First World War: Lost Voices from the Middle
    Eastern Front* (Stroud: Tempus, 2006). A more old-fashioned military
    history is C. H. Dudley Ward, *History of the 53rd (Welsh) Division (T.F.)
    1914–1918* (Cardiff: Western Mail, 1927).

2. Diary entries of 1 April and 18 July 1917. Although there were other local men named William Davies, this could be William Davies of Roger Street, whose brother David John Davies had signed up for the 3rd WFA at the same time as Richard.

3. Martha Hanna, 'War Letters: Communication between Front and Home Front', in Ute Daniel, Peter Gatrell, Oliver Janz, Heather Jones, Jennifer Keene, Alan Kramer and Bill Nasson (eds), *International Encyclopedia of the First World War* (2014), *http://encyclopedia.1914-1918-online.net/article/war_letters_communication_between_front_and_home_front* (accessed June 2017), p. 6.

4. See Appendix 2.

5. See 'Llandilo', *Carmarthen Journal*, 9 June 1916, 8 and *http://www.cwgc.org/find-war-dead/casualty/113061/LLOYD,%20ALFRED* (accessed January 2018).

6. See 'Toll y Rhyfel', *Y Goleuad*, 4 August 1916, 7 and *http://www.cwgc.org/find-war-dead/casualty/111031/LOUGHER,%20DAVID%20WILLIAM* (accessed January 2018).

7. Sir Rosslyn Wemyss, commander of the East Indies and Egyptian Squadron.

8. Richard's sister Hannah (Nance) was living with Mrs Williams in Montpellier Terrace, Swansea.

9. Cf. RE1918-06-03a (ch. 8).

10. This individual cannot be identified, although he might be the J. John commemorated on Caersalem Newydd's Roll of Honour.

11. This must be David Rees, his mother's youngest brother. There is another mention to 'Uncle Dai' in IE1916-06-08 (ch. 4), but nothing is known of his war service.

12. For details of Lena Ashwell's concert parties, see Margaret Leask, 'Lena Ashwell's Modern Troubadours – Entertaining the Troops, 1915–19', *Popular Entertainment Studies*, 5.1 (2014), 8–27.

13. The *Penny Pictorial* was a weekly illustrated magazine owned by Lord Rothermere that carried some war news but was mainly concerned with detective and adventure stories.

14. The British Army's advance upon El Arish in December 1916 was well reported in Welsh newspapers, e.g. 'After two years British occupy El Arish', *SWWP*, 30 December 1916, 2.

15. See Appendix 2. Richard's diary entry of 27 January notes that he met him and gave him a tin of pears.

16. Evan Samuel Rees: see Appendix 2.

4

Ivor Eustis at school, 1914–1916, and in north Wales, May–November 1916

When the war broke out Ivor was seventeen and a half years old. Once the summer holidays were over, he returned to Gowerton County School, the school attended by those pupils resident in the Swansea Rural District who had passed the entrance examination. In September 1914, Ivor received the news that he had passed the Senior Certificate of the Central Welsh Board examinations, but he remained at school for another year and a half, not just to study but also to take his place in various sports teams. After he joined the army in May 1916 he was sent to Kinmel Park, north Wales, to train, and he was stationed there (except for a short stint at another training camp) for almost another year and a half. This chapter will consider how the school community understood the war while Ivor was there, and then review the first twenty letters that have survived from his time as a soldier.

It is clear from many of Ivor's letters of 1916 to 1918 that he held Gowerton School in very high regard. In three of the letters from his first month in the army Ivor refers to a favourite teacher, Mr Jenkins, and in one he describes striving to write him a letter that would create the right impression. Two years later, when he was stationed in France, he eagerly awaited news of his sisters' attempts to gain entrance to the school and when Lottie was successful, his letters are full of joy. Thus it is worth examining the evidence that is available regarding how the war was talked about at his school while he was there.

The school produced a magazine at the end of each term, *The Gowertonian*, and it appears that the first mention of Ivor in this publication is in the cricket report at the end of the summer term of 1914.[1] Browsing through the issues of the school magazine, it is clear that the institution prized academic as well as sporting ability, and showered praise upon those alumni who gained admission to one of England's prestigious universities. Although the curriculum and ethos of the school clearly emulated an English public or grammar school, there was also a recognition of its Welsh location. The school's motto is in Welsh – 'Mi ddylwn, mi allaf, mi fynnaf' ('I should, I can, I will'). Perhaps a sixth of the material in the magazine is in Welsh (poetry and prose), and the report of the school's St David's Day celebration of 1914 proudly notes that all of the recitations and songs (except 'God Save the King') were in the Welsh language.

There is a dramatic shift in tone and content in the December 1914 issue of *The Gowertonian*. The editors note, 'As this is the first issue of the magazine since the outbreak of the war, it has been considered appropriate that it should be as far as possible a war number.' The inclusion of a Roll of Honour listing those former pupils who have 'joined the Colours at the call of their King and Country' is published 'with great pleasure' and the number of names (forty-three) is described as 'very gratifying'.[2] Amongst a host of articles that are war-related, there are essays explicitly dealing with the question of the war's purpose in both English and Welsh. A rousing patriotic poem by 'Aim High' is entitled 'England's Honour'.

The following edition is dominated by the war to almost the same extent. There are three more names for the Roll of Honour and congratulations for the five former pupils who have been promoted. 'Aim High''s poetic contribution to this issue is entitled 'England', and there is further poetry in praise of Kitchener, to go with a potted biography of Britain's Secretary of State for War. There is also space for other material, including mention of Ivor's name as one of the scorers in the school's rugby team.[3]

The July issue contains a little more non-war-related material, including extensive reports of the school's cricket team. Captained by Ivor, they had an impressive season: his personal highlight was an innings of 87 against Ystradgynlais County School.[4] The magazine also contains a blatant attempt to shame those young men who were of age but who had not enlisted to volunteer. This Welsh-language article imagines a conversation between such a man and a wise old resident regarding the necessity of volunteering now. The language is saturated with references to the righteousness of the cause: those Welshmen who take part will have their names honoured by future generations.[5] Another piece of evidence from July 1915 comes in a local newspaper where one of Ivor's classmates, Elfryn Stephens, was praised for his 'splendid spirit of patriotism' for offering to 'take the place of any local postal servant desirous of joining the colours'.[6]

The first deaths of former pupils are recorded in the issue of December 1915. Donald Davies and Tom Mitchell are listed as 'Fallen on the Field of Honour': the editors declare 'we are proud to say that they gave their lives for their King and Country'.[7] There were thirty-six further names of Old Gowertonians who had volunteered. The tone of some articles was shrill, perhaps betraying a sense of panic. A two page article 'If——?' set out in graphic terms the consequences of a German victory in the war: how the 'vile hordes' that had overrun 'a great part of Europe' would make Englishmen 'a servile band of despicable followers of German heroes'. The repeated conflation, or confusion, of 'England' and 'Britain' in this article does not leave any room for Welsh sentiment.[8]

This, then, was the way that the war was being talked about and understood as Ivor remained at school in the second year of the war. He was awarded a supplementary certificate by the Central Welsh Board in September 1915, and qualified for matriculation to the University of Wales: yet, he remained at school in the spring of 1916, as his name appears in the rugby report of April 1916.[9] In this issue, 'Aim High' contributed 'To the Sons of Wales', which urged the young men of Wales to volunteer:

'Tis not in your own country
Your homes you can defend
The battlefield is Europe,
And there the strife must end;
Then forth with mighty valour!
Strong in your freedom's might,
Follow your Prince to battle
And nobly join the fight![10]

The Roll of Honour in the *Gowertonian* of July 1916 commemorates two who had fallen in battle, including David Arthur Mort, a near neighbour of the Eustis family, who had been a teammate of Ivor's in the Mynyddbach rugby team of 1913–14. Then it lists seven names of former pupils who have joined the army, including Ivor Eustis and Elfryn Stephens, both of whom had joined the 12th RWF.[11]

No paperwork has come to light to show exactly when Ivor and Elfryn joined the army, but from their regimental numbers (Elfryn was 46143; Ivor was 46144) we can estimate it was the second half of May 1916. This was, of course, after the introduction of conscription, the Military Service Act having been passed by Parliament in January, and coming into force on 2 March. Ivor had turned 18 in March 1915: thus he chose not to volunteer for the armed forces for a period of over a year, while eligible. There is no evidence that he resisted the call-up, but neither is there evidence that he put his name forward while he had a choice in the matter.

The first item to be preserved in the family archive from Ivor as a soldier is a postcard to his mother, postmarked 26 May 1916, sent from Kinmel Park. This was the largest army camp in Wales, being where the new recruits for most of the units of the Welsh Army Corps were sent for training. Construction was begun at the camp in November 1914, and the facility expanded enormously during the course of the war, eventually consisting of twenty sub-camps and a host of facilities. A narrow gauge railway was constructed to transport people and goods to and from the mainline at Rhyl. Local newspapers contain reports that 15,000 soldiers were to be sent there in February 1915, and that there was room for 40,000 by June 1915.[12] A study of the camp paints a picture of an unhealthy and unhappy place, with reports of suicides and desertions as well as a range of fatal accidents and illnesses.[13] As will be seen, Ivor's correspondence does have plenty to say about issues of health, but in general the tone that he conveys to the family back home is one of reassurance.

This first postcard was issued by the Lancashire YMCA, and has an image of three soldiers poised ready to fight. Ivor wrote:

IE1916-05-26 Postcard

Dear Mother,
    Just to tell you that if you have not sent that box, you need not do so, because I have just been given one by a

chap who is leaving for Bedford. I am sorry to trouble you. I received your letter today and I was glad to get it too!

I find it a bit of a job to get up at 5.15 in the morning, not so much the actual getting up as the keeping awake during parades when we drill at 5.30 without a bit of breakfast until 7 o'clock. If we stand very long to attention I find my mind wandering and my eyes closing.

I will write again – Ivor.

There are a further twenty-nine letters extant written by Ivor at Kinmel Park over the next sixteen months, together with one he wrote while on a training course at Altcar (November 1916). Most of the earlier letters are undated, but it has been possible to estimate the month, at least, of every one. Much of the content of these letters is rather mundane – particularly so when there were many letters exchanged in a short period of time. There is much regarding food and a few references to money. There are also many requests to send things to the camp, as seen in the beginning of the first letter to have survived:

IE1916-06-03

Dear Mother,

Just a few lines again to keep up my reputation as a begger. This time I want some shirt buttons and some cotton to sew them with. I had three shirts when I came here, two good ones, and one second rate. Well now I have only two buttons between the lot, so that about a dozen will be quite welcome.

I have intended sending those cufflinks and the watch chain back all last week but each time I was unable to do so owing to various circumstances, so I'll do my best to send them today.

I have been expecting a letter from you these last few days but not one has arrived yet. When you write don't put the date (like May 2nd) but write the day (as Monday or Tuesday). You see, since I've been up here I have forgotten all about the date and everything, and so has everyone else. We never reckon further than 7 days in this camp, in so many days before the next pay day.

The letter goes on to ask 'Does Auntie Charlotte want Dick's letter back? if so, she can have it any time'. This is the first of many references to the sharing of letters in the collection. He also enquires whether his schoolmaster, Mr Jenkins, has called.[14]

Within the same envelope is a letter written the following day: both were posted together. This begins with a request for his mother to send him more paper, before he explains how he writes his letters.

IE1916-06-04

I am writing this in the hut now, as I have done all the latter letters. I have brought a bottle of ink, which I keep with the stationary in the box you sent with the cake; it is much better to write here if you choose your chance properly when most of the boys are out. Now at first I used to polish my things and set my bed between 8 and 9, then write letters till lights out; but we have to be in by 9.30 so that while I was writing the boys came home one by one, each kicking up a row as he came; then at 9.30 all the boys were in, so that you can bet there was some noise there. However, I have got to know little things one by one and I make a better choice, and the result is I have a clearer head to proceed with the job. I remember one letter in particular; it was to Mr Jenkins (Llangyfelach); I had tried about four times and each time I had to abandon it. However at last I determined to stick it to the end; and accordingly I started a letter straight after tea one evening, amidst all the chatter and the rattle of about 30 boys feeling healthy after a meal and exercising their lungs to the utmost. Well I got no further than beginning when I had to give up; I put the letter in the box and went out for a stroll. After about an hour and a half I returned and resumed the job of the letter; but before I had the pen in my hand properly, in came a crew from the canteen and started playing about. Well I made up my mind to stick it to the end and a terrible job it was too. At last I finished but goodness knows what the letter was like.

I noticed a few dozen mistakes when I read it over, and I had half a mind to tear it up and write another, but I thought that if I did, the next would be quite as bad so I posted it forthwith. I have received no reply so I guess I have forgotten the address to which a reply could be sent, or some other such silly mistake. Thus you see it was a difficult task at first.

Now however, I know better. I see my chance when it comes and I take it. For instance this morning (Sunday) we had a church (nonconformist) parade to a YMCA hut where the service was conducted, we returned about 10 and then the hut was nearly empty, because the other boys were on parades later than ours so that they have not returned, so that under these circumstances I can write to my heart's content. However I can hear the band playing which means that the Church of England parade is returning from Abergele, where their service was held, so that I had better dry up.

Ivor

The next extant letter was posted on 8 June 1916, and it is the first of the collection to engage directly with military matters. The great naval Battle of Jutland was fought on 31 May–1 June 1916, and it is clear that the family, not knowing Gabriel's whereabouts, were concerned that he could have been involved in the engagement. Ivor gives his Aunt Charlotte a calm and logical explanation of why she should not worry.

IE1916-06-08

Dear Auntie Charlotte,

I have just received your post card and I hasten to make the earliest reply.

First of all you want my opinion about the Naval fight. Well honestly, I am quite confident that Gib was not concerned in the awful slaughter for various reasons. If you notice Admiral Beatty sighted the enemy when <u>he</u> was cruising not far from Denmark, and he sighted the enemy <u>15 miles away</u>; after a while the enemy fled home, getting further and further away from the place Gib usually goes. Another thing, in a battle of such magnitude as that, a boat such as Saxon would be passed by as not worth wasting shot on, and in a running fight, it would soon be left behind.

Then again if Gib had started on the journey he spoke about previously, he would not have been near the place of action, because his course was much more to the north. So you see that everything points to his being clear of the fight, and I hope this opinion will be confirmed later.

So Willie Evans is safe, is he? I am very glad of that, and that the news came early, because his ship the Lion must have been right in the thick of it.[15] You have not explained much in your postcard about the why and wherefore of the return of the Evans', nor much about Uncle Dai but of course there was not much space on that card, though as it was a case of 'multum in parvo' ('much in little') as they say in Latin. Mr Jenkins has called then? I should very much like to hear about him, how long he stayed and what he had to say. You can write a book on that subject if you like; it will interest my [*sic*] greatly. I enclose Dick's letter for you; you needn't send any others along, but just let me have the pith of them as they come, and I shall be satisfied, because I have started writing to him and Gib myself. One thing I should like to know is, how long the letters take to reach him, and how much to return.

The letter finishes with thanks to Charlotte for sorting out some business at home.

The next two letters in the collection can be dated from their envelopes: both were posted on 10 June 1916 (a Saturday). They are written on YMCA paper, from 'Kinmel Park', and they deal with similar subject matter, although the tone of the second letter, to sister Hannah, is markedly different to that in the first letter, to his mother.

IE1916-06-10a

Dear Mother,

Just a few more lines of news. In the first place I have been inoculated today and to tell the truth I feel a bit bad after it. There were 150 of us under treatment and you can see the doctor had some work to do. After this we get two days excused duty and I can tell you that we need it too. But there is one good comfort, that is that you know that there are 149 others besides yourself who are in the same state. All the doctor did was to pinch the skin of the left arm between his forefinger and thumb and stick a kind of needle in, then at the same time injecting some fluid into the arm. This was quite painless, and after dinner (an hour after it was done) I scrubbed my bed and my share of the floor, without having any pain at all; but after a time my arm began to get stiff and to ache when I moved. Then I felt a bit sick, and that's how I am now; no real pain, but I feel sick and weak. I know from what the older boys tell me that it will be all right after the first two days, so I'm making the best of it. I suppose I will be no worse than the hundreds who have been inoculated before.

The night I wrote the last letter, Thomas Henry Matthews came over here to see me. His hut was only a quarter of a mile away from mine, but we never knew of each other until Polly wrote him a letter to tell him that I was here. As for myself, I always thought he was at Birmingham, that was all the last I heard of him. He is going away to Liverpool tomorrow, and he's coming over tonight to bid me goodbye. He looks all right, and other things point to the same. He has been convalescent all the time, which means that he did not do any drill, being on a kind of sick duty.

I had another visitor today in the person of Gabe Williams, he came over to see me, having heard from home that I was here.[16] His quarters are on the other side, about a quarter of a mile from here, so you see, I have been three weeks between him and Thomas Henry and never run across either of them until they heard from home that I was here. He seemed to be all right, but with a great deal less swank than when I last saw him. From what I hear, he expects to go out to France before long and of course I wish him the best of luck. Well this is all at present, so I conclude, hoping that they are all right down there, and that the effects of this inoculation will have been over by the next time of writing, with the best love

from Ivor

P.S. Don't forget to send that exercise book. I am ready for it

Thomas Henry Matthews was a cousin of the Eustis brothers – reference was made to him in Richard's letter of September 1914 – and 'Polly' is his sister, Margaret Hannah. He had been evacuated from Gallipoli in November 1915 suffering from dysentery, and was sent for recuperation first to Birmingham and then to Henley-in-Arden V.A.D. Hospital.[17] At this point in his army career he had been transferred from the SWB to the RWF. He was not sent to the front again, but was medically discharged in July 1917.

Although much of the same ground is covered in the letter Ivor wrote the same day to sister Hannah, there is more of a swagger in its tone. The envelope is addressed to Hannah c/o Mrs Williams, Montpellier Terrace (on the western side of Swansea, close to the town centre). It appears that Hannah was living there as a home-help, or possibly a maid.[18] Note that whereas in the very first letter in the collection, Richard addressed his younger brother Ivor as 'Dear Kid', now Ivor is doing the same to his younger sister.

IE1916-06-10b

Dear Kid,

I should like to know what has become of you lately, because I have received no reply again to the last 500 letters I've written to you. Fancy not writing to your beloved brother, with all the time you have to spare (not much for me, I'm afraid). So you just hurry up and scribble me a line or I'll be down there and then look out. You haven't seen me since I became a soldier, have you? Well, I'm the most brutal, merciless bully that ever trod this old camp; a look from my fierce countenance would kill an ox, so I'm sorry for the Germans I'll meet out across the water.

Well, I have a little news to spout out. First, I've met Thomas Henry Matthews who has been convalescent at this place for the last four months. He dwelt at a hut about a quarter of a mile from mine but I didn't see him anywhere until he came to see me the other night. He looks well and in the best of health something like myself only not half so fat though he is quite as big around the waist as father was. So you have some idea of my proportions.

Another fellow came to see me today – Gabe Williams from Cwmbwrla. He also appeared to be all right though he looks slightly diminutive when compared with myself. He is a queer person, talks so nicely that sometimes you make a mistake and forget that you're talking to a man and say 'What size do you take in socks?' or something like that, which is more applicable to a flapper than a soldier. I think he's going away before long to France and I expect I shall meet him out there, when I'll be inspecting the forces (I suppose that you have heard that Kitchener is dead?).[19] As to myself, I feel rotten – I was inoculated this morning and now I know it. I have since called the doctor all the names in my vocabulary but I'm sorry to say I am no better after all because I think I feel very bad, I shall probably peg out in the night. I've been writing letters since the operation and this is the 35th so you can see that I've been busy. I expect you know that Gib was all right and was safe from that affair on sea. I bet you feel quite proud of the fact that you have three <u>big</u> brothers fighting for you and other such nice things. Well no more this time so I conclude with the fondest love from

<u>Ivor</u>

The word 'flapper' in this letter is interesting: most people would associate this word with the 1920s and the Jazz Age, conjuring up images of independent-minded young ladies with short skirts, bobbed haircuts and a cloche hat. Judging from Welsh newspapers, the word was relatively rarely used in 1916, with twenty-seven occurrences in the digitised collection of Welsh newspapers, but it did already have the meaning of a flighty young woman who defied the conventions of the age.[20]

The next, brief, letter is only dated 'Tuesday', but its contents indicate that it was written three days after the previous letters.

IE1916-06-13

Dear Mother,

I have received your letter all right and it found me in the best of health and spirits, having fully recovered from the inoculation affair, though it laid me rather low for two days. I thought that it must have been against overwork that they inoculated me, because I felt so lazy and sick, that I had no desire to get up off my cot; but it disappeared quite suddenly during Sunday evening and on Monday there was left only a slight stiffness and pain in my elbow on moving it; I hope you enjoyed a good holiday because I have nothing to say against the way I spent mine, for I had a most glorious time at Colwyn Bay; it was really fine. The weather has been a good deal cold since I've been up here and I notice that the wind is always blowing from the north and comes here straight from the sea, which we can see about 2 miles away from the camp. No more now, except that I shall be busy for a long time now, so don't expect more than about one letter a week, but <u>you</u> can write as many as you like – Ivor

The next letter is dated 'Thursday', and from its contents it is clear that it dates from either nine days after the previous letter or, more probably, two days later.

IE1916-06-15

Dear Mother,
        Just a few lines to let you know that I am all right and in the pink of condition. I thought that I would be busy this week but I made a mistake, for as a matter of fact we are having the time of our lives. Yesterday for instance we only did about two hours drill in the morning then we were sent to the back of the camp for bombing instruction but there was nobody there to meet us so we obeyed orders by sitting down on the grass, basking under the trees. Nobody came till [~~nearly~~] half past 12 when a passing officer asked us what we were doing there and when we told him he told us to go and have dinner. Then after dinner, the Brigadier General came to inspect some men on draught and as our instructor had to go and attend to him, leaving us to ourselves all the afternoon. So you see we get a gay time of it here, listening to the band all day long, or marching about the country whistling or singing as we march.
        I posted the registered letter with the chain and cufflinks for Auntie Lizzie on Tuesday and I expect you have

had them by now.[21] Also, have you got my clothes yet? you never said you had received them. I think after that everything will be clear and nothing will remain to be sent home.

I hear that Grace is not well there – well I hope she will be right by the time this reaches her. How is Danny now? and Bess Ann. I needn't ask about Lottie <u>she'll</u> be all right no matter what would happen.

Well I haven't much more to say except that I am in the best condition possible and as happy as a lark, so I conclude with the hope that all at home are the same.

Yours with best love

Ivor

The next letter, dated 'Tuesday' has reference to Will Evans being home, after the Battle of Jutland. As there are newspaper reports of him being at home on 21 June, it is likely that this letter dates from 27 June 1916.

IE1916-06-27

Dear Mother

Thanks very much for your letter which I received today. Auntie Charlotte seems to be in a bad state with her cold, though she never mentioned it in the letter she wrote me on Sunday. We seem to be keeping the kettle boiling all the time, though we are rather far apart, for after Grace had it, I had a dose, and then comes Auntie Charlotte. It is just like her, to write a letter full of news without a word about herself being in a bad state of health. As to staying at home, you seem to forget that poor Aunt Charlotte is not like I was at school, the least excuse being sufficient to keep me at home. I wish people at home would acquaint me of any bad news at home <u>at the earliest opportunity</u> not let me know that the event is over. For instance Grace has been ill, and I was told that she was much better in one letter without my knowing that she was ill; now there's Auntie Charlotte again. So if anything takes place like that please let me know as soon as you can, I would like it much better than not being told.

We are still having an excellent time here and still very good food (except now and again). Today our breakfast was not up to my liking because it was made up of sardines for one thing and you know, I think, that I don't fancy them. But for dinner we had a fine plateful of meat potatoes, beans, cabbage and 'crwstyn' [*crust*], with plenty of excellent gravy. Well I pitched in and ate a healthy meal with a vengeance, but though I enjoyed it very much, I was sorry in an hour later, for we had to do physical drill after dinner throughout the afternoon, and you can bet that the waist of my trousers was more tight than comfortable. So you see, it does not always pay to enjoy yourself. The inoculation (second) is a thing of the past now again for I am as well as ever today again. So Will Evans is home again is he? I expect the 'Lion' is being made up again after the fight; it must have been a hot time of it, but I'm sorry he does seem to be so well [*sic*].

I think I shall go and have a nap now, though it is only 7 o'clock, for I am rather tired after the days work, and a bath, and washing socks, and the <u>dinner</u>.

No more, with love, from Ivor

One trusts that the comment regarding Will Evans's health is a slip of the pen, and that the word 'not' has accidentally been omitted.

The next letter to have survived, dated simply 'Friday' was written in the summer of 1916 (when gooseberries were in season), just after Ivor had been promoted to lance-corporal (or 'Lance Jack' in army parlance). He states in a later letter (IE1918-12-17 (ch. 13)) that this promotion took place in July 1916, so this letter most probably dates from that month.

IE1916-07-a

Dear Mother,

Just a few lines in reply to yours, while I have the time. I have been very busy throughout the week as Orderly Corporal. I have never done this job before because only Lance Corporals do it; and it is the business of one lance corporal each week to look after the food and general needs of the whole company. In reality it means being the handy

man for 'C' Company – about 300 men. So you see that so
far, the stripe has been more of a load to me than anything,
but never mind, orderly corporal finishes tomorrow, so that
I will not have to bother any more. But there is much about
it – I cannot have two stripes without having one first, so that
I must put up with the extra work now until something else
comes my way.

What is more to my discomfort is the fact that I have
had to move out of the old home, No 2 hut. The captain
came round the huts to inspect them a few days ago and
he found that they were all very untidy, with the exception
of No 2. Now in some huts there was only one N.C.O.
in charge, so when the captain kicked up a row about the
huts, all the Lance corporals in No 2 had to move to other
huts to help the corporals there. We drew lots as to who
should remain in No 2 and Stephens won, so he is alright.
All the others had to go. I was placed in No 3 hut, which is
undoubtedly the worst in the company. The men here are
of the worst type and very dirty, and what is more there
are only two or three decent chaps in the whole hut. I was
very sorry to have to leave No 2, as I had settled down
comfortably and had made a home of it. Then again there
were in No 2 a party of the very best kind of men and of
these, one was corporal in charge of the hut, four were
Lance corporals (myself one), one had first class musketry
(very rare), and the other two were marksmen. Tonight we
are going to be invited to a dinner given by the first class
musketry man, in honour of his achievement, at Rhyl.
Stephens and another Lance Jack from Anglesey are on a
musketry brigade course this week and next; then there will
be an examination at the end and if either of them gets first
class, he is to stand the remainder a feed again. So you see,
success in the army costs a lot; for instance when I had this
stripe, I had to treat hundreds of chaps to lemonades at the
YMCA. I had saved a little money but now I am broke to the
world, I have not a penny in my pocket. Its a jolly good job
that it's pay night tonight, or it would be hard up on me. I
thought at first that it would be an easy job to save money in
the army but I find out that it is not. What takes most is the

fact that we don't get supper here. No matter how much we eat for tea (5 o'clock) we are quite as hungry at 9 as we would be otherwise. So we go up the YMCA for a cup of tea & a cake to start with, and you end up with a tight strap around your waist which means that you are hungry no more. Then again, sometimes there is half a ton of pepper in the dinner and you have to go to the YM after it, to get your mouth and tongue into a decent state. So you see that money runs through our fingers.

There's one thing I want you to send me every week if you can, that is gooseberry tart, 'paste goosberris'. I see every body up here getting them from home, some having currant tart or raspberries, so I thought that as they are rather plentiful down there you might make one every week for me. **I'll pay the postage**; so in the next letter I shall enclose half a crown for the first. You needn't send the plate, only the pie, pack it up in a box and send it up. It draws water to my mouth simply to think of it. No more now as the bugler is blowing 'Orderly Corporal' for all he is worth which means that I am wanted at the Battalion Orderly Room. He is still blowing, the poor chap must be tired

yours affectionately

Ivor

There is no doubt that the 'Stephens' referred to here is Ivor's schoolmate Elfryn Stephens: there are further references to him in the next extant letter and in that of 5 November 1916.

As there are gaps in the collection, there is no record of Ivor's response to a significant occasion at Kinmel Park on Sunday 19 August 1916, when a Nonconformist place of worship was opened at the camp. The first sermon in the hut was preached by the Rev. John Williams Brynsiencyn, perhaps the most enthusiastic recruiter from amongst the Nonconformist clergy, and certainly the most notorious. He delivered his keynote sermon, 'Cyfiawnder a ddyrchafa genedl' ('Righteousness exalteth a nation'). At the end of the service, Lloyd George addressed the soldiers in both English and Welsh. It was in Welsh that he delivered the rousing finale to his speech in which he dealt specifically with the attack of the Welsh Division on Mametz Wood (9–12 July 1916). He declared, as the

4.1: Ivor Eustis as a lance-corporal

soldiers cheered their appreciation, that the Welsh Division had 'accomplished much with honour to themselves and the land to which they belonged'.[22]

The next surviving letter must have been written shortly afterwards, for it mentions the reorganisation of the battalion which took place in late August 1916. It is dated 'Friday' and has been preserved in an envelope with the postmark 28 August, indicating that it was most probably written on 27 August 1916.

IE1916-08-27

Dear Mother,

There was a great deal of excitement here today when
the crowd left for Litherland: there were about 200 of our
men going, all of them trained soldiers, that is, men with
over 12 weeks service. You see, the authorities are getting
all the service men together to form a new battalion to go
to the Front, men from many battalions, the RWF, Welsh,
Borderers etc, but when they arrive at Litherland, they will
be given a number – 64 – instead of their cap badges, which
is the number of the new battalion. There is a rumour about
that the same will happen to the remainder of the 12th RWF
instead of being called the 12th RWF in future we will be
the 62 Reserve Training battalion, so that we shall do away
the cap badge and wear a 62 number instead. I was placed
on the list for the move, but the Musketry Officer had my
name crossed out owing to his being unable to allow any
instructor of his to go. The same happened to Stephens and
another chap, so that now it looks as if I shall not go out for
some time again. I can tell you that I've been very lucky to
have had the First Class Musketry Pass, otherwise I would
have been out by this time, because I have been placed on
the list of two drafts this last week, one for Mesopotamia
and the other for Salonika but on each occasion my name
was erased at the command of the Musketry authorities,
so that in one way the bit of hard work I did at the brigade
school has repaid me well. I expect there will be a large
number of recruits here before long, for as it stands now
that the Litherland lot have gone, the camp seems rather
empty.

Well I have not much more news, so I wind up.
Thanks for the parcel. Here are some views of Rhyl which
perhaps you would like to have, or perhaps Hannah might
take an interest in them. I bought them last night at Rhyl.
This reminds me of another item. Last night we (Stephens
& I) ran across one of our old masters at Gowerton –
Mr Adams – the mathematics master; he was up at Rhyl for

the sake of his health. We had a long chat with him on the
Promenade and he ended up with a cordial invitation to us
to call at the Bank, St Asaph where he was staying.[23] This
is only about 3 miles from here and we go there very often,
sometimes on Sunday nights when we go to the Cathedral
which is a very old and historic building. As for Mr Adams
he was the same good old sort as when he kicked our
backsides for acting the goat in class; we reminded him of
that and he laughed heartily, saying that he was sure it did us
no good and that we deserved far more than we got.

> Well no more now.

> Ivor

The discussion in this letter of how Ivor's expertise as a musketry
instructor meant that he was not sent to a fighting front is significant, for it sets the scene for what happened over the following year.
As will be seen, there were other occasions when Ivor's name was
removed from the list of those drafted to be sent to action because
he was required to train the recruits at Kinmel Park.

The next three letters from Ivor in the collection were written
on 20, 24 and 25 September 1916. It is not possible to identify the
Phil Evans mentioned in the first two letters, but the fact that he
was expected to call indicates how a comrade's home leave could be
utilised as a way to reinforce the connections between the soldier
and his home. Although it would be but a poor substitute for the
presence of Ivor himself, had Phil Evans called at least the family
would be able to have first-hand news of his progress. There are
further indications in these letters of the connections between the
three Eustis brothers, and how information about each of them was
shared.

IE1916-09-20

Dear Mother,

> A few lines in reply to yours which I received
yesterday. I thought I had told you that I would send those
boxes home when I wanted you to send me something, and
I seem to be doing well on Army food now, so I don't want

to trouble you on that line. You know, I would not ask for anything unless I was hard up, and I would far rather you sent the stuff to Dick and Gib than send it to me because they are more in need of it than I am.

I am very sorry to hear that Granny is unwell, but as you say it is not to be expected for her to enjoy good health always and I believe she has not done so badly lately. I suppose it has been caused by the cold weather, if it is the same down there as it has been here this last fortnight. It has been raining off and on all the time, besides being very cold, especially in the mornings when we turn out for the first time. It is dark every morning yet they don't turn on the lights; then down the field instead of the usual marching and drill, we do everything at the double – that is, we run instead of walk in order to keep ourselves warm, otherwise we would surely freeze. They say up here that the winter they get at Kinmel is very cold and wet and that they get a very rough time of it; judging by the present weather, it is probably quite right too, for though it is only September we are having rotten weather, but today is quite a change, being mild with a bit of sunshine.

I expect that by now you have had a visit from L/cpl Phil Evans, a brother to Rees Evans; I think I have mentioned him before. He was going on his final 6 days leave last Saturday and he promised to call. He is a good old sort is Phil, very much like Rees in his ways, and we get on well together. No more this time as I conclude

affectionately yours
Ivor

IE1916-09-24

Dear Mother,

I received a letter from Dick on Friday with which was inclosed three other letters which he asked me to post for him, which of course I did. He deplores the number of flies which are there, and from what I gather, they are a perfect nuisance. I have not received any news from Gib this last three weeks, and previous to that I used to hear from him rather regularly. Have you heard from him lately? and what did he have to say.

I see that my friend Phil Evans did not call to see you, then. I think I have written to you before about him. He promised to call last week when he was home on leave but now that he has returned he says that he did not call, owing to his time being so short. After all, six days is a very short holiday to be home on after being away for about 4 months. His pass went down to the Orderly Room marked 'Special' which meant that he would get another leave before he went out to the Front; however when it returned it was changed to 'Final' and he is now on the list for the next draft. There is one chap going with the next draft (on Monday to France) who is quite broken hearted because he has to go. He was a leader of the choir in some chapel in Bangor before the war, and he appeared to be a religious man; he was a good sort all round, until he was put down for draft, when a great change came over him immediately [??] after he failed to join the signallers (in order to try and dodge the draft). He is now a very selfish, spiteful chap, very sour and as downhearted as possible, in fact it is a pity to see him. He was telling me this morning when I was trying to cheer him up a bit, that he couldn't help feeling so sad, it was his disposition to be so. I told him to try and buck himself up as it was of no use grumbling over anything, but it was of no good. I never saw a case like it before – you can bet I won't be like that when I'll be going out.

How is Granny getting on, is she any better now? I hope she is and that she'll soon recover. No more this time, perhaps I'll write again soon. – Ivor

P.S. They have promised me leave before the war is over!

The next letter, written on YMCA paper, contains Ivor's new regimental assignation: 62nd Battn, T.R. [Training Reserve] Regt. 'C' Com[pany]. It also names the Bangor choirmaster who was fearful of going to the front. Although it is only dated 'Monday', there is no doubt that it was written on 25 September, for Sir John French visited north Wales on Thursday 28 September 1916.

IE1916-09-25

Dear Mother

A few lines as promised. There has been some great excitement here tonight when the draft was leaving, for they were a jolly crowd with one exception. We are not many left in 'C' Company but as many as there were there gave them a rousing cheer as they marched off from our lines, down to the battalion square. All of them were quite happy as they lined up, though we knew that they were sorry to leave us, as much as we were sorry to see them go. They were willing to go most of them and they were quite merry while they were waiting the time for leaving but when we shook hands with them for the last time, the tears were very near the surface in one or two cases, though they were old hardened veterans. There was one however – John Roberts (the choir conductor) who had been brooding over it for days and since Saturday morning he never ate a morsel of food – old fool as he was.

There is a great fuss up here this week for there is going to be an inspection by Field Marshal Sir John French on Thursday afternoon. Every body has got some extra work to do, especially us poor warriors; cleaning is going on on a grand scale, every nook and corner of the camp, and every scrap of anything in it. Every man in the Battalion had to turn out today with a full pack, all the cooks, policemen, postmen, band, orderly officers, in fact every body in the battalion.

I myself have had a very hard time of it today; I am orderly corporal this week again, and just before going to bed last night the order came out that all must be on parade. The result was that I had to put my tackle together and clean it this morning besides carrying on my duties and feeding the old rebels. However, I got everything off all right, after sweating myself till my shirt was soaking. General Picton-Campbell was supposed to inspect us but he did not turn up; I had to go on parade with a full pack (what I haven't done this last month or so) and then had to dash away at 3.30 this afternoon to attend to some more duties. No more now till the old gentleman comes. How is Grannie today? Ivor

The next surviving letter, dated simply 'Wednesday' was written prior to Ivor returning home on leave, but after he had been promoted to the rank of corporal, meaning that it must come from early October 1916. Once again there are discussions of health issues, and Ivor seeks to allay the family's fears that his clothing is inadequate.

IE1916-10-a

Dear Auntie Charlotte,

I received your letter tonight just after arriving off parade, so that it was a good foundation for my tea, to hear that Granny had recovered so well and that everyone else is all right. There's no doubt about it that it was a serious case this time, and that it was really hard lines on poor old granny to be the victim of such a bad attack. Let us hope that she will be saved from another such illness for a long time. As to myself and my complaint, I'm afraid that you think that the affair is much worse than it really is. All I suffer from now (this week anyway) is a cold in the head, and a 'tight' chest <u>on getting up in the morning, on going to bed</u> and also if I happen to wake up during the night (which is not very often). This only happens at the times named and only for a few minutes, but longer in the morning, lasting then for about half an hour, when I also have a bad cough. Throughout the remainder of the day I am alright, what I believe is the matter is that I have an old cold at the bottom of my chest which I cannot get rid of. I went to the doctor yesterday about it, the cough being a little bit worse; well all he put on the report after examining me was – 'Cold, light duty, 1 day, and on this verdict I could have laid down on the bed all day ('light duty' being equal to 'excused duty' for NCO's) but I chose to go on parade as usual. The worst of laziness is that the more soft time you get, the more you want, and this doesn't agree with one's comfort in the Army. So you see, there is nothing to worry in the least about, it is only a slight inconvenience.

As to my clothing, that's all right. I have three pairs of socks, two pairs quite whole & in good condition as regards quality, while the third pair has two holes in the toes which I shall repair as soon as they return from the wash (Saturday).

Indeed, I pride myself on my ability to darn socks, and scrub floors. Then I have three good shirts, without a blemish (one of them is hanging up to dry at present, having been washed after I fell into a trench up to my armpits in mud. There was a mess, I had to wash everything except my hat, and at the last 5 minutes of the afternoon it happened too, worse luck, for if it had taken place first thing, they would have sent me to change and I would have had the afternoon to myself, but as it was I had to do all the changing etc in my own time). Then my two underpants are in good condition, though I might say they were not made for me more likely for someone the size of Herbert Evans.[24] Then two very good pairs of boots, which can be repaired at any time for nothing, two good trousers, & tunics, a new overcoat and also I have a woollen cap comforter which can be utilised as a night cap if need be. I believe the fault lies in the old huts because it is of no avail to wrap yourself up if there is a few dozen draughts knocking about.

Then there is the matter of a second stripe. Well as a matter of fact, I had intended to spring a surprise on you when I came home by swanking with two stripes, but now, since you ask me, I better let it out that I have been since promoted and am now a full corporal. There you are, you are the very first one I've told, not even Dick nor Gib. I might as well finish it now I suppose since I've let out that much so here you are in black and white. I intend coming home the same time as Gib and for that end I have been working this last month or more, when Gib suggested it. I could have had leave a long time ago if I had wished but if I had leave then, I would not be able to have leave when Gib came, so I waited patiently and it has been hard work too I can tell you, more so because all along I knew that I would be forfeiting 6 days leave out of 12 in order to be home with Gib. So you can do what you please with it now, either let it out or keep it secret, which you like, for there's no-one else in the know, I think I've done well this time so I conclude with

love to all,

Ivor

Ivor and Gabriel managed to arrange their home leave at the same time in late October 1916. There are in existence pictures taken in a

Swansea studio, which must date from this time. A posed photograph shows Gabriel and Ivor in their uniforms (Ivor with the two stripes of a corporal) together with a sister – one cannot be sure whether she is Hannah (b.1900) or Elizabeth (Bess) Ann (b.1902). Another (confusingly) shows Gabriel and Ivor having swapped uniforms. Both of them sent a letter home immediately after arriving back with their units, with rather mundane details of the train journey back to their bases.[25] One aspect of Ivor's letter which is different to the others is that at the top of the YMCA paper he gave the address as 'Kill-men Park', but after this, the entire tone of the letter is deliberately monotonous, to highlight the fact that nothing has changed in his army routine and thus to allay any of his mother's fears about his safety. After describing the train journey back to north Wales and the meal of boiled eggs and bread he had at Rhyl, he continues:

IE1916-10-28

The supper went down alright and after a few mins rest I was ready for the bus, which eventually took me back to the same old camp, with same old huts, the same old guard room with the same old clock – which registered 12.30 Midnight when I handed my pass in. Anyway, up I went to our hut and was lucky enough to have a fire in the stove. I then hunted up the hut for a bed and at last found one – somebody else's – and slept in it. Before I knew that I was asleep somebody dragged me out of bed and said it was time I was on parade. Yes I was in the same old style, and dressed in the same old togs, and then went on the same old parade. Afterwards the same old breakfast appeared, with the same old smoke & bacon and I ate it with the same old appetite. Then I went through the same old routine. Now I'm in the same old YM, writing the same old letters. Frankly, I felt rotten all day – never felt the same in my life before. Nevermind I'll wash the same old face now, and go to the same old bed, to dream the same old dreams, so Good night – Ivor

P.S. I had a letter from Dick awaiting me. But there was very little news – the same old style from the same old Dick,
Ivor

4.2: Gabriel (left) and Ivor Eustis, with a sister

4.3: Ivor (left) and Gabriel Eustis, having swapped uniforms

The next surviving letter, dated simply 'Thursday', can be dated to 2 November 1916 as the content fits in with the subsequent letter, written on 5 November.

IE1916-11-02

Dear Mother,
        I received your letter on Monday but I'm sorry I have not answered it sooner. I have been having a splendid time of it this week thanks very much to our doctor. I was a bit lazy on Monday morning so I reported sick and went to see the doctor. You know I had a slight cold when I was home, which was coming out on my lips. Well, the doctor asked me what was the matter with me and I said that I felt very bad indeed, that my head was simply splitting, my arms were stiff, I had a rheumatic feeling in my legs, that I suffered from heartburn, that my stomach was bad, and that I was not half well myself. Well, he examined me, asked questions about this and that & I told him all sorts of tales. He tested my chest and found that I had a bit of a cold so he said 'All right, you'll have to do light duty for a few days and he gave me a bottle of medicine and some pills, saying that it was a case of Bronchitis without a doubt. But I could hardly believe it, but it was no use giving your self away, so I said to him very gently that 'Light Duty' was no good to me as I would have to go on parade as usual. 'Oh! is that the case?' he said, 'Very well, you are excused duty for a week' and this nearly knocked me down. I couldn't believe it – I had to kick myself to see if I was awake. Really it was ridiculous, and when the report came, my case was 'Bronchitis – excused duty one week.' Ha! ha! ha!! I've not stopped laughing over it yet – It's simply incredible, because I have no more Bronchitis than the Table has, but of course, the doctor knows best, Ha! Ha! So you see I've got a week to myself; I was never so successful in my life. Why, I'm as fit as a fiddle, now that I've drank a drop of that medicine, the little bit of cold that I have is quite gone, and there's nothing the matter with me – still, a week's rest will do me good I suppose.

You need not be in a hurry about sending the things I left behind. I'll let you know later what I want. No more this time

with love

from Ivor

The following letter was written on the Sunday evening:

IE1916-11-05

Dear Mother,

Just a few lines to let you know how things are getting on in this old place. My week's holiday is nearly at an end and I shall soon be compelled to go on parade again as usual, but it is needless to say that I shall probably have 'Bronchitis' again when the chance comes, ha! ha!! There is a strong rumour about that there are 108 recruits to come to our company some time next week, and I hope to goodness that the rumour will become true, because we are all sick and tired of doing the same things day after day, with such monotony. We are only about 20 men in the company now so that the duties come round much oftener than they would if we had plenty of men.

There have been many rumours before, for instance last week we all thought that we would be moved to Wrexham, and afterwards that we have to shift to Pembroke Dock but nothing came of either. But all the same, I think the recruits will come very soon, because we have been expecting them for so long.

When did you hear from Dick last? I have not heard from him for a long time now, not since the day after I arrived home on leave. Has he been in need of money afterwards?

Then about those things I left behind – the only things I want you to send to me are the knife, fork and spoon – they are the only ones that I need, the other trash can be kept down there as relics of war. I would like to get the knife sharpened too if possible because the meat you get for dinner, although nice, is not what you can call 'tender' by any means in fact it is very often the case that some boys go to dinner armed with a razor to cut the meat.

It's a bit dry here now that both Stephens and Phil Evans are away. Phil is at Oswestry on a general course and will probably be there for a few weeks again, but it doesn't matter much all the same because there are plenty of decent chaps in the company in fact they are mostly all fine fellows with a few exceptions.

We had excellent singing in chapel this morning in the Free Church Hall. The place was full of soldiers and when you get a crowd of boys like that together they don't half let it rip. The chaplain – the Rev W. Llewelyn Lloyd – gave a strong sermon and let us have it right and left because he considered that we did not attend the services in the week days often enough. Of course, that only applied to some.

There are some new people again in the YMCA (where I am writing this) and of course as they are beginners, things don't run so smoothly as before. For instance they have run short of envelopes and the pens and ink, have not been changed this last month. Consequently I have had to use Mr Davies' stuff, and they come in very handy in cases like these.[26] Well no more this time so goodbye, with love from Ivor

The Rev. William Llewelyn Lloyd of Anglesey had served as chaplain to the 16th RWF on the Western Front, and following a period in hospital in London he was posted as one of the chaplains to Kinmel Park by May 1916. He was a Calvinistic Methodist: there was also a Baptist, a Congregationalist and a Wesleyan Methodist to cater for the spiritual needs of the Welsh Nonconformists. The quality of the singing by the congregation in the Free Church Hall was also noted by a visiting minister at one of the mid-week meetings.[27]

The following day, Ivor sent another brief letter home.

IE1916-11-06

Dear Mother,

I've been booked for Altcar next course which starts next Monday so that I shall probably start on Sunday night;

and what is more I shall probably be home again somewhere around Christmas on leave; but Christmas is a long way off yet, and in the meantime I have the job of going through the course successfully. I shall most likely be rather busy this week preparatory to leaving.

The place, from what I gather is not far from Liverpool and if I get the chance of course I'll be able to trot around now and again, to see the place. I have already booked one weekend in Manchester to the brother of one of the chaps who is going with me, so there is also a chance of seeing that great city.

Ivor went on to ask for Bess Ann to send him some stationery and the book *Chemistry for Matriculation*. He did indeed leave Kinmel Park the following Monday as the next letter in the collection was sent home from 'School of Musketry, Altcar, Nr Liverpool'. After describing the journey there, he continues:

IE1916-11-15

Although we were in Liverpool for many hours we did not see half the town because it is such a big place. One thing struck me very much, that is the dense fog which prevailed all the while we were there and as a result when we were crossing the Mersey we did not see any big boats at all, though I expected to see a monster or two of the Mauritanian type but as it was I had no such luck. This place in itself is rather dreary but it is very convenient, for though there are only two houses within sight of the school, the railway station is only 5 mins walk, besides Hightown and Formby are only about 1+½ miles away. I shall probably spend the weekend in Liverpool. The routine is altogether different from that at Kinmel Park, the main thing being that we don't get out till 9 o'clock yet we finish at 4 o'clock in the afternoon. All the same, they are extremely strict in the matters of discipline though we get any amount of freedom while off duty. I'm very busy just now and shall probably be so for some time as we have a huge amount of notes to write out. I am planning to leave the hut I was placed in, to come to this place where I'm writing from – that is another lot of huts after the style of officers' quarters with cubicle room for two only which is far better than a crowded hut. Then I shall be with Sgt John who came with me from Kinmel Park and we are very pally. The food is excellent, even better than at Kinmel and it is likely to remain so as we have officers on this course as well as NCO's. Well no more this time

from Ivor

These letters from 1916 allow us to trace the development of Ivor Eustis from a schoolboy to a young soldier. They establish a number of themes that will remain prominent in the letters of 1917 and 1918, such as Ivor's concern for his own health and that of his family. As Ivor was throughout this period in a training camp, there is nothing here regarding what was ultimately the soldier's principal task, of facing the enemy in battle. Yet there are indications that the business of putting one's life in danger was present in the family's thoughts. Clearly the folk back in Mynyddbach had real fears for Gabriel's safety when they heard of the great naval battle in June and it took Ivor's clear head to rationalise the situation and to allay their fears. It is obvious that Ivor was glad that he had avoided the draft to Mesopotamia and Salonika. However there is also a sense of youthful bravado or naivety in some of his remarks. Ivor's comments reveal disdain and a lack of sympathy for the attitude of the Bangor choirmaster who was terrified at being sent to France, and he was sure that he would prove himself to be more of a man as he declared 'you can bet I won't be like that when I'll be going out'. Also, the disparaging comments about the lack of Gabe Williams's masculine attributes smack of a boastful youth, strutting about to impress others. In mitigation, one might note that this letter, to 'kid' sister Hannah, has a playful tone at its start, and perhaps his attitude betrays exuberance rather than arrogance. Note that Ivor suggests that she should feel 'proud of the fact that you have three big brothers fighting for you'. He had thus graduated from being one of the boys, dependent upon his parents and others for protection, to being a man, responsible for protecting his family.

Notes

1. *The Gowertonian*, 3.6 (July 1914), 28.
2. 'Editorial'; 'Our Roll of Honour', *The Gowertonian*, 3.7 (December 1914), 1, 5.
3. 'Football Notes', *The Gowertonian*, 3.8 (March 1915), 27. Two others who scored for the team who also feature in this book are Trevor James and Elfryn Stephens.
4. 'Cricket Notes', *The Gowertonian*, 3.9 (July 1915), 24–7. See also 'Local School Cricket', *Llais Llafur*, 26 June 1915, 5.
5. 'Ymddiddan am y Rhyfel', *The Gowertonian*, 3.9 (July 1915), 20–1.
6. 'Loughor schoolboy postman', *CDL*, 29 July 1915, 5.
7. 'Editorial'; 'Our Roll of Honour', *The Gowertonian*, 3.9 (December 1915), 2.
8. 'If——?', *The Gowertonian*, 3.10 (December 1915), 6–8.
9. 'The C.W.B.', *HoW*, 25 September 1915, 4; 'Gowerton Intermediate School', *Amman Valley Chronicle*, 16 December 1915, 6; 'Football Notes', *The Gowertonian*, 3.11 (April 1916), 21.
10. 'To the Sons of Wales', *The Gowertonian*, 3.11 (April 1916), 22.
11. 'Our Roll of Honour', *The Gowertonian*, 3.12 (July 1916), 22.
12. 'Huge camp at Kinmel Park', *North Wales Chronicle*, 19 February 1915, 8; 'The Abergele camp and aliens', *Denbighshire Free Press*, 12 June 1915, 5.
13. Robert H. Griffiths, *The story of Kinmel Park Military Training Camp 1914–1918* (Llanrwst: Gwasg Carreg Gwalch, 2014).
14. There is also a brief mention of Stanley Richards, presumably the same as the man on one of the Mynyddbach Rolls of Honour.
15. *HMS Lion* was the flagship of Vice-Admiral David Beatty. A hundred seamen were killed on board during the battle.
16. See Appendix 3.
17. 'Treboeth Borderer Invalided', *CDL*, 10 December 1915, 7.
18. Cf. the reference to Miss Williams as her 'mistress' in RE1916-10-12 (ch. 3).
19. Lord Kitchener, Secretary of State for War, was drowned when *HMS Hampshire* sank on 5 June 1916. The news was reported in the *CDL* of 8 June 1916.
20. *www.newspapers.library.wales/home* (accessed September 2017): search performed on all the instances of 'flapper' in 1916. See the reference to the 'impetuous flapper' (*SWWP*, 17 June 1916, 3) or the 'frivolous flapper' (*Carmarthen Weekly Reporter*, 29 December 1916, 3).
21. Auntie Lizzie is presumably John Eustis's elder sister, Elizabeth Jane.
22. 'Mr Lloyd George at Kinmel', *North Wales Chronicle*, 25 August 1916, 3. Other newspapers carried detailed reports of the occasion, such as

'Mr Lloyd George ym Mharc Cinmel', *Yr Herald Cymraeg*, 22 August 1916, 8 and 'Welshmen and Mametz', *CDL*, 21 August 1916, 3.

23. Oliver Adams MA had a sister who lived in St Asaph: see 'Mr J.H. Adams, Y.K., Cilgerran', *Y Goleuad*, 3 December 1915, 10.
24. A portly gentleman from Treboeth: see Gethin Matthews, *Gwrol Ryfelwyr Caersalem Newydd* (Treboeth: Treboeth History Society, 2014), p. 18.
25. Cf. GE1916-11-01 (ch. 5).
26. Possibly this is the Rev. James Davies, minister of Mynyddbach: he sent ink tablets to Richard Eustis at this time – see RE1916-12-20 (ch. 3).
27. Rev. O. L. Roberts, 'Noswaith yn Kinmel', *Y Tyst*, 22 November 1916, 6–7.

5

Gabriel Eustis aboard
HMT Saxon, to February 1917

After Gabriel left Bristol for his training in the signal school in Crystal Palace in November 1914, there are only snippets of information about his movements for the following two years. According to his service record, after training in the signal school in Crystal Palace Gabriel was transferred to the Wireless Training School located at 'The Firs', Clapham Park, in March 1915. A group photograph shows Gabriel with other seamen, most probably at one of these two training centres. The men have a badge on their right sleeve which denotes the rank of 'ordinary telegraphist' – the rank at which Gabriel entered the service.

On 1 May 1915 Gabriel was transferred to the muster roll of *HMS Dido*: this was the depot ship for one of the squadrons that was responsible for enforcing the naval blockade upon Germany and her allies. The service record does not state which ship or ships Gabriel served on for the next few months.

The purpose of the naval blockade was to prevent Germany and her allies from receiving supplies of any kind from the rest of the world. The naval blockade was a long-standing tactic of the Royal Navy, which could use its enormous resources to throttle the supply-chain to enemy countries. There were, however, enormous difficulties both in political and practical terms during the First World War. The trade of neutral countries with Germany needed to be halted, which of course led to a hostile reaction from traders from those countries, and thus potentially a clash with their governments. In practical terms, there was an enormous area of sea to be monitored, though the focus was upon the unfriendly waters of the North Atlantic. As John Fisher puts it, 'the Allied

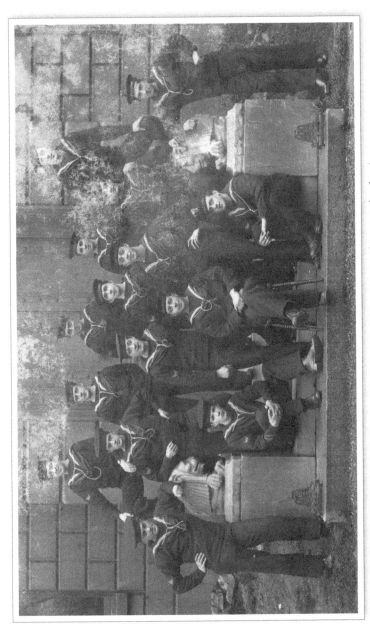

5.1: Gabriel Eustis (ninth from left) in a group photograph of trainees

blockade of the Central Powers was global, but the key area was in the Atlantic between Scotland and Iceland'.[1] Thus the 10th Cruiser Squadron, which covered this area of 220,000 square miles of sea, had an important, delicate and difficult task to do.

During the year 1915, the squadron chased and examined 3,098 ships, of which 743 were found to be carrying contraband, and were sent into port.[2] As well as being responsible for preventing merchant ships from reaching German ports, the squadron had other difficulties to face. It is clear that they were not provided with the newest and best-equipped ships, and two vessels 'foundered in circumstances that suggested they were not seaworthy enough for the job'. The German U-boats posed threats throughout the war and seven ships of the squadron were sunk by enemy action in the three years to December 1917.[3] The circumstances called for the deployment of a large number of smaller ships that were suited to operating in the North Atlantic, and so the Royal Navy requisitioned a number of trawlers. One of these was the *Saxon*, 120 feet long and with a fishing crew of nine, built at North Shields in 1907. On her arrival at Milford Haven she was described as an 'up-to-date steam trawler'.[4] After being requisitioned in September 1914, this ship was converted for use as a minesweeper, with the addition of a 12-pounder gun. Later an anti-submarine weapon, a 7.5" bomb thrower, was also installed.

Based in Scotland these small ships patrolled a vast area of inhospitable sea. In their role as scouts, it is obvious that the telegraphists on board had a vital responsibility, relaying information to larger ships that were within broadcasting range. The *Saxon* was involved in an incident off northern Norway in August 1915, rescuing survivors when *HMS India* was sunk by a torpedo, and delivering them to safety in Narvik.[5] It is unlikely that Gabriel was involved in this, as a later letter from the *Saxon* suggests that he joined the ship in September 1915.[6] This letter of September 1918 also says that it was exactly three years since he was at Archangel, the Russian port in the White Sea. It seems that Gabriel initially joined the crew of the *Saxon* as a supernumerary, and after his promotion to the rank of telegraphist on 30 December 1915, he was officially posted to the ship on 1 January 1916.

There are very few specific details as to his movements for several months thereafter. A letter has survived written by Gabriel's shipmate Bunty on 4 April 1916, when both were on home leave. This confirms that *Saxon* was based at Aberdeen at that time. One could deduce from Ivor's comments in a letter of June 1916 (in which he allayed his aunt's fears about Gabriel's involvement in the Battle of Jutland) that the *Saxon* was due to sail in the far North Sea, or perhaps on another journey to the White Sea.[7] Ivor noted in October 1916 that he had arranged his home leave to coincide with Gabriel's, and it is clear that this is what happened. Ivor's letter home describing his journey from Swansea back to Kinmel Park was written on 28 October: a letter written by Gabriel from the 'Aberdeen Sailors' Home' describes his journey back to Scotland on 31 October. The brief letter finishes:

GE1916-11-01

Let me know how things are going at home as soon as ever you like & if you have not already done so, send those fags to Dick.
No more this time as I am in a hurry, so
Bye Bye,
Best Love to All,
Gib

A picture has survived of Gabriel alongside two of his colleagues from *Saxon* which was taken at Oban (in western Scotland). On Gabriel's sleeve is the telegraphist's badge with the star above to denote that he has passed to the rank of telegraphist. The next two letters from Gabriel to have survived in the collection were written from aboard *Saxon* at Oban on 2 February 1917.

GE1917-02-02a

Dear Mother,
Just a few lines on the chance of being able to post before we return to the above place. I received your letter of January 7th, also Dan's, Lottie's & Grace's. I'm glad to see that they enjoyed their Christmas alright. From all accounts 'Mab i Dad a Mab y Mam' [*Father's Son and Mother's Son*] is getting quite a little man now & I hope he will have no

5.2: Gabriel Eustis (left) with two shipmates

occasion to 'mitch' from school this year. When is he going
to have his photo taken again? I had intended taking him
myself last leave but you know what a hustling time it was.
However, if he is not taken before, I'll see to it next leave.

I can't understand why Dick says he has 'had no
letters from me for some months now' as I write to him
practically every time I come in. Still seeing the way letters
have to go to reach him some are bound to go astray I
suppose. We have not been in port since Jan 12th & are not
likely to get there before Feb 18th or 20th & therefore have
had no mails this last three or four weeks, so I can't say
whether there are any letters from him or Ivor this time.
I suppose when our mail does come there will be quite a
budget of letters for me to answer, & as I have some of my
last lot to answer yet, I shall have to 'work late in the office'
each night or else engage a lady typist. We had a rather lively
time of it after we left on Jan 12th, a nice bit of sport with a
touch of excitement so the time seemed to pass fairly quickly.

Well Mam, I am enclosing a little of the ready, to start
making up for lost time. I also enclose a few trifles for the 'wee
yins'. As for the pudding you needn't worry about me Mam as
I can buy all I want now though prices are high at our base.

I close with Best Love & Wishes to All, there being no
particular news this time.

Gib.

A postscript at the top of the letter adds 'Will write to Lottie &
Grace when I get in.' A letter to Daniel was included with this letter
to the mother. This is written in highly colloquial Welsh – the little
brother would have been just under five and a half, and although
he would have been learning English at school it is clear that Welsh
was the natural language for Gabriel to communicate with him. He
addressed the letter from 'Y Box Sepon, Ar y Mor' [*The Soap Box,
On the Sea*].

GE1917-02-02b

Well Capten Dan, shwd mae'n mynd gyda ti nawr ers
lawer dydd? a shwd mae pethe'n disgwyl yn Heol Daniels

ar hyn o bryd? Fe geso i dy lythyr di wrth Mam ond smo ti
wedi gweyd shwd leikes di dy bwdyn 'Dolig. Odd Dick yn
gweyd bod y pwdyn yn y pink, sawl platted fites di o' no
fe? Fe fites i fale a oranges a grapes a cnai spo fi jest a bosto
Dydd Nadolig, ond na'r gwitha, o'n i mas ar y mor a weti'n o
ni ddim gallu mynd i un Eisteddfod a ffili cal game o football
na dim byd. Glywes i fod Daddy Christmas wedi dod a lot
fawr o pethach i ti do fe?

Ma fi'n ala swllt a thair iti, ag wy'n gobeitho doti di
y swllt yn y bank Band of Hope. Aros di spo fi yn dod lawr
to, a i naf i ti ganu yr hen ganwn [ganeuon]. Faint o football
wyt ti'n wareu nawr, a sawl pêl sy gyda ti yn gyfan nawr.
Shwd mae'r hen Joe y cu yn beafio ddar ma Ivor yn Rhyl, odi
e'n grindo peth iti'n weyd wrtho fe nawr. Faint o gwên bach
sy gyda ti nawr a shw mae'r White Hope a Jack Johnson?
Rhwyn gweld bod ti'n dwli am tomatoes a chunks eh? Pan
dwa'i lawr tro nesa fe gawn ni chunks a tomatoes i de bob
dydd cawn ni?

Well yr hen Foy, cofia di garco Mam a Nad a Mamgu a
Dadcu, a nw gyd spo fi a Dick a Ivor yn dod nol ar ol wado'r
hen Germans. Bit lot fawr o fwyd a cadw'r bola bach yn
llawn spo ti tyfu'n ddyn mawr fel Nad. Dim rhagor nawr,
Gib

[*Well Captain Dan, how are things going with you
now after such a long time? and how are things looking at
Heol Daniels at the moment? I got your letter from Mam but
you have not said how you liked your Christmas pudding.
Dick said that the pudding was pink – how many plates of it
did you eat? On Christmas Day I ate apples and oranges and
grapes and nuts until I was fit to burst, but the worst thing is
that I was out at sea so I was not able to go to an Eisteddfod
nor have a game of football or anything. I heard that Father
Christmas brought you a lot of things, didn't he?*

*I am sending you a shilling and threepence, and I
hope that you will put the shilling in the Band of Hope bank.
Wait until I come down again, and I will make you sing
the old songs. How much football are you playing now, and
how many balls do you have now. How is old Joe the dog*

behaving now that Ivor is in Rhyl, does he listen to what
you tell him now. How many chicks do you have now and
how are White Hope and Jack Johnson? I see that you love
tomatoes and chunks, eh? When I come down next time we
will have chunks and tomatoes for tea every day, won't we?

> *Well, old Boy, remember to look after Mam and Dad*
and Grandmother and Grandfather, and all of them until
myself and Dick and Ivor come back after smacking the old
Germans. Eat a lot of food and keep that little tummy full
until you grow up into a big man like Dad. No more now,
> *Gib]*

These letters of 2 February 1917 indicate that Gabriel was part of
a wider family conversation in this period, most of which has been
lost. Each of the younger members of the family at home sent and
received letters, and we can assume that, as in the letter to Daniel,
the message Gabriel relayed was appropriately tailored to the recipi-
ent. Thus Daniel's letter is replete with references to tasty food and
playing football. The sentence towards the end of the letter, in which
Gabriel imagines coming home to do his duty of looking after the
family after he and the two elder brothers have beaten the Germans
('walloped' is another appropriate translation for 'wado' offered
by the dictionary) tells us a lot about how Gabriel understood his
role. He and the other two had a duty to see their job through, but
Mynyddbach and family were present in their thoughts and central
to their future plans.

Notes

1. John Fisher, 'Neither fish nor fowl: Mercantile seamen on armed merchant cruisers in the Great War', *International Journal of Maritime
   History*, 28.3 (2016), 496–512, n. 1.
2. Julian Thompson, *Imperial War Museum Book of the War at Sea 1914–18*
   (London: Sidgwick & Jackson, 2005), p. 164.
3. Fisher, 'Neither fish nor fowl', 500.
4. 'Milford Haven', *Pembrokeshire Herald*, 8 November 1907, 2.
5. Thompson, *War at Sea*, p. 163.
6. GE1918-09-10 (ch. 10).
7. IE1916-06-08 (ch. 4).

6

Richard Eustis in Egypt, March 1917–January 1918

The ten-month period from March 1917 to January 1918 was a momentous one for the forces of the EEF. Having secured the Sinai Desert and all of the territory that had previously belonged to Egypt, with three decisive victories against Ottoman forces at the Battles of Romani (August 1916), Magdhaba (December 1916) and Rafa (January 1917), the Allied forces had reached the boundary with Palestine. By the beginning of January the railway (essential for bringing in supplies from Egypt) had reached El Arish, and construction continued to the east. In his diary on 1 March 1917 Richard noted that 'The R.E. are laying the railway down at the rate of 1½ mile [per] day'. By the end of that month the EEF was ready to launch an attack on Gaza: the First Battle (26 March) came so close to proving a success that it led to the fateful and mistaken decision to try again. After the disastrous Second Battle of Gaza (17 to 19 April), the commander-in-chief of the EEF was relieved of his command, to be replaced by General Edmund Allenby. For the troops on the front line there was a period of stalemate and trench warfare for several months until an Allied victory at Beersheba (31 October) was followed by successful attacks upon Gaza, which led to a wholesale retreat of the Ottoman forces. The EEF pushed far into southern Palestine and Jerusalem was taken in December 1917.

There are eight letters extant from Richard in this period, beginning in August 1917. These give very few details of his military duties and activities, although in the letter that he sent to Ivor, in which he boasts of how they gave 'Johnny Turk the damnest hiding he ever had in his life', there is a clear pride in the achievements of the 53rd (Welsh) Division.[1] For the family at home Richard describes the biblical sites he saw in Palestine, such as Beersheba, Bethlehem and Jerusalem, although the photographs he took and sent home are not extant.

It is not until January 1918 that the letters home give the first reference to his sweetheart, Mary Lizzie Morgan, with the mention of sending 'a little brooch to Morriston'.[2] However, Richard's diary for 1917 shows that their long-distance courtship was continuing. On 24 September Richard looked through the diary and counted twenty letters sent to her that year. At a time when his situation was changing and he was moving through an unfamiliar environment, the link with home provided stability: an anchor for his non-military identity and also a platform upon which he could imagine building a future.

The destruction and dangers of war were visible for Richard as his unit moved east. The diary notes several attacks by enemy aeroplanes, such as on 10 March when two Taubes came over, and the shrapnel from the anti-aircraft guns 'was dropping like rain all around in our camp'. They encountered Turkish prisoners and refugees from the Turks, who were 'in a hell of a state' (24 February). Richard spent several days on water duty, but was mainly busy with his packstore duties and taking charge of ambulance convoys. On 24 March they were on the move again:

> Marched off at 4.30 p.m. On Camels. Marched till
> 12 midnight. Through a large Arab village. No doubt now
> that we are well in Palestine. Different country altogether.
> Most interesting march we've had on this stunt. Camped in
> an orchard of oranges & almonds. Beautiful. Hope to see
> Jerusalem before long.

This was the build-up for the EEF's attack upon Gaza, in which the 53rd (Welsh) Division took a prominent part. On 26 March Richard's day began with reveille at 3.15 a.m., after which he loaded the camels. The principal entry in the diary is not easy to read, but Richard gives another account of the day towards the end of the diary, although the early part of this entry is also difficult to decipher.

> the way the 4th Welsh went into it was a sight for the gods
> over a ploughed field into the Turkish trenches. Absolutely

mown down. We arrived on the scene just after the charge.
I took two squads after the 7 RWF & 4th Welsh. Piles of
Turkish dead. I went through the Turkish Headquarters to
fetch Capt Fletcher.[3] Told he was dying, so took another two
cases back. Terrible place. Turks at our heels. Retreated from
Advanced Dress Station at dawn. Carried patients about
10 miles back to base, arrived there at 3.30 p.m. Had to leave
some wounded behind. Pitiful. Crying for us from all sides,
but couldn't see to them as we had a loaded stretcher. Carried
them back to Deir-el Belah. Never felt so tired in my life.
Soon was alright again. Sight of blood & dead don't affect me
at all.

On 30 March, Richard noted that many cases were still dying in
his hospital. He was 'just getting over the exhaustion ... We have
not seen bread for about 14 days. No sleep for the last four days.'
Nevertheless, routine was re-established soon enough. Rugby
returned, with two games against the New Zealanders in the first
week of April (one victory and one draw). Enemy planes were
sighted and shot at. A new addition, the gas drill, became part of
the routine. However long Richard's New Year resolution to abstain
from drinking had lasted, it was certainly over by 9 April: 'Will
James got hold of a jar of rum. All merry.'
    Then on 14 April:

Turkish Bombardment ... Shelled the R.A.M.C. to blazes.
Several casualties in adjoining Ambs. Saw 6 buried together.
Tea. Digging Funk-holes.[4] Cocoa & turned in. Heard a deuce
of a row about 10.30 p.m. Went out and saw the tanks for the
first time. Hideous looking things. Aubrey Harris Morriston
driving one of them.[5]

The following day:

Packed off & moved with a convoy of camels. Hell of a
trip. No cover & peppered with H.E. [high explosives]. Will
James & S. Rich hit.

In another part of the diary there is a note:

April 15th W. James wounded – Thigh   – Shell
   "   "   S. Rich   "   Upper Arm   "
April 20th W. James died at Kantara[6]

There was no time for Richard to mourn as he was in the thick of
the action of what is known as the Second Battle of Gaza. He was
sent to the front-line positions of the 160th Brigade at midnight
on 19/20 April, and was out again at 2 a.m. on 21 April to pick up
a party of wounded. His diary entry for that night reads 'Slept all
night. First night's sleep I've had for nearly a week.'

For the following weeks there are periods of inactivity in the
intense heat, interspersed with short bursts of action and danger.
Richard was busy sending letters back to Wales and received a variety in return, including a parcel on 3 May from Mary Lizzie which
contained a piece of wedding cake from her cousin's wedding. On
4 May: 'Reading till lights out. Then three Taubes came over us with
bombs and machine guns. Hell of a sensation. They did no damage
here.' Then, after 'Lying about' for much of the following day:

> G. M. & I went over to the Red House. Beautiful orchards,
> full of apples, oranges, lemons & pomegranates, apricots,
> melons. Had been shelled to blazes. Back to tea. Mail in.
> Had a parcel from home, biscuits & fags from Gib. Beautiful.
> Turned in. Aeroplanes again. No firing.

The dismal routine of life in the overwhelming heat prompted this
entry in the diary for 17 May: 'Sick of this life. Hope we'll shift
tomorrow to have something to do.' On 26 May Richard reports
that they packed up and marched for 5 miles towards Beersheba.
June and July were relatively quiet months, with occasional reports
of strafing by Taubes. On 14 June Richard wrote 'Weather getting
hotter every day. My skin almost black through the heat of the
sun.' He suffered from a sprained wrist in early July and a bout of
sickness in the middle of the month, but was recovering as rumours
went around that they were to be granted leave. On 20 July, 'Capt
Richards told me in Welsh that we were going tomorrow', and after
'a hell of a journey' they arrived in Kantara early on the morning of
22 July.[7] Richard visited William James's grave, and then proceeded
via Ismailia to Alexandria, where he arrived at 9 p.m. His diary

indicates that he and his comrades made the most of their four days in the city, meeting old friends and making new ones, including a crew of King's Own Scottish Borderers (KOSB). A photograph has survived portraying Richard in a borrowed glengarry which must date from this trip.

Richard also sent some silk to Mary Lizzie on 26 July, his last full day in the city, which culminated in a 'Rare night. Nearly set the hotel on fire.' They left Alexandria at 8.30 on the morning of 27 July and arrived back with their section at 7 p.m. on 28 July. The comment in the diary is rather unexpected: 'Glad to be home again. The old familiar boom of the guns to be heard as soon as we landed here.'

They were on the move again on 3 August, amidst rumours of 'Another scrap brewing'. Their new location was close enough to the sea for swimming (11 August: 'Very heavy surf. Fine fun'), but also close enough to Turkish positions for artillery shells to fall

6.1: Richard Eustis in a glengarry

occasionally. Given that Richard and his friends had now served for the four years they had originally signed up for as territorials, there was much speculation that they would be given home leave. On 13 August Richard had a 'Vivid dream of home' and five days later he lay in bed 'hoping for leave to the U.K.' There was much mail sent and received in this period, to and from the regular correspondents and also some new ones. Richard wrote to Dai Harris and David Thomas Morris (friends from home serving in the Royal Navy), to one of his new friends in the KOSB and to two Treboeth men whom he had met while serving in Egypt, Trevor James and Abraham Rees Morgan. The latter was serving as a chaplain with the 24th Welsh Regiment, and had been in Egypt since February 1917.[8] Both of these are mentioned in the next extant letter.

His diary tells us that on 26 August his mouth was sore from dental treatment and synovitis in his wrist was causing him trouble, but these matters do not crop up in two letters he wrote to the family at home. Both were addressed simply 'Palestine'.

RE1917-08-26a

Dear Mother

I was very pleased to receive your letter dated Aug. 2nd and was glad to hear that all are well at home there. So you have received the photo, well I daresay that by the time you have this one, you will have received the other photo which I had taken in Alexandria. Let me know what you think of it.

So Dai Evans is to be called up eh? Well, he is young and healthy, so I don't see what he has to complain about. Besides, he ought to be jolly thankful that he has escaped it these last three years.[9] Aunt Charlotte mentioned the Eisteddfod in her letter, which I received the same time as yours and it strikes me that it must have been quite a big thing.[10] No mother, Dd R. Thomas & I are not together, because his section went out to relieve our section, so that now he is out while I am at the base. I don't know how long it will be, but I have quite a good job now, being in charge of the hospital by night. Who could be that fellow home from Egypt who said that he had been speaking with Dai

& I before he came home. Do you know his name by any chance? I should like to know who he is …

Well, mother, you know I had rotten teeth? I have been to the dentist to have them all out. I was with him yesterday when he took three out for me. I have to see him Thursday again to have some more out. Of course, I feel quite alright except that my mouth is sore after it but I suppose it will be alright in a few days. I have been pretty free from toothache since I'm out here, but the war might end soon now, so I am trying to have a set of teeth before I leave, which of course won't cost me anything. I had a letter from Ivor the other day saying that all was well with him except that most of his pals were being drafted away to other battalions, and that he was feeling pretty lonely. I haven't heard from Gib for some time, but I expect a letter from him every day now. I wrote a few lines to A. Rees Morgan the other day telling him where to find me, for the chances are, that he will have more time to look for me than I'll have to look for him. I should like to see him, seeing that all the other boys have met him. I also wrote to Trevor James, for I haven't seen him for some time. One of the patients in our hospital mistook me for Johnny Eustis (Clydach) and then asked me if I was related to him. Do you know what has become of Johnny? Has he joined, or is he still at home? Send me his address if you know it.[11]

Well I have no more to say this time, Mam, except that I and the other boys are quite well, hoping that this will find you the same.

Love to all

From Dick

The reference to the photograph in this letter is most probably the one of him in the glengarry. In the letter to Aunt Charlotte, below, written at the same time, he makes reference to other photographs he sent that have safely arrived home. It is highly likely that this refers to the two photographs showing desert scenes which are the only ones that remained with the collection of letters. On the reverse of the smaller group photograph, Richard has written 'Having our mid-day meal. Blanket for tablecloth.'

6.2 AND 6.3: Two desert photographs

RE1917-08-26b

Dear Aunt Charlotte

I received your letter dated Aug 7th the other day, along with one from mother, and I was very pleased to receive them. Glad to hear that all are well at home there, but very sorry to hear about poor old Uncle Sam. I hope he will soon be alright again. I'm glad you received the snapshots safe, yes, I'm the one drinking out of the mug. Mother mentioned the Eisteddfod in her letter but as that was dated Aug 2nd, she couldn't give me the results. It must have been quite a big affair, and as you say competition must have been keen amongst the local choirs.

Poor old Grace! She seems to be suffering a great deal from toothache. As I said in mother's letter, I have started parading to the dentist, to get all my teeth out. You see, I'm hoping that the war will soon be over now, so I'm trying to get a set of teeth, before leaving them. So Dan is as full of mischief as I was. Ha! Ha! Ha! I haven't heard from Gib for some time now, but I expect a letter from him almost every day. I hear from Ivor oftener, and when he writes his letters are worth reading. He has the gift alright, for he writes 12 & 14 pages every time. I'm sorry to hear that he missed the trip to Dublin, for it would be worth having. I sincerely hope he shall remain in England till all is over. So Mamgu & Uncle Sam are going back to Cae Parc?[12] Back to the old house, I suppose? Well, no doubt it will be a great deal better for Uncle Sam, more so, as he is so ill. I'm very sorry to hear about his being so ill, for he has been a real pal to what he terms 'bechgyn John ni' [*our John's boys*]. So Dd N. Griffiths has been gassed now again?[13] That will delay his wedding now, I suppose. I'm afraid Uriel is going to be sadly disillusioned, if he thinks he can have his own way, every time he changes his mind about joining and having exemption. Of course, good luck to him, the longer he'll keep clear, the better off he'll be. You needn't worry about my work, for it is only my number I've changed. I don't think there is any danger of being combed out here, for as you know, there is a vast difference between R.A.M.C. and

Field Ambulance. Naturally, we are in the field, just behind the Infantry, but what they are after are the fit men who are in the Base Hospitals, especially in the towns here. So Willie Rees is home on leave from the Soudan? I haven't heard a word from him since we were down on the Suez Canal, somewhere about last November. I wrote to him from there, replying to his letter, but I never heard any more about him.

Well, things are pretty quiet with us at present, but we don't know what day we'll be into it here once again. Dai R Thomas has been down 'ar lan y môr' [*by the seaside*] at El Aresh for a week and he is due back tomorrow morning. There are strong rumours of leave to England now, for men who have been out here for two years, so as my time is up as well, I rather fancy my chance of coming with one of the first batches. I don't know when it is going to start, the sooner the better.

I have no more to tell you this time so I conclude.
Love to all from
Dick
PS All the boys are quite well and happy under the circumstances

Comparing Richard's private thoughts, as recorded in his diary, with the content of these letters shows how the messages that he seeks to convey to his family at home are nuanced. Neither of these letters contains any information on the Turkish shelling nor the threat from enemy aircraft. Richard brushes off the troubles he is having with his teeth and does not mention the pain in his wrist. The focus is very much on allaying the fears of his mother and aunt, and engaging them in a conversation about family members, local events and the activities of mutual friends. By referring to Dai R. Thomas's visit to El Arish as him going 'ar lan y môr' (the title of a popular Welsh song), it is made into something comfortable and familiar.

Richard had three more teeth out the following Thursday (30 August). The next day G. M. Williams was admitted to hospital with sand-fly fever and a temperature of 104°; Richard was admitted with the same disease on 2 September, with a temperature of 103.4°. As he recovered, he was sent to 'rest camp' at El Arish, where he was able to swim for much of the day: 'Having a rattling good time.

Fine rest' he wrote on 13 September. Four days later he returned to his unit, where he had more teeth removed. (18 September: 'Hell of a job. Had three out. Nearly drove me mad. Suffering terribly.') He was put on a light diet and given light duties in the packstore. More teeth came out the following week and Richard was paying weekly visits to the dentist through the month of October. There were new pastimes, and from late September chess becomes a craze (29 September: 'I have chess whacked. Beat the one who taught me to play'). Older activities resumed: soccer and rugby returned to the schedule of events. Some activities endured and every week there were letters to or from home or Mary Lizzie. There were further encounters with old friends, for example with the Rev. Abraham Rees Morgan (19 September) and Trevor James (2 October).

There was a lot of movement in late October prior to the EEF's attack upon Beersheba on 31 October. Richard's unit was not involved but they heard about it that day: 'Hell of a battle going on. Good reports. We have given the Turk a real hiding this time. Fighting all day. Gained all objectives.' The next day Richard was up at 3.30 a.m. for a 7 a.m. start for a march to Beersheba, where they arrived at midday. There followed an exceptionally busy period, and many of the diary entries for early November report that he is 'Dog tired' and sleeping 'like a nail'.

> [6 November] Slept all the morning. Dinner. On hospital.
> Busy. Struck hospital. Marched off 10 miles. Put hosp up.
> Got a convoy in straight. Very busy & dog-tired.

> [7 November] Turned in 5.30. Slept till dinner. On hosp. Fine
> news. Huge victory. Special mention of 53rd Division. Tea.
> But it has been terribly hard work. Working 18 hours a day.

> [8 November] On at 6 a.m. Haven't shaved for 4 days.
> Congratulations read out from Allenby, Chetwode, Mott &
> Vernon.[14] Highest praise I heard. Gained everything. Gave
> Turks a hell of a swiping [??]. Wholesale massacre. Still
> receiving wounded & Turkish prisoners.

Richard wrote letters to his mother, Mary Lizzie, Gabriel and Aunt Charlotte on 9 November, but none of these have survived. The extant correspondence resumes with a significant run of letters written as the 53rd (Welsh) Division was part of the Allied move into Palestine, which culminated with the capture of Jerusalem. On 14 November Richard wrote to his aunt again, from 'Beersheba Palestine'.

RE1917-11-14

Dear Auntie Charlotte

I was very pleased to receive your letter the other day, dated Oct 16th, and am very glad to learn that all are well at home there. I daresay that by now you have received my last letter which I sent you a few days ago, telling you of what I have seen here up to date and what I know about this part of the world. I am very pleased to note that you mention the date of my letters, for by doing that, I can see at a glance, whether you receive all my letters, or not.

Well, as you say, that Gib is a lucky bounder, to have five weeks leave, all of a run like that, but good luck to him, let him make the most of it. Yes, I daresay Uriel is beginning to understand a thing or two about army life by now, besides, he has a good champion in Ivor, but there is another side of it which I sincerely hope that he, or Ivor will never see. So we must hope for the best. From what I understand by your letter, Ivor is going in for a further promotion in the Non-Commissioned Rank. All well and good, as long as he doesn't push himself abroad, and from his promises to me I can trust him not to be too forward in that respect, but I know it is asking a great deal from a boy of his spirit. I am very sorry to hear that Uncle Sam is just the same, and no better, I sent him a letter a few weeks ago, in which I enclosed one of the photographs, which I had taken at Alexandria, to cheer him up a bit. Have you heard whether he has received it, or not? You might enquire, and if he has not, I shall write him another.

Yes, Dai R. Thomas is still a corporal, for he has not moved more than myself, since we had these nearly two years ago. Never mind, I daresay you know that it hasn't been our fault, and as long as my conscience remains as clear as it is at

present, I don't care if I never have another stripe. So young
Thos. J. Cole has been sent to France, eh?[15] Poor little fellow!
I heard that the authorities had 'pinched' two C.O's from
the district there, but I will not express an opinion one way
or the other. So Dd Thos Morris is home on leave?[16] Lucky
boy, I hope he'll have a good time. I am very glad to hear that
Dad's cold has cleared away. It is a funny thing, but I have
almost forgotten what a cold is. I don't think I have had what
you might call a proper cold since I came out here. Besides,
we have had so much experience about hospital work and
we have access to so much stuff that should we feel below
par, we know by the symptoms what will put us right again.
Therefore we seldom worry the Medical Officer with various
ailments. Of course we are not supposed to take anything
except what the M.O. prescribes, but you have an idea what
a lot of boys there are, they won't go to an Officer and say
they have a headache, but simply take a pill for it. Well I
daresay you have read all the fighting we've done out here
lately, well, this morning our Colonel called a parade, and
explained the position to us. It was very interesting indeed.
Seeing that it was such a huge success, there was no harm
in telling us of the plans, of what part was allotted to each
Division, what they expected, and what actually took place.
Then he told us of the work done by our own Brigade and
it made a fellow's blood tingle, to think that he had taken
part in such a splendid victory. Well, today I witnessed a few
honours being given by the General. It was quite a big thing,
all the battalions lined up in a square, and the recipients in a
line in the centre.

 Well Auntie Charlotte, you mention in your letter
about preparing Christmas parcels. Well I don't want
anything at all; I have a splendid sleeping helmet (which is
seldom used since Suvla Bay) which I wouldn't part with for
ten pounds, because it served its purpose during the blizzard
at Gallipoli; undoubtedly the most severe cold I have ever
experienced, or ever likely to see again. As for gloves or
socks, it would be a waste of time & money to send them
to me, because I should never have cause to use them as
the weather is so hot here. Of course we are supplied with

any amount of good socks for they don't allow darning, for fear of injuring the feet for marching. So you see how it is, you can tell Mrs Davies that I am not in need of anything, thanking her all the same for her kind intentions. If you send a Xmas parcel from home, let it be of cigarettes and unperishable eatables. You see what I mean Auntie Charlotte, anything from Mrs Davies would only entail a long-winded reply, and I don't feel up to it at present. So W. Rees never came near Mynyddbach then?[17] I remember that he could play the violin, when he came to visit us once when I was home. Never mind, he is well over a thousand miles away from me, so I have no chance of running across him, so you need not worry.

During the battle up here, Sammy Rees brought in a wounded Turkish officer, and seeing that Sam was so tender with him, dressing his wounds, etc. he (the officer) gave Sam his watch and chain. It is a very pretty little thing, solid silver, double cased like the one I left at home, and marked with Turkish figures, with the name of a firm in Constantinople on it. Sam values it very much, for it is a beautiful little memento.[18] I hope you will be able to see it when it is sent home. I have no more to say this time hoping that all are as well at home, as this leaves me at present, so I close with love to all

from

Dick

It is instructive to compare the letter above with the one that follows, written on 20 November. This is the only letter to have survived in the collection that Richard sent to Ivor when both were serving. Parts of this letter cover much of the same ground as the letter to Aunt Charlotte, though the tone is rather different.

RE1917-11-20

Dear Ivor,

I was just beginning to wonder what had become of you when your letter dated October 10th arrived two nights ago. I am glad to hear that all's well with you & that you are still in that land called Blighty.

Well Ivor, the yarn was quite true about my having
had a touch of fever, but by fighting it, I am pleased to say
that it left me without a trace of anything about a week or so
later. Don't worry kid, illness won't bowl me over, unless it
is one of those diseases accompanied by an eight inch shell
plonking you one in the pot, then I'm afraid I shall have to
give in. I am very sorry to hear that you are in trouble again,
owing to those flappers; you'd better watch yourself for
stripes are easier lost than gained, not that it would make any
difference to you, or I, I know, but to the folk at home, who
are so ignorant of Army life just think of what it what mean
[*sic*] to them. If you remember when you had two days C.B.
to them it was two days gaol, and if you lost your stripes,
you would think that you must have murdered someone, or
done something equally serious. I heard all about Gib's series
of extensions, but I am very sorry to learn that they put you
out of pocket so considerably, but you can see it was no fault
of Ginger's. By what I understand, the exchequer ran very
low when he was at home, but of course, that was only to be
expected after a run of five weeks leave. Don't you think so?
Well kid, I daresay you've heard & read all about that little
stunt we had here recently. I went through that little lot,
but I am fortunate this time again, in not bumping into any
of those little Turkish pellets. Ha! Ha! The unit has had
another two Military Medals again, so you see the honours
are slowly increasing. One of the recipients is a very old pal
of Uncle Sam Eustis, being Sgt Will Bowen from Manselton
or Forestfach or somewhere near there.[19] There is no doubt
about it that we have given Johnny Turk the damnest hiding
he ever had in his life, this time, and I daresay you have
read all about the advance we have made in Palestine here.
It was terribly hard work while we were at it, but it passed
off alright, the 53rd as usual coming up to scratch. We are
now having a quiet little rest after it, but God only knows
where we shall go to next, and what's more, I don't care. I am
already itching to be on the move again, for the old Johnny
Turk has retired a hell of a distance, and I should like to see
what's doing. I am very glad to hear you say that Uriel is
'exaggerating', possibly, in time, he may come to be able to

look after himself, and fight his own battles. Keep him clear
of the women, Ivor, for I've heard that one or two from the
district there, have dropped into it. No names, no pack-drill.
        Well Ivor, being so near, I wonder if I'll ever have
the chance of seeing Jerusalem. By what I understand, we
are only about two days march away from it, where we are
at present. Not that I am interested in the Biblical side of
it but just idle curiosity. I daresay it is like all other Arab
towns and villages, nothing but a heap of mud-huts and one
swarm of flies, but still I should like to have a glimpse at it.
I would also like to see that phenomenon, the Dead Sea, fed
by fresh-water rivers, having no outlet and yet as salty as
hell itself. Funny, isn't it, eh? Well I have no more to tell you
this time hoping that you've been able to scrape through that
trouble again and that you are as well as your humble, also
all the other village boys who are out here.[20] I often see Trev.
James have you heard from him at all? He says he has written
to you.
                No more this trip with the best of Luck
                        from Yours
                            Dick
P.S. Haven't had the mags yet but I suppose they'll turn up
one of these days

One aspect of this letter which causes complications in its interpretation is Richard's reference to Ivor's problem with the 'flappers'. Ivor
used this word in a 1916 letter in the sense of a 'flighty woman'.[21]
Given the context that Richard's comment follows a discussion of
illness, it could be interpreted as a warning to avoid prostitutes.
Alternatively, it could just be a case of the big brother pulling his
little brother's leg, after the youngster has discovered that men in
uniform are attractive to some young women. Later on in the letter, Richard's instruction to Ivor to keep their cousin Uriel 'clear of
the women' hints that there may be some playful teasing going on.
As this is the only surviving letter from one to another from their
period in uniform, we cannot judge how it fits into the rest of their
correspondence. However, it is unclear when Ivor received this letter: by the time it would have arrived in Kinmel Park, he had left
'Blighty' and was in France. None of the letters that Ivor received in

France have survived in the collection, so it is likely that this letter was sent on to the home address, and therefore may not have been read until Ivor visited home in the last month of the war.

This period in late November 1917 appears to have been busy but not unpleasant for Richard. He had plenty of duties in the packstore, but also time for chess, football and rugby. Then on 30 November it was time to pack up the camels again as the unit was on the move, with a march of around 22 miles. Four days later, there was another seven hours' marching, to reach Beersheba. By now the weather was very cold and wet: 'Glad of our greatcoats' is a comment on 7 December. Rain or no, almost every day saw a game of soccer. There are no reports of incoming mail in the diary for three weeks until he received a letter from his mother on 14 December: it is clear that he wrote the following letter earlier in the day.

RE1917-12-14

Dear Mother,

Just a few lines to let you know that all is well with me at present hoping that this will find all at home enjoying the best of health and spirits. I have not had a letter from you this last two or three weeks but I'm expecting one now almost every day. Of course, I don't grumble, because I know that you have to write to Gib & Ivor as well as me, but it is very awkward to write a letter, unless you have a letter to answer; at least I find it so, for I have nothing to say. The weather is getting colder here, now that the winter is upon us, and we have had quite a lot of rain lately. We are having a fairly easy time at present doing practically no work, except footballing to keep muscles in good condition, and ready for anything that comes along. I daresay that you know long before this that we have taken Hebron, Bethlehem and Jerusalem, three very historical places and I hope to see them shortly. As far as I understand, they have not been shelled at all, so, I shall, possibly, be able to see them as they have stood for years. No doubt they will be interesting to see if only for the fact that they are so famous, and date back for so many centuries. Perhaps I shall be able to say more about these places after I've seen them. Beersheba is very picturesque, lying as it does, in a hollow, between the hills and to see the sun setting behind it is quite a sight. The town itself is very pretty with its red-tiled buildings, also there are little public gardens dotted all over the town, each with a little fountain in the centre. Well mother, my watch has gone beyond repair, so I would be very pleased if you would send me another of the same type. Mine got full of sand while we were on the desert, and I saw it was no use sending for another for I would not be able to keep the sand out of it, but now that we have left the desert behind, I shall be able to take better care of it, also it would be very handy, so I shall be very thankful if you send one along. If it were possible for me to buy one here, I wouldn't worry you about it.

Well I have no more to say this time, but I will write again as soon as I receive a letter from you.

Love to All

from Dick

Richard's unit was on the move again shortly afterwards, marching through the Judaean hills for two days. He slept in a cacolet (which he spelt 'cacholau') – a seat fitted to a mule or camel for carrying the wounded. They reached Hebron on the afternoon of 18 December, and Richard had the first opportunity to sleep on a mattress for a long time. However, the following day they were off again and on 20 December they went through the 'most terrible move I remember' in the 'Perishing cold' and rain before arriving in Bethlehem. The next day they moved on to Jerusalem. The entry for 22 December notes: 'The old Holy City out of bounds. Can see the Mount of Olives quite near. Also the great Mosque of Omar. Hope to explore the town soon.' A lot of alcohol was consumed over the next three days, though Christmas dinner was 'Bully and Biscuits. Miserable.' However, the fighting recommenced late on 26 December, and Richard witnessed the battle on 27 December:

Field & H.B. [heavy battery] all around us. Terrible din going on all the morning. Hardly any casualties yet. Saw the Dead Sea and all the front. Fine sight. Tea. Took some Turkish (w) [wounded] in. In a hell of a position. 14 Guns lined up in front of us. Hell of a din. Very little sleep

[28 December] Took some wounded in 6 a.m. Breakfast.
Very cold. Quiet till dinner. Saw a terrible bombardment and
a creeping barrage. Wonderful work. Tea. A.D.S. [advanced
dressing station] went out. Working till 3 a.m. clearing
wounded. Turks & Bedouins mostly.

The following day Richard reports a Turkish retreat, although sick
and wounded were still arriving at his unit. On New Year's Eve, he
had another novel experience, when he borrowed a motorcycle and
learned how to ride it. Thus ends the available day-by-day account
of Richard's activities, but there are three letters extant that he wrote
home in the next month which give further details of his activities.
The first, dated simply 'January 1918', was sent from Jerusalem:

RE1918-01-a

Dear Mother,
          Just a few lines to let you know that I received your
parcel and letter the other day and was very pleased to have
it. Everything was alright except a few of the biscuits, which
turned because of the fruit you put in one corner of the tin.
Of course, when you think of the time it has taken to arrive,
we cannot complain. Although the food was a little plain
when we were on the move, being only bully & jam and
biscuits for about five or six weeks, now that we are settled,
the food is everything you could wish for, including an issue
of Australian butter, which is as good as any I ever ate. We
get bread every day also, so you see, there is no need for any
more parcels. The fags were very acceptable for we cannot
buy any here, and one cannot live very well on the Army
issue alone, for it is not enough. I daresay that we shall have
Y.M.C.A. and Canteens here now before long, then we shall
be alright.
          Well, Mother, after all I've heard of this beautiful (?)
city, I am greatly disappointed with it for it is as dirty as any
other town or village out in these parts. Of course there are
a few ancient, historical places here, but there is a high city
wall around the ancient Holy City, and only twelve of us
are allowed in there at a time, and even then, an officer must

take us in. I went in there a day or two ago and went all around most places of interest there, including the Garden of Gethsemane, the Great Mosque of Omar, Tomb of Solomon, Temple of the Holy Sepulchre, etc. I have also seen the Mount of Olives, Mount Calvary, Mount Zion, the Dead Sea and part of the Jordan. Also we marched through Bethlehem, there is a church to be seen, where it is supposed that Christ was born. They have erected a church on the site of the old stable and have a star worked into the floor to show the actual spot where He was born. This is called the Church of Nativity. Inside the City wall, I should think that things are just the same as they were hundreds of years ago, the streets if you can call them such are so narrow that you can shake hands from one side of the street to the other. Well since we have been here, we have had miserable weather also plenty of rain, but fortunately, we are in buildings in the town so we are alright.

Mails have been very slow lately, having been held up for a while I daresay, until things are straight here. I suppose they will all come up together one of these days.

I have no more to tell you this time so I close with
love to all from
Dick
Will write again in a day or two

On both of the following letters, written on YMCA paper, Richard gave the date as 'January 9ᵗʰ 1917', but they are clearly from 1918.

RE1918-01-09a

Dear Mother,

I was very pleased to receive your letter dated November 28th and am glad to hear that all are well at home there. I heard from Stephens that Ivor had been sent to Ireland, and that he would not be very long before going to France.[22] Well I sincerely hope that he will be as fortunate as Gabe & myself have been, as regards health, etc. I often wonder how he managed to stick there so long. I'm glad to hear that he had a few days before going out anyhow. Mails have been rather slow lately, but one can quite understand it seeing that we have been so busy here for the past few weeks. Never mind, I daresay they will turn up together one of these days. I haven't heard from Gabe for some time now or from Ivor, but I daresay I'll get a letter from both when the mails come up. I sent Hannah a little brooch from here a few days ago, just a little souvenir of Jerusalem. I have also sent Auntie Charlotte a little Olive-wood bound Bible. It was like this, we were only paid 10/- a day or two before Xmas, but I managed to have £1, so I couldn't very well send anything all round to you, but we may have another pay before we leave Jerusalem, so perhaps I'll be able to send a few things home.

The weather here is terrible at present, but fortunately we are in a building but on the way up here we were marching by day, sleeping out in the night in the rain. Often we were starting [the] day's march soaking through to the skin and sleeping out in [???], that night. But thank goodness we are now in a house and the wet weather will soon be over, then we shall be alright again. The food is not all bad here now, as we are having any amount of bread, butter, jam, fresh meat and vegetables, so you can see, we are not doing at all bad.

We only arrived here a day or so before Xmas, so we spent Xmas on bully beef & Biscuits, which was not very pleasant. Never mind, we will make up for it when we return home again, after all this is over. This is the fourth Christmas for me to spend away from home and I needn't tell you that I am sick and tired of it.

You say you have heard rumours of leave for us out here, well mother, I don't think there is any chance of leave for us until everything is over, so don't build any hopes on our coming home just yet. Although we are time expired we will not have any leave, except the £15 bounty. I have no more to say this time so I close with

> Love to all
>> from
>>> Dick

RE1918-01-09b

Dear Auntie Charlotte
        Just a few lines along with this little souvenir of
Jerusalem, hoping that you will not be offended with it. I
should have liked to send something all round to the folk
at home, but we were only paid 10/- about 2 days before
Xmas. I managed to have £1, but as you know, a pound isn't
much to buy presents with, so all I could do was to send
you this, a little brooch to Morriston & one for Hannah. I
am living in hopes now that we shall be paid again before
we leave this old city. I have seen almost all places of interest
here, and on the whole I am disappointed with it, after all I
had heard of this famous old city. Of course, things [are] a
great deal more miserable because we happened to get here
during the wet season, and it is a wet period, raining day
after day regular as clockwork. Well, we marched through
Bethlehem about two days before Christmas, and we could
see what is called the Church of Nativity, built over the old
stable where Christ was born. I haven't had a chance of going
inside it yet, but Dai R. Thomas has been inside and he says
that things are exactly as they have been for hundreds of
years, and that almost all denominations keep guard over
the manger in turns. I shall certainly go to see it if I have half
a chance. I have been inside the ancient city of Jerusalem,
which is surrounded by a high city wall, and we are only
allowed in there in parties of twelve, accompanied by an
officer. It is very quaint and a typical Biblical picture; I have
seen the Garden of Gethsemane, the Golden Gate, the Great
Mosque of Omar, Solomon's Tomb, the Temple of the Holy
Sepulchre, Mount Zion, Mount Calvary, Mount of Olives, the
Dead Sea, part of the river Jordan, etc, etc. But I don't think I
could tell you much about any of these places, except describe
them as they stand. The wood binding this little Bible is made
from [is] Olive-wood from the Mount of Olives, and it was
the best little memento I could see in the town there. Let me
know if you receive it alright and undamaged.
        I have no more to tell you this time, so I close with
love to all
                from Dick

The 'little souvenir' that arrived at Laurel Cottage was a Bible: the brooch was received by Hannah, though we cannot know for certain whether Mary Lizzie received hers in Morriston.[23] Whatever photographs Richard took in Palestine have not survived, although those that were sent home by his comrade (Evan) Samuel Rees are extant.[24] Both of these men had been brought up in the Welsh Nonconformist tradition, and had thus attended Sunday schools where they would have been taught about the history and geography of the Holy Land.[25] The names of the places that they visited were familiar both to them and to their families back home, and so the descriptions and photographs of these sites had a particular resonance. Samuel annotated his photographs and wrote messages on their reverse which located them within the biblical narrative, such as his photograph of Bethlehem which has an 'x' to mark 'the actual place where the barn or stable was situated', where Christ was born.[26] Even though Richard candidly states in his letter to Ivor that he is not 'interested in the Biblical side of it', he is very keen to see the sites, to describe them to his mother and aunt, and to send the latter a present that she will treasure.

Notes

1. RE1917-11-20, see below.
2. RE1918-01-09b, see below.
3. Lieut. Horace William Fletcher: see *http://www.cwgc.org/find-war-dead/casualty/1645174/FLETCHER,%20HORACE%20WILLIAM* (accessed January 2018).
4. Funk-holes: dugouts for shelter.
5. See Appendix 3.
6. *http://www.cwgc.org/find-war-dead/casualty/474872/JAMES,%20WILLIAM%20CHARLES* (accessed January 2018). See 'The Scroll of Fame', *CDL*, 30 April 1917, 2, and a photograph of William James, 'Local Heroes', *CDL*, 3 May 1917, 4.
7. Richard only names George M. Williams and Jack Llewelyn in the party: it is not clear how many others went with them from the unit.
8. Ieuan Elfryn Jones, 'A Welsh perspective on army chaplaincy during the First World War: the letters of Abraham Rees Morgan MC', in Michael Snape and Edward Madigan (eds), *The Clergy in Khaki: New Perspectives on British Army Chaplaincy in the First World War* (Burlington, VT: Ashgate, 2013), pp. 57–73.
9. This Dai Evans cannot be positively identified, but he is referred to again in RE1918-08-22 (ch. 11) (at which time he still had not been called up)

and he is most probably the same as the Dai Evans mentioned in Dai Harris's letter, DH1918-12-17 (ch. 13).

10. The second eisteddfod to be organised by the local Soldiers' and Sailors' Support Fund was held in Treboeth on 4 August 1917, with a concert on the following day. See 'Treboeth Eisteddfod', *HoW*, 11 August 1917, 5.

11. John Eustis was a second cousin of Richard's. It is not known whether he joined up, but two other second cousins from this branch of the family did serve in the army, with the surname spelt 'Eustace'. Gabriel Eustace survived, but his brother James Henry Eustace was killed in the Battle of Loos in September 1915.

12. Mamgu: grandmother, Ann Eustis. Cae Parc is the local name of the area around Parkhill Terrace.

13. See Appendix 2.

14. General Sir Edmund Allenby, commander of the EEF; Lieut.-General Sir Philip Chetwode, commander of XX Corps; Maj.-General S. F. Mott, commander of the 53rd (Welsh) Division; Brig.-General H. A. Vernon, commander of 158th Brigade.

15. See Appendix 2.

16. See Appendix 2.

17. Most probably the William Rees mentioned in RE1917-08-26b, see above.

18. It is very likely that this chain is the one still in the family's possession. It is now attached to the medal that Evan Samuel Rees received from the Mynyddbach Treboeth and District Soldier & Sailor Reception Fund. See *https://www.peoplescollection.wales/items/387696* (accessed January 2018).

19. See Appendix 3.

20. 'Your humble' is short for 'your humble servant': see also the use of 'yer' 'umble' in DH1918-12-17.

21. See the discussion in ch. 4.

22. This is most probably (Thomas) Grongar Stephens, who was serving with the RAMC in Egypt, having volunteered at the start of the war. Grongar's brother Elfryn had enlisted with the RWF at the same time as Ivor and trained with him at Kinmel Park.

23. RE1918-03-20a (ch. 8).

24. These are available via the *People's Collection Wales* website: see *https://www.peoplescollection.wales/collections/388562* (accessed January 2018).

25. Samuel attended Caersalem Newydd, which translates as 'New Jerusalem'.

26. *https://www.peoplescollection.wales/items/388341* (accessed January 2018).

7

Ivor Eustis in north Wales, 1917

Following the sole letter from Ivor's time at Altcar in November 1916, there is a gap in the collection until the beginning of 1917. Ivor had hoped that he was to have leave around Christmas 1916: perhaps he did. There is then a run of eight letters he sent home in January and February 1917, one from March and then another gap until there is one from July and two more from September.

By this time, Ivor was firmly ensconced at Kinmel Park, and despite numerous indications early in the year that he was eager to leave, his skill as an instructor meant that he had to stay to train the new recruits. Many of the pre-occupations of 1916 are present in the letters, such as food, health, money and home leave. The letters also indicate how information about other family members was pooled, with Ivor reporting on the news he had received from his serving brothers.

The first letter of 1917 was sent on 5 January, with Ivor giving his address as 'C' Coy, 62nd T R Battn, Camp 1, Kinmel Park: the same address as his other letters from north Wales for that year.

IE1917-01-05

Dear Mother,

I received the washing and your letter this morning quite safely, and I shall let you have a similar packet next week to do, because I know that if I send them to the wash I shall never see them again.

This is the last day of my excused duty lot and I shall not be sorry to go on parade again because with the training I've had it is more of a job to do nothing than to go through a hard day's work. Well I have just received a letter from Dick, which has been delayed two days owing to somebody making a mistake and sending it to B company instead of 'C'. Dick seems to be having a good time of it now, having returned to the remainder of the boys. He is looking forward to a fine Christmas as he writes to me; he includes with it a letter for you, which I am sending on with this.

Well, Mother, I know you will be pleased to hear this:- I've been again promoted and now I wear 3 stripes instead of two. There will now be a great change from what I've usually been going through. In future I shall have all my meals at the sergeants mess instead of with the rest of the men. Plenty of swank now! ha! ha! fancy eating grub on a tablecloth and what's more a waiter to attend to you. You see there will be no need to fight for a meal now everything will come around decently.

Well I have little else to say except that I recovered nicely from my cold, and everything is all right again. So no more,

with love from

Ivor

The next surviving letter was written on 14 January.

IE1917-01-14

Dear Mother,

A few more lines to let you know how things are going on here. I am glad to say that everything just now seems at its best, with one exception, that is that our prospects of getting leave are getting more and more remote, and in fact at present, there is hardly any chance at all of getting leave. That is the only drawback there is at present because everything else is all right – the food is very good and continues the same as when I first came here for my dinner.

There is a draft leaving here for India, either tonight or tomorrow and I'm sorry to say they have stopped me going with it. I tried hard to be allowed to go but they would not let any of us go. There are 78 going all together – all of them more or less recruits because they have only been here 5 weeks. Nothing would please me more than to be allowed to go with them especially as they are going all the way to India. We were very busy today until dinnertime helping them put their things together. They did not know how to put their equipment together, so you can guess how much they know about their job. They will probably do about a month or 6 weeks training on board ship and they will have some more time to get used to the climate. By that time they will have probably finished the regulation 14 weeks training. There is a rumour of another draft going next week so that there may be a chance of going on that. Anyway, I'll do my best.

I have sent the usual things home to be washed again and in the parcel you will find a woollen glove which Auntie Charlotte asked me to send home, so that she can make another one in place of the one I lost Christmas week.

How are things at home now? how is Danny standing the winter? It is very cold up here, and though it's been dry the last three days, one cannot depend on the weather. As you probably guess, it is all mud here from one side to the other and the least drop of rain causes a few more feet of mud.

Well I have no more this time so I conclude
with love from
Ivor

A little under two weeks later, Ivor wrote to Aunt Charlotte. He began by thanking her for the gloves and then passed on the 'good news' that he has been awarded a first class for the musketry course. He continued:

IE1917-01-27

One of the instructors at Altcar was a chap who had
been at Gowerton the same time as me for years. He was
from Gorseinon, and when war broke out was at Cardiff
University, and doing well too. He was telling me that he
did not know what he was going to do after the war, and I
replied that I did not know myself what I was going to do.
I shall certainly have to begin all over again. It is somewhat
premature to talk about the end of the war at present, we
must remember that my tour of France is not done with
yet by any means. There is some rumour about that all
NCO's who have not been out, will be abroad by the end of
February, but I don't know how much truth can be attached
to it.

I am going to see our Quarter-master about making an
allotment; there will be no addition by the Government, but
all the same, every little bit helps.

I am having a fine time just now, only doing about
4 or 6 hours a day and a few hours night operations
occasionally. Naturally this is not exactly to my liking as
it makes me lazy, and you know what follows. I would far
prefer a hard day's work to an easy one. Well there is hardly
any news, this time, so I conclude with best love & good
wishes from

yours affectionately,

Ivor

The eagerness to leave Kinmel Park for India which Ivor
expressed in the letter of 14 January might seem as though he was
keen to avoid the Western Front, but in the following letter there
is a passage that is rather surprising. Ivor suggests that both he
and the men stationed at Kinmel who have already served on the
Western Front were impatient to go to France. This letter, written on Church Army Recreation Hut notepaper, was simply dated
'Tuesday', but the date on the sketch makes it certain that it was
written on 30 January.

IE1917-01-30

Dear Mother,

I have just received the parcel with the gloves from Auntie Charlotte and of course there was a letter with it. I am very sorry to hear that Dad is down with a cold, especially as it is so bad as to cause him to lose some days from work. It is probably a direct result of the cold weather you are having down there; it is also very cold here, though it's a good job it's dry. The ground is as dry as a bone this last fortnight and it has been freezing all along. As it is, it is only our hands & faces that suffer and I can tell you they do get it too, especially our hands, because we have to carry the old rifle about with us all day long, and in the morning when we start out for the park, the rifles are not on our shoulders five minutes before our hands are quite numb, but now that the gloves have come, it will be all right.

I've been having quite a good time of it this week so far, quite a lazy time. Yesterday I did two hours work in the morning and two in the afternoon, while today I had the whole of the afternoon to myself. When I do work, it is not very hard, because the men I've got with me now are all Expeditionary men, that is, men who have been out to France two or three times and are ready to go again, and as you can see, such men as these want very little teaching. They are nearly all sick of this place, though they have only been here a month or so, and they would gladly go back to France anytime. So would I, though I know there is no hope for me.

So Dick has shifted again. From what he tells me, his finger is not so bad as the famous 'fellwm'.[1] I am still looking out for a letter from Gib. The sketch included is of my corner, my bed-sitting-dining room & coalhouse combined. With love from Ivor

The sketch has survived. It was done on the back of a target and is entitled 'Not at Home'.

7.1: 'Not at home', by Ivor Eustis

The next letter, to Aunt Charlotte, is undated but was written
the following day as the event it refers to, the opening of the Church
of England Hall, took place on 31 January 1917.[2]

IE1917-01-31

Dear Auntie Charlotte
    A few lines while I am waiting for dinner. Things
are just the same as usual here except that the weather has
been still worse, bad as it was before. Really it surprises me
that it can be so cold here. The fire buckets which are kept
outside the huts have long ago been frozen up and on Friday
the order came that the ice was to be emptied, the buckets
refilled and placed <u>inside</u> the hut. This was done in our hut
straight away, the buckets being placed each end of the huts,
but on Saturday morning the buckets were frozen again, a

layer of ice about an inch thick being found in each case. Ha! ha! this is the standing joke of the camp now and in future the buckets must be kept near the stove. Also they have at last realised what it is like with the men, as that there will be an extra blanket issued out to every man at 2 o'clock today. That will be a total of 4 blankets, a mattress and a pillow and the recruits are feeling it badly too … I have a thick jersey in my kit bag, but as long as I can keep in my present state of health without it, in the kit bag it shall remain.

They are opening still another recreation hut today for us, and according to the boys who have been there, it beats all the others. There is now within 100 yards of our hut, 3 such [????] – the Wesleyan Institute, the YMCA Hut and this new one – the Church of England Hall. Then about 400 yards away is the very popular Free Church Hall (Nonconformists) and another YMCA. Then about the same distance away are two picture houses and a 'Church Army Hut'. So you see as far as this is concerned Kinmel Park is well blessed; but you must take into consideration the huge size of the Camp – where there are about 30 to 40 thousand men.

I am expecting letters from both Gab and Dick every day for I have not received one from either for some time. Busy, I suppose, for like myself their time is not their own.

No more this trip, from your affectionate nephew, Ivor

In the next letter to have survived, written on 11 February, Ivor again makes it clear that he is agitating to get sent out of Kinmel Park, although Gabe Williams, who has experienced the front, is not.

IE1917-02-11

Dear Mother,

Just a few lines to let you know that I am enjoying the best of health at present and to hope that everyone at home is the same. The weather has taken a turn for the better and the frost has disappeared to a certain extent, though not completely.

I was down at the Rifle Range at Rhyl all last week, teaching these youngsters how to shoot and on the whole it

was quite pleasant, although it meant getting up early and a
bit harder work than I've been doing lately. We started out
at a quarter to seven every morning and marched down to
the Range, 5 miles away and it was very cold on the first day
(Monday) until about 11 o'clock when we had the full benefit
of the little bit of sun there was. We had breakfast each day
at 6.30 and a dinner when we returned about 3 o'clock in the
afternoon. It was a long stretch between meals, I must say,
for we only had a cup of cocoa in between, but all the same
this was nothing to make a fuss over, especially as we had a
dinner enough for a dozen when we returned. You bet we
made a meal of it, too.

There is one thing I forgot to mention in my last letter,
that is that 'Will Jones y Saer' [*Will Jones the Carpenter*]
wishes to be remembered to father. I came across him last
week and of course he was glad to see me, if only that I
came from Mynydd Bach. I was taking him and another
man around the park in the course of duty, and noting
that he spoke with a South Wales accent, I asked him if he
came from anywhere near Swansea – you see, I seemed to
recognise his face though I could not remember who he was.
Well of course when he heard that I was 'Mab Jack Eustis'
[*Jack Eustis's son*] he was thunderstruck. He said that he was
speaking to Father just about Christmas time when he was
home on leave. He has been out in Mesopotamia, and then
was brought back to Litherland and from there to Kinmel
Park to our Battalion; but not exactly to this Company.

I have not seen Idris Evans yet,[3] and it is not likely
that I shall too, for as I said before, this is such a huge place
– for instance there were 12,000 men on Church of England
Parade alone this morning, while 6,000 had to be dismissed
as there was no room for more. So you can guess the size
of it. Gabe Williams is still here and is in the best of health.
He is sick and tired of this place like myself, but he does not
want to go out again, he says. There is no chance of my going
out, again, after all the promises they made. It seems that the
colonel has nothing to do with it – it was the Brigadier Gen.
who ordered all Altcar men to be kept here until they can be
replaced. Well, this is the lot this time, with love from Ivor

The following Sunday Ivor wrote home again and (not for the first time) reassured his mother that he was keeping up his attendance at chapel.

IE1917-02-18

Dear Mother,
 I've just come back from chapel and it is now only 10 o'clock, so you see I've been a good boy today again. I haven't been so bad lately all the same, for it's 5 weeks since I missed church parade last. I received the parcel last night and everything was all correct, though the letter was rather short, wasn't it? I also got a letter from Dick, which I have been expecting this long time. He seems to be moving about quite a lot lately, marching from one place to another, all the time, and it must be hard work too, for out there it is hot enough to make a 'tafell o dost maes o gefn dyn' [*a slice of toast from a man's back*], and again they have not got good roads there like we have at home for it's all sand for miles and miles. It does not seem to affect Dick very much now though, because he is now quite used to it, and like myself he doesn't trouble much what happens, as happy as the day is long, and this is by far the best way to look at things, for once you start looking for complaints and start grumbling at your luck, you'll never finish.
 There has been a grand change in the weather here this last week or so and the frost and cold we have been having lately has now disappeared completely and it is nice and mild every day with a clear sky all around. I had a rather nice trip to Crewe to fetch a prisoner. I've been to Crewe before on my way home and so the place was not entirely strange to me. This is what they call 'escort duty' in the Army and it is not half a bad job too. Of course we did not pay our railway expenses for we were provided with a free warrant and again we did not pay for a night's lodging neither, for we spent the night at the 'Soldiers and Sailors Rest' which is just outside the station, and that free of charge. They have a 'Visitors Book' there where every soldier who calls there is invited to put his name down; I remember putting mine down on the

night I came home on leave, when we had to wait at Crewe for about an hour and a half to get a train, and that was about 1 o'clock in the morning so you see how very useful these institutes are for soldiers travelling.

We have had about 50 more recruits to our company, men who have been transferred from the Army Service Corps, so it looks like more work for us to make soldiers of them. Also about 150 of the same lot came to A Company last weekend and they will have to be put through a course of musketry also, so that together with what we've got already there will be somewhere like 300 men to be put through it in the next few weeks and as far as I can guess we shall be kept rather busy for about 6 weeks or 2 months again. This will not be so bad now that the weather has improved such a lot. I'm glad to know that old 'Eustis bach' is getting on so well, as Auntie Charlotte says. Is Joe still there?[4]

Well no more this time, so I conclude with love from
                    Ivor
PS. I wrote to A. Charlotte a letter in middle of the week, but I forgot to post it.

This is the only reference in Ivor's letters to performing escort duty. It is quite probable that the prisoner he was escorting was a conscientious objector, for at this time those men who were deemed fit to serve but refused could be taken to training camps and subjected to military discipline.[5]

It is clear that money was always tight at Pengwern Road, and Ivor's next letter to his mother, written the following Sunday, makes reference to the latest financial problem. It seems that he had applied to have part of his pay remitted to his parents, but that this had not yet happened.

IE1917-02-25

Dear Mother
                    I received your letter on Wednesday and I am sorry to hear that things are not quite up to the mark down there. It was rather unfortunate that father hurt his wrist, but accidents will happen always and I suppose we shall have to

put up with it. I am sending you as much as I can spare of what money I have to keep things going. Don't you worry about me. I am all right and I can manage pretty well for the rest of the week, because I've still got another 2 shillings. We must all make sacrifices during these times when the price of everything is going up and I am quite ready to do my share of it. There does not seem to be much work done with regard to the allowance affair although I have given all particulars to our quarter master sergeant, the man who is in charge of our pay and things. I gave him all the information he wanted, but I have had two pays since, and they have not kept anything out of either of them yet. I had half a mind to see him about it tomorrow but there is a rumour about that there is another man coming to take his place so I am letting things slide until everything settles down properly.

I see that the weather is just about the same down there, but I am glad to say that there has been a great change in the climate here, and I have decided to give up wearing the singlet because I can now do without it all right. It will save money on postage and what is more important, it will save you extra trouble in washing it. So when you receive a parcel for washing do not send the singlet back, only the socks and handkerchief. Well no more this time so I close with love from
Ivor

There is then a gap in the collection, with no more surviving letters from Ivor to his mother for five months. The only letter from this period is one to Aunt Charlotte from the end of March 1917, written on YMCA paper. It is concerned, like so many of the brothers' letters, with home leave: Ivor had tried to get permission to go home while Gabriel was there. The letter ends with a (surely tongue-in-cheek) request for Charlotte to write to the commanding officer to request that Ivor be allowed leave.

IE1917-03-31

Dear Auntie Charlotte,

I could not get leave after all my efforts, and as things are at present I don't even think I'll ever get leave again until the war is over. I first of all tried to get a week end leave (for last week end) but I was told by the Captain that leave is only granted now under special circumstances, and that even then the consent of the Brigadier General has to be obtained. Well I thought to myself that I'd bother him again this week, in the hope that he'd be in a better humour but after all it was no good – it was the same tale again.

Ivor explains that after failing to be granted home leave he received a message saying Gabriel was travelling back to Scotland on the Friday, so he tried to arrange to meet him at Chester, but in vain.

It is a ridiculous state of affairs in regard to the stopping of weekend leave. These were stopped because the railway companies could not find conveyance enough. but yet you can get a late pass to anywhere you like in the Kingdom, you can even get a late pass from after duty Saturday until 11.30 same date and also from reveille Sunday morning until 11.30 Sunday night, but they won't give you a pass from after duty Saturday until 11.30 Sunday. Isn't it a ridiculous system? But it's like everything else in the army, governed completely by red tape. Would you mind writing to our C.O. asking him to grant me 6 or 8 days leave to do the garden, telling him that I've been in the habit of doing it these last few years? It's no use my asking. Please, with love from
                    Ivor

The next extant letter gives an indication of the day-to-day frustration and tension that Ivor faced as a well-educated young man in a junior position in an inflexible bureaucratic system.

IE1917-07-30

Dear Mother,
            Here we are again at the end of a busy week. It was not half as busy as I thought it would be, for of course I was thinking of my last experience on that job; do you remember last Christmas, what a busy time I had then? and they kept

me at it for a fortnight too. But this week it was not half
bad, and in fact, if it had only been my own work I had to
do, I would have had an easy time of it, but they had tons of
work at the office and I had to give a hand there, and I soon
became the best man there.

I think I wrote a long time ago that there was one man
whom I simply could not get on with him at all; this was the
Sergeant Major of our company. He is an old man of about
50, who has been in the Army about 30 years, and I tell you
he is about the biggest rogue I have come across yet, and
I've come across a good many during this last twelvemonth.
Well, he and I have always been 'fel ci a chath' [*like a dog
and cat*] to one another. Naturally I had as little to do with
him as I could because I knew the first chance he would get
he would have me up before the captain on the least offence
and this he did more than once though I fortunately got off
each time all right. However, this week he had a new Quarter
master, who was absolutely no good in his office, one of
those who handles a pen like a 'raw' [*shovel*]. Well, he had
been behind with his work last week and the old Sgt Major
was 'fel cwyd o wenyn' [*like a bag of bees*], like a bear. He
noticed me sitting down, doing nothing in the office for I had
finished my own work, and no sooner had he done that than
he jumped down my throat, saying 'what the dickens did I
join the army for, to sit down doing nothing?' and he used
fearful language. He immediately set me to do things and
of course I soon cleared up his mess for him and he seemed
quite pleased. Well I had to carry on after that all the week,
and wonderful to relate, the old gent gradually changed and
slowly became quite friendly towards me, so that by the end
of the week, we were the best of pals. I am not trusting him
further than I can see him, because no one knows when he'll
change and go for me again. Ha Ha!!
          Good luck for the holidays – Ivor

No letter from Ivor in August 1917 has survived, although one
was received by Hannah on 14 August. In a letter she wrote that day
to their mother (she was then residing in Montpellier Terrace), she
wrote 'I had a letter from Ivor this afternoon. He's alright.' There

is nothing in Hannah's letter to indicate that she was upset, but it is clear from the next extant letter that something had happened in the meantime. This letter also shows that Ivor had a brief period of home leave over the summer.

IE1917-09-09

Dear Mother,

I had a letter from Hannah yesterday in which she seemed to be in a state of war with everybody. I take it that she saw the letter I wrote to you and as a result she has sworn vengeance on everybody, and nobody in particular. Leave her to me and I will put her right. Another thing, although you have not written to me about it, I have just found out that Dad has been idle for some weeks lately, and even while I was at home on that week-end leave nobody mentioned a word about it to me. Everyone seems to be keeping it as a secret as if it were something to be ashamed of. I know that father is not willing for you to go complaining to us boys and all that, but that is all nonsense. How would he like us to say nothing when anything happens to us; for instance, suppose I fell sick or something, and did not write home about it, I am sure he would not like it. Please let me know next time or I will consider it very unfair of you.

I had a great surprise this morning. I was writing some stuff in the hut, when I noticed a youngster laughing in the door – I looked at him for a moment and then he called me out – Ha! Ha! Ha! It was Uriel, and I did not know him till I went out to him. He remained here for some time after, before he went to dinner promising to come back afterwards; so I am expecting him every minute now. He arrived here last night about 6 o'clock. He is with the 59th Training Reserve Battalion, which occupies No 8 camp about half a mile from ours. I expect he will let you know all about Kinmel Park now. He tells me he was kept at Cardiff for three days before he came up here, so that he has seen a bit of the Army before.

I have been very busy this last week and that is the reason why I did not write sooner. I had to do Orderly Sergeant this week again and that occupies all my spare time.

We are booked down for the Range next week, so that
there is still more excitement in store for me. No more
with love to all
Ivor

Uriel Rees was the brothers' cousin, who lived next door to Rees
and Elizabeth Rees, their mutual grandparents. Uriel was obviously
close to his elder cousins, all three of whom mention (at different
stages) that they had received letters from him. He is mentioned
again in Ivor's letter from three weeks later:

IE1917-09-30

Dear Mother,
    Just a line or two, to let you know how things are
going in this part of the world.
    I have been busy this week, both during the day and in
the evenings. Last Saturday I was told that I was to start on
what they call a 'General Course' at No 20 Camp about a ¼
of a mile from our own. I was very much puzzled as to what
was in store for me, till Monday morning the whole problem
was solved, when I had to begin from the very beginning
and do recruits drill all over again. It was a bit dreary at first,
but after about three days of it things began to look brighter.
Anyway, to cut a long story short, I may say there is nothing
new in the course at all, simply what I have taught hundreds
of recruits to do myself. I was getting tired of the job I was
on, lately, for this reason. We had a Captain who knew very
little about Musketry, but whenever he came on parade, he
always put his finger in the pie, telling us to do this and do
that according to what <u>he</u> thought on the matter. If he left
us alone to carry on in our own sweet time and do things
properly it would be much more interesting both for us and
the recruits.
    It was he that put me on draft last, about a fortnight
ago, but my name was crossed off again, as usual, and he
could not have his vengeance on me, as he would like too
[*sic*]. And what is more – that gentleman will very soon be
out of harm's length, because he is going on draft on Tuesday.

Well, I expect you are making Gib comfortable just now – that is why I don't bother you very much with letters this week Ha! Ha! Ha!! giving Gib a chance – the best of luck to him. No more this time, for Uriel is here & he will want some entertaining.

Ivor

This is the final surviving letter written by Ivor from Kinmel Park. However, in another family archive a photograph has survived which must be from either October or September 1917. Ivor (who can be seen seated on the floor, on the right) has written on the rear:

IE1917-10-a Postcard

What do you think of these boys?

All from No 11 Hut – Uriel knows most of them by now.

I'll answer your letter as soon as I can – a bit busy just now.

with love to all
Ivor

Details are very sketchy about the next turn of events. We can glean from two of Richard's letters and one of Gabriel's that Ivor was still in 'Blighty' on 10 October and had home leave for a few days at around this point, but that he was in Ireland by late November or early December.[6] He was posted to Limerick, home to the 3rd Battalion of the RWF, and which was used as a staging post for RWF reinforcements bound for service overseas (despite the extra travel involved). Ivor travelled on to Southampton, en route for France. He wrote a brief postcard in a cafe in the port at 4.30 p.m. on 6 December:

IE1917-12-06 Postcard

Dear Mother,

Arrived at Southampton all right and just settling down to a feed. Been around the town to see what it is like,

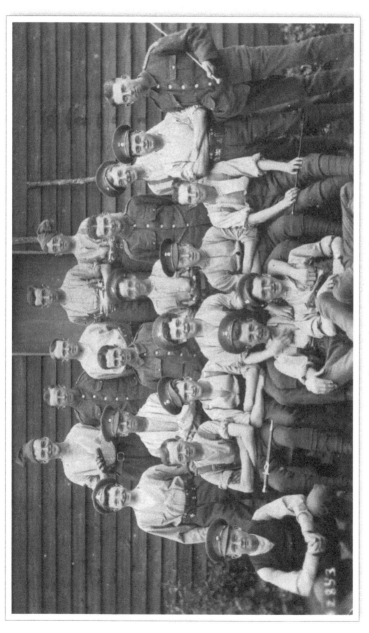

7.2: Group photo, Kinmel Park

and found it all right – quite a change from Ireland. I'll write again as soon as I finish the next move.

Until then, ta! ta!

Yours affectionately,

Ivor

There is little evidence here as to how Ivor viewed his imminent relocation to France. He had been impatient to leave earlier in the year, but by the end of September to be put on a draft to leave Kinmel Park was seen as 'vengeance' on the part of the officer. There are hints of stoicism in these letters, such as in his declaration in February that it was best not to grumble and that he was not much troubled by what was to happen. This ties in with the underlying optimism that comes through in a number of these letters. Ivor is able to overcome the freezing weather or the hostility of the old sergeant-major, and can take comfort in the fact that the vengeful officer is about to be sent away. As ever, one has to bear in mind that one overriding purpose of these letters was to reassure the family back home that Ivor was coming along well.

Notes

1. Properly spelt 'ffelwm': whitlow – an abscess in the soft tissue near a fingernail or toenail.
2. 'New Church "Hut" for Kinmel', *North Wales Chronicle*, 2 February 1917, 2.
3. See Appendix 2.
4. Joe: the pet dog. 'Eustis bach' [*Little Eustis*] is Daniel.
5. One such conscientious objector, court-martialled at Kinmel Park on 23 February 1917, was John Day of Nantyffyllon: see 'Maesteg notes', *Merthyr Pioneer*, 24 March 1917, 4.
6. RE1917-11-20 (ch. 6); RE1918-01-09a (ch. 6) and GE1917-11-20 (ch. 10). His family were unaware that he had moved on from Kinmel Park when they posted him a letter there on 10 December.

8

Richard Eustis in Palestine and Egypt, February 1918–June 1918

In the collection there are nine letters sent home by Richard Eustis between February and June 1918. These were all headed simply either 'Palestine' or 'Egypt', and as we do not have the benefit of Richard's personal diary, it is not usually possible to be sure where he was stationed. After the capture of Jerusalem in December 1917 there was a lull in the offensive while the EEF consolidated its position, and the poor weather prevented any further advance. As in the previous letters home, there are precious few details of his military actions and responsibilities. All we can glean is that in June he was involved in 'out-post duty': he only mentions the danger he was in from enemy aircraft after he safely returned to base.

Richard's letters also show how his plans for the future were changing, and he is considering what the future holds for him. He wrote to Aunt Charlotte, 'I doubt very much whether I shall go back underground again' and there are multiple references to marriages back home, such as 'It seems to me that all the boys at home there are getting married one by one.'[1] Homesickness is evident in a number of these letters, as there was no prospect of any home leave.

At the time of writing the following letter, 20 February 1918, the EEF (but not Richard's unit, the 53rd (Welsh) Division) was involved in capturing Jericho, to the north-east of Jerusalem and close to the River Jordan.

RE1918-02-20

Dear Mother,

Just a few lines to let you know that all is well
with me, etc. I have not had a letter from you for about a
fortnight, but I am expecting a few letters almost any day. I
have only had one letter from Ivor since he went to France,
but I am expecting one every day also from Gib. I have not
heard from him lately. Never mind they will all turn up
together one of these days, then I shall have as much as I can
do to answer them.

Do you remember Gib falling into the gasometer at
Mynyddbach long ago? Well, I had a similar experience a few
days ago, Ha! Ha! Ha! I am on an Anti-Malarial Squad you
see, and part of my work is to clear all pools and wells, to
prevent the breeding of mosquitoes. Well, I sounded a pool
the other day, with a view to filling it in. After finding that
it was six or eight feet deep, a stone gave way under me, and
into the pool I went, head over heels. Ha! Ha! I looked like a
drowned rat when I got out of it. Fortunately, I had a change
of clothes to get into, so I have not suffered any ill-effects
from it. Ha! Ha! Gib won't half laugh when he reads about
that little lot.

I received that little parcel from Auntie Ann the other
day, and it was very acceptable, too.[2] I was very pleased to
have it especially the cigarettes, for we have to depend on the
Army issue now as we cannot buy any. And as you know,
I would just about be without food, as without fags. I shall
write Auntie Ann a letter as soon as I can thanking her for it.
Well mother, I have remitted three pounds to you. I daresay
they will notify you about it, then you can go and draw it
from the Post Office. I would like you to let me know, what
you have for me at home there, for I don't know where I
stand. Did you get my letter asking you to send me one of
those Ingersoll Crown watches again? I wrote to ask you
about it somewhere about Christmas time, but the letter
must have gone down. But if you cannot see your way clear
to send it just let me know.

All the village boys are together at present, Dai
and I living in the same room. They are going to hold a
celebration here on St David's Day, and they have persuaded
me to give one or two Welsh items. Ha! Ha! I daresay it will
be 'some' concert. We have a piano here, so it ought to go
off alright. Dai had a little bottle sent out to drink Oliver's
(his brother) health. He got married sometime ago. So of
course I had to have a mouthful and wish him all that he
could wish himself. He and I were very thick when I was
home there. It seems to me that all the boys at home there
are getting married one by one. Good luck to them. I have
no more to say this time but as soon as I have a letter from
you, I will write again.

   So I close with love to all,
     from
      Dick

There is no report of how the St David's Day celebrations went,
for the next surviving letters were written on 20 March, by which
time Richard was stationed close to the Suez Canal, back in Egypt.
Like the previous letter, the next one contains some thoughts about
matrimony.

       RE1918-03-20a

Dear Mother,
   I was very pleased to receive your letter dated
February 8th, and I am very glad to hear that all are well at
home there. I am also glad to hear you say that you have
received six or eight letters during the same week, but I
daresay that after a spasm like that you will have to go a few
weeks without one. I haven't heard from Gib or Ivor for
quite a long time, but I am expecting to hear from them every
day now. So the village turned out en-fete [*sic*] to welcome
the boys from France, eh? I shouldn't think that Tommy
Mathews has met Ivor yet, for Ivor hasn't been out there
so very long has he?[3] I am very glad to hear that you have
received that photograph of me on the Mount of Olives. Yes

I do look a bit rough, I admit, but during that time it was terribly wet and cold up there.

As you see by my address, I am now back in Egypt, in fact, down on the banks of the Suez Canal. I have explained to Auntie Charlotte how I came to be down here, so I needn't repeat it to you. Probably you will be able to see the letter with Aunt Charlotte. I had a letter from her along with your letter and she gave me some of Dan's history. How he brings everything out in school that he hears at home. And Ann Morris has been threatening him already, eh? Ha! Ha! He is beginning young. She also told me that you often have visitors there, and that you are not likely to keep either Ivor, Gabe or myself long, after we come home again, for there are three already claiming us.

I shall be very glad to get the watch Mam, for out here, one cannot buy them under three or four pounds, and even then they are no good. Have you received that £3 I sent you some time ago? I sent it through the army authorities, by what they call a remittance form. Probably they will notify you about it, and tell you what Post Office you can draw it from. If you get that alright, I may be able to send some more home. I am all on my own down here now, not one of the village boys being near. Still, I daresay they are alright, or I would have heard from one of them. You can address my letters to the unit, for I shall probably be back there in a week, or two at the outside. Only, in future I shall be Pte instead of L[ance] Cpl.

I had a letter from Nance the other day saying that she had received the little souvenir I sent her from Jerusalem. I sent Auntie Charlotte a little Bible from there, too, and I sincerely hope that she will get it alright. I have had my teeth put in at last, so now I am alright once again. How are things going in the village there? Still the same as usual, I suppose, except that there are a great number of the boys away from there. Sam Rees was down in Alexandria about a week ago, and who do you think he met? Only Clement Mort, Pen-y-Bank.[4] He is in some R.A.M.C. mob at Alexandria and from what Sam says, he was looking tip-top. I did not know

he was in the Army. Well if ever I get down that way, I shall
try to see him. There are one or two Morriston Boys down
there too, that I should like to see. I have rather a good job
at present so I shall be able to write pretty often, that is if I
can have anything to write about. It is quite a long time since
I was down this way before. Our unit started marching up
from here on January 1917, and I marched all the way with
them up through Hebron, Bethlehem and through Jerusalem.
After sticking all the wet weather up there, it was rather hard
lines to be sent back here for so trifling a thing. Well, Mam,
I have no more to tell you this time, hoping that all at home
there are as well as this leaves me at present
Love to all from
Dick

On the same day, Richard sent a letter to his sister Hannah.
He began by acknowledging her letter of 3 February and worrying
whether Aunt Charlotte's Bible had arrived, before continuing with
an explanation of how he was sent back to this base.

RE1918-03-20b

Well Nance, I am at present down on the banks of the
Suez Canal again. I was sent to the dentist at Jerusalem for
my teeth, and after putting them in instead of sending me
back to my unit, they sent me to the Base Depot. I have been
here for nearly a fortnight, but I don't know what day I may
be sent back to the unit again. By being sent here, I had to
revert so you can address your letters to the same address,
except that now I am a Pte, instead of Lance Cpl.
I have not heard from Gabe or Ivor for some time, but
I am expecting a letter from each of them almost every day.
Never mind, they will all turn up together one of these bright
mornings. So Gabe's boat is on Convoy work now instead
of Patrol work. Quite a nice change for him isn't it. And
Dai Harris was home on leave after being torpedoed, eh?
He is very fortunate to have leave, for I have been out here
nearly three years and not had a single day yet, and I have no

hopes of leave until the end of the war. That's cheerful isn't it? Never mind, it may come to an end now shortly, then we shall all be home together once again. But according to a letter I had from Auntie Charlotte, neither Gabe, Ivor or I will remain at home for long as there are three girls trotting up home pretty often enquiring after us, Ha, Ha. It came as a surprise to me, for I didn't know that Gabe or Ivor had anything to do with them. Don't worry but once we come home again, we will soon square up matters, and settle down once more to home life.

Of course, after four years of it, I have got quite used to this life and I don't worry my head about it. When I came down to this camp, there was not a single chap here whom I knew, but that did not worry me, for I soon made a few friends and now I am quite alright. I had a letter from Mam the other day saying how things are there and giving me all the local news. I have not heard from Morriston for about a fortnight, what's wrong I don't know. Letters are very slow arriving here lately, possibly having been delayed somewhere on the way. But I daresay they will all turn up one of these fine days.

I have no more to tell you this time hoping it will find you well, also all at No15 Montpelier Terrace. Give them my best wishes, hoping they are enjoying the best of health and spirits.

No more with Love from

Dick

P.S. I have received your letter dated Feb 10th. I will reply to it in a day or two.

The mention of Morriston in this letter is of course a reference to Mary Lizzie. Richard's anxiety at not receiving any letters for two weeks shows how important the connection with loved ones was for men who had been away from home for so long, and how even a few days without communication could make them worry about what was going on.

Richard was still stationed in Egypt four weeks later, when the following letter was written.

RE1918-04-14

Dear Mother,

Just a few lines to let you know that I received
your letter dated March 5th a few days ago but I'm sorry I
couldn't reply to it sooner. Well I am very glad to hear that
tadcu[5] is quite alright again, also that all at home are quite
well. It is a long time since I did any gardening, and when
I come home, I'm afraid you will have to teach me all over
again from the beginning. But never mind I shall soon learn
once I come home. It is very little garden stuff we get out
here. We sometimes get lettuces but not very [often??].

Richard then worries, once again, that the Bible he sent to Aunt
Charlotte had not yet been delivered.

It was a beautiful Bible, too, bound in real
Olive-wood from the Mount of Olives. Yes Mam, I
have received the watch quite safe, and it is keeping time
beautifully. While I am down here, I can keep the sand out
of it, but once I go up the line again I shall have to take great
care of it. It seems very funny to hear you say that you have
been put on rations. Honestly Mam, I think I am better
off out here, than you are at home there. So don't worry
about sending me anything, if you get any fags or anything
like that, send them to Ivor. Look after him, and if there is
anything you cannot get for him let me know to see if I can
do anything for him here. Possibly, I may be able to get a few
things here which you cannot get at home.

I daresay there was 'tipyn o swank' [*a great deal
of the posh*] with you in Richard Hughes's turnout with a
'Fedog a Shawl' [*apron and shawl*]. You say that Dan keeps
on asking when am I coming home, well, I wish I could tell
him but we must wait and see, and hope for the best. Let
me know whether he had the little note I sent him in Auntie
Charlotte's letter. Tell him that I received his letter and was
glad to have it. So Tommy Thomas is coming out this way is
he? I shall try to see him. I have met Bryn Thomas Vicarage

Road, Morriston out here. You know him or at least his
mother 'Mab i ferch Daniel James [*the son of the daughter of
Daniel James*], Caemawr'.[6]

I am expecting to go back to the unit now any minute,
for a few of the boys have been wounded (none from our
village) and I have already been put on draft to go up. So by
the time you receive this letter, I shall be back amongst them
once again. Let me know when you receive that £3 I sent
home, then perhaps I shall be able to send some more.

I have no more to say this time except that I am
posting a letter which I wrote up the line before I came down
and I forgot to post it, so you might as well have it now.

No more this time with love to all at home from

Dick

By the time the next letter was written, on 5 May, Richard was
back in Palestine. The campaign in the east had been directly affected
by events on the Western Front, where Germany had launched a
major offensive in March. As a consequence there was a desperate
need for experienced troops back in Europe, and so many units of
the EEF were sent to France. Although the 53rd (Welsh) Division
as a whole was not despatched, many of its battalions were, to be
replaced by units from the Indian army. Given the disruption to
the force, and the weakening of its attacking potential (and the fact
that the Turkish forces were also weak and depleted), there were no
major battles in this period.

RE1918-05-05

Dear Mother

I was very pleased to receive your letter dated
April 10th and was very glad to hear that all was well at home
there. I am very sorry to hear that letters are slow in arriving
there, but I daresay they will all turn up together. I daresay
say that by now you will have received my letters saying that
I have had my watch, and it is keeping time very well. Well
Mam even a Field Card is very acceptable from a place such
as Ivor is in, for it tells you that all is well with him, and that
is the main point isn't it?

You have done quite right to keep those things that
Miss Walters gave you to send to me for as I have said before,
I have more clothes than I can wear now, and when we move
from one place to another, we have to carry everything we
possess, on our backs.[7] Also, when anything gets the worse
for wear, we only have to take it to the stores and they give
us a new article in place of it. So you see, the less personal
property we have, the lighter we are on the march. As soon
as Dd. R.Thomas & the other boys receive the parcels I will
acknowledge it exactly as if I received it, so say nothing.
Honestly Mam, I think that I am living far better than you
people at home for we get any amount of good plain food,
and also there are tons of oranges here and we are able to buy
these at a rate of 12 for 3d. They have been much cheaper,
still, I manage to eat 10 or 12 every day and fine big fruit they
are too. The only thing short here is cigarettes, we can not
buy any fags up the line here so we have to depend entirely
on the issue we get, which isn't much. I don't want you to
send me a parcel of fags, but a very good plan would be to
put a packet of Woodbines in every letter you send, that
would not put you out of your way, would it? But if Gib or
Ivor want anything at all, let them have it, and if you cannot
see your way clear to give them anything they want let me
know to see if I can manage it. I always keep a couple of
pounds on my pay-book now, in case of emergencies, ever
since I sent to you for that £3 in 1916 and I hope that by now
you have received the £3 I sent you in February through the
Army Authorities.

So you have heard that all the Band boys are coming
home on leave? Well, I am afraid that there are four of them
out here who will not come home on leave, although I mean
to do my utmost this summer to try it, but at present I'm
afraid that things are looking black indeed. Still, don't worry
Mam, it is bound to end some day, and as long as the three
of us are enjoying the best of health, we shall all be home
together some day again for good. Of course, anybody in
France has a fine chance of time-expired leave, but we have
no hopes out here, I suppose it is because we are too far
away. Gib has been very lucky as regards leave hasn't he?

I daresay he has been home on leave about six times now, lucky boy.

So Dan has gone to the big school eh? Well he must be some swank now? Auntie Charlotte must feel at a loss now then, having lost every one of us. She has had one or other of us for a long time now. It reminds me of the days when Gib and I used to go there. When you took the pair of us one day against our will. Ha! Ha! So Lottie is trying for Gowerton? I hope she will pass for it will make all the difference to her life. And poor old Uriel is in France? Well, a fellow can hardly realize it, for when I was home, he had only just left school, and to think that he is in France. I daresay we shall see some changes, when we come home again, what with all that have been married, and everything, and the alterations made in the old village there.

I have heard that Tommy Thomas, Mynydd Cadle, is out here, and Dd R. Thomas has had one or two letters from him, but we have not seen him yet. So you don't think the war will be over till 1919? Well I honestly think that this year will see it all over, anyhow, and then we shall all be home once again. Well Mam, things are going very well with me at present, rather quiet for shells, but we have one or two enemy aeroplanes over every day, but they don't have much time to do any damage; of course they come over sometimes about five o'clock in the morning, and drop a few bombs, but I think we have them beat now. While I was down at Kantara, my sleeping partner was wounded by a bomb so now I am in a dug-out on my own, Dd Rees Thomas living about ten yards away from me, so we spend a great deal of our time together. Sammy Rees is out in advance with one of our sections, but he is quite alright and only yesterday we had a letter from him. I was asking a chap out of Trev. James' crowd how he was getting on? And he said that Trevor was going down to Cairo or Alexandria on leave for a week. There are some rumours here that they are going to start short leave to Egypt for us again, so I may go down in about two months time. Now if you'll tell me what you would like from there, I may be able to get it. I cannot think of anything suitable myself, but you may be able to suggest something.

I don't think I shall be able to go before I receive a reply to this letter, if you'll mention anything.

We have a party here still, and Dai and I are with it. We are giving concerts all over the place here and are enjoying ourselves the same time. Of course they don't ask us for a concert without having a feed for us after it is over. So you see we are doing well. I posted a letter to Ivor in Auntie Charlotte's last letter, because I don't know his address, so I would be very pleased if you would send me his address. I hear from Nance pretty often, too, and she seems to be doing well and has struck a good billet. I hope she will stick to it, for they seem to be very kind to her. I sent her a letter last week. I also wrote to Gib. Letters are very slow in coming from Morriston, why, I don't know. They must be going astray or something. How is Uncle Sam getting on? I hope he is recovering from that rheumatic fever? I sent him a letter some time ago, but I have not heard about it whether he received it or not. I know Sam is not fond of writing, but at least, I expected Polly (merch [*daughter of*] Auntie Margaret) to send a Postcard to say that they had received it.

Well Mam, I have no more to tell you this time, hoping that this will find you all well at home there as it leaves me, so I conclude with

Love to all

From Dick

A week later Richard wrote a wide-ranging letter to Aunt Charlotte. This contains remarks on news from home, thoughts on his future plans, some nonchalant comments about the number of casualties recently suffered and indications of how Richard rated the relative risks of the different theatres of war.

RE1918-05-12

Dear Auntie Charlotte,

Letters are terribly slow arriving here, but I received yours of the 8th April today and am glad to learn that all's well at home there. Well one cannot expect much from Ivor in the way of letters, for he hasn't the time to write now the

same as when he was at Rhyl. Still as long as you receive
Field Cards from him, that is the main thing, isn't it. I am
glad also to learn that Gib is alright, and I daresay that by the
time you get this, he will be home on leave again, the lucky
boy. So poor old Uriel has gone out now again? Well I would
much rather see him go to India or Italy than France, but
there, why worry? All we can do is to hope for the best. As
you say, he has not had much time in England before going
into the real thing.

Well I have written several letters saying that I have
received the watch, also Danny's letter, and I enclosed a note
for him in one of your letters, I daresay it has turned up by
now. I'm sorry I cannot oblige him about the tricycle, at least
not just yet, but as soon I come home, we'll see what we
can do for him. The same as father said about Nance, he'd
buy her a piano, 'paish binc' [*pink petticoat*] etc Ha! Ha! I
don't suppose she has had them yet. Never mind, she may
stand a chance yet, when the boys come home. So Dan has
been transferred to the Ysgol Fawr [*big school*]? I daresay
he is some swank now. I doubt whether I shall know him
when I return, for four years make a big difference in a little
youngster like Dan. I was just telling mother in my last letter
that I have not put a foot in a garden since I left home four
years ago, so when I return I shall have to begin all over
again, for I have forgotten all about it. As you say, I sincerely
hope that I will be home in time to enjoy those cabbages,
especially if they have any red cabbage there for pickling. I
have not tasted any of them since I left home. The nearest
thing I had were the pickled almonds in Cambridge. A real
good old-fashioned feed would do me the world of good just
now, just after the style I had at home there. But we cannot
grumble for we have plenty of good food, but none of the
good old favourite dishes we used to have at home Bara-lawr,
Paste Gig, Cawl Pen [*laverbread, meat pie, broth*], for
instance, I could just about square a few items like that now.
I know the David Matthews you mean, who got married.
They are all going one by one. So they are going to comb out
the mines again, are they?[8] Yes, I daresay there are a number
of youngsters there, who wouldn't be missed. I doubt very

much whether I shall go back underground again, for often
these years I am beginning to like life on the surface. I think
I shall look for a job as tram-conductor, or postman or
something like that. Well we have been rather unlucky as a
unit lately for we have been the subject of two air-raids in
eight days. During the first one, we suffered two men killed
and five wounded, and in the second we had five killed and
twenty wounded. Not one of the village boys were touched.

I have just heard that Walter Evans has gone to Italy.[9]
I wonder how he will get on there? I hope he will be a little
more fortunate than he was on the Peninsula, anyhow. There
must be a tidy crowd from Mynyddbach and Caersalem
abroad on foreign service now compared to the number who
were away at the end of 1914. There is some talk of leave to
Egypt here again, that is of course a week or two in Cairo
or Alexandria. Still if I can manage it, I think I'll go down
the Nile this time, down to Thebes, Luxor and Assouuan.
Dd R.Thomas went down there last year and quite enjoyed
himself, but I did not have a chance of going. Still, I may be
able to go this year. Well Auntie Charlotte, I have just learnt
that a letter I sent you, also to Ivor on April 21st have been
damaged at sea. They may be delivered or they may not. It is
rather a pity for I had enclosed a few snapshots of Jerusalem,
Bethlehem, Hebron, etc. I am enclosing a few in this one
again, hoping that this time they will reach you alright. I have
quite a decent little collection here but I cannot send them
all together in one letter so I am sending a few at a time. I
will try to explain on the back of each photograph what they
represent.

I have no more to tell you this time so I conclude
hoping that all are quite well at home there, as this leaves me
at the time of writing

With love to all

from

Dick

He added a postscript saying that he would send more photographs by registered post, but unfortunately none of these has been
preserved.

Richard wrote two letters from Palestine on 3 June 1918. Although comments on some matters are present in both letters, there is not too much direct repetition. Richard was aware that his writings would be shared, so that there was no need to say things twice.

RE1918-06-03a

Dear Mother,

Just a few lines to let you know that I have received your two letters dated April 14th & 16th respectively, also one from Auntie Charlotte somewhere about the same date. I'm very glad to learn that all are well at home there, also to say that things are going alright with me at present. I am sorry to hear that mails are so slow reaching you and the same this end. I received your letter about the shirts from Miss Walters and you did quite right in keeping them back, for even if you sent them out to me I am not allowed to wear any private shirts or clothes of any description other than the things they issue out of the stores here. So make what use you can out of them. About that talk of leave to the band boys. Our time is up at the end of this month but there are no hopes of leave for us boys in Palestine here. Those in France may get it, but we shall not. All we shall get is the £15 bounty, £10 of which is put into the War Loan for us and the other £5 to our credit on the pay-book, and we will be lucky if we get that. I'll try my best to have leave but I don't think I have much chance.

I had a Field Card from Ivor the other day, but I don't know his address now, so I cannot write to him directly. I have enclosed one letter for him in one of yours, so that you can address it to him, and I have also asked you for his address some time back. But I haven't had it yet. I will enclose one for him in this one again and you can send it to him. Then send me his address as soon as you can.

I heard in Auntie Charlotte's letter that quite a crowd have been called up from the village there again. All youngsters, too. As you say, it is rather a pity that they should go while the likes of Harry Watkins should be left behind.

I am very glad to hear that you have received the £3 I sent you some time ago. Will you let me know what Post Office you drew it from? Was it Landore? Did you have to go down there for it or did you have it from the Tirdeunaw Post Office? I have had the watch and cigarettes some time ago, but as yet I have not had the Morriston cigarettes. But there, I daresay they will turn up one of these days. I shall acknowledge that parcel to Miss Walters exactly as if I had received it, so I suppose that will do them alright.

I heard that Dan was in the Ysgol Fawr. Quite a big affair in his little life. I daresay he is some swank now. Has he had my note about the tricycle yet? I'm afraid he will have to wait awhile for that, but we will see what we can do for him when the boys come home. Things are going alright with me here. I have a little party of twelve doing out-post duty. We have been here for over a week now and by what I can hear we shall be here till the end of June. We have a very nice little camp in amongst the fig-trees, we do our own cooking. I have built an oven, so we are doing well. There is a little village about half an hour's walk away and we can get any amount of eggs there at the rate of four for a shilling. So we have a few variations in the food line now. Jam tart, rice puddings with any amount of eggs and milk in it, roast beef & potatoes, besides what stews and things we can cook on the fire. I think I shall be able to show you a thing or two about cooking when I come home again. I had a letter from Johnny Phillips yesterday. He has been slightly gassed in France, but he is getting over it. I have no more to tell you this time except that all the village boys are alright. Will you address the enclosed letter to Ivor.

No more with

Love to all from

Dick

RE1918-06-03b

Dear Auntie Charlotte,

I was very pleased to receive your letter dated April 16th the other day along with two from Mother. I am

very glad to hear that all are well at home there also to say
that I am alright and in the best of health & spirits. I'm sorry
to hear that letters are so slow reaching you there for they
are exactly the same this end, as you can see when I have
just received yours of April 16th and it is now June. I had the
Field Card from Ivor and I enclosed a letter for him in one
to Mother because I do not know his address. I can quite
understand him not being able to write as often from France
as he did from Rhyl, but we cannot blame him for that, can
we? As you say, he is our chief concern now, and I would
give anything to get him away from there but all we can do
is to hope for the best. Yes, I have heard that poor old Uriel's
also in France, but if he is still at the Base there is no cause
to worry. So you don't think that Mother will keep us long
after we return again? Well, it does not look like it, according
to your letter, if you say that there are three or four ready
to pounce on us as soon as we come home. Well I heard in
one of Mother's letters that she had received my remittance
so I don't suppose there is any need to make any enquiries
about it now. I know that many people have been done out
of money like that, but now Mother has had it, well I may
be able to remit some more. We are expecting short leave to
Egypt again, so I am keeping a few pounds on my book for
that. Then we shall see how things go afterwards.

So they are still combing out at home there. I am sorry
to hear that those youngsters will have to go, for they will
find it a great deal different to home life. Yes, I have received
the watch some weeks ago, and it is keeping time beautifully.
Yes, I heard that you received the Bible and I was very glad
that it turned up, for I was afraid that it had 'gone West,'
when it did not arrive together with the other stuff. Still, all is
well that ends well. So Mr Higgs has taken Dan in hand, eh?[10]
Well, I hope that he will do better than I did, otherwise there
are many hidings awaiting him, Ha Ha.

Things are going alright with me at present, being out
on out-post duty, with an officer and eighteen men. We are
doing well in the food line, cooking our own food. I have
built them an oven, for they had no idea how to set about
it, and now we turn out all sorts of delicacies, such as rice

pudding, bread pudding, Cornish pies, etc. So you see, we
are well away, doing fine. We have a very nice little camp in
a grove of fig-trees, our bivouacs being placed under a tree
out of the sun, and of course for 'camouflage'. We are having
a very quiet time, with very few shells coming over, and we
may be here for a few weeks yet. All the village boys are
alright here in the best of health & spirits. Mother was saying
in her letter about leave for the band boys as time-expired.
Well I am afraid that we don't stand a dog's chance for leave
from here. There are men here who were time-expired
eighteen months ago, and they are still here waiting for leave.
Of course, I shall do my utmost to come home on leave, but
I am not building any hopes on it, for I don't think it can be
done. All we shall get is the £15 bounty and we'll be lucky if
we get that. I have no more news to tell you this time, hoping
all are well at home there so I close with

> Love to all
> from
> Dick

Richard was still in Palestine when he sent the next letter in the
collection. At this point the letters which arrived safely were taking
three or four weeks to travel from Wales to the East.

RE1918-06-25

Dear Mother
        I was very pleased to receive your letter dated
May 28th which I received a few days ago with one from
Auntie Charlotte. I am very sorry to hear the letter had been
in the water but it is better to receive them like that than not
at all. We heard that they had been sunk so I never expected
you to get them. I hope you were able to understand at
least a part of them. Yes Mam, the watch is keeping time
beautifully. Now that we are on cultivated ground a watch
doesn't need such careful watching as it did while we were on
the desert. So Ivor had to send his watch home to be mended,
eh? I am sorry to hear that Gib has not had his leave yet,
but never mind, I suppose it has only been postponed for a

few days. I am sorry to hear about the death of Jack Jones, for it will mean a great deal to him with eight little children. So Glyn Evans lives opposite our house now? Where has Mrs Evans gone? I am glad to hear that you had a good time Whitsun time at Gelly-wastad.[11] I wouldn't mind being there myself for it seems to me that there was quite a nice little crowd there.

I sincerely hope that by now you have received my letter telling you not to send me any shirts, for we are not allowed to wear anything except the clothes and shirts issued to us through the Army. Dai Thomas & Ivor Lewis have received them, I know, but they cannot wear them, so they only mean extra weight to carry in our pack. As for that rumour that we are coming home it is all nonsense, so don't take any notice of it. I applied for leave to come home a few days ago but I have just learnt that there are no hopes of it, so the best thing I can hope for now is a week or so down in Cairo or Alexandria. That will be a nice change from field life. Yes Abraham Rees Morgan is in France for his Division left here some time ago and are now in France. Sammy Rees has not gone to the Royal Engineers yet, but he is expecting his transfer to come through almost any day. You ask for particulars as to how I lost my stripe. Well I was sent into hospital for artificial teeth, and instead of sending me back to my unit when they had finished with me they sent me from there down to the Base, on the banks of the Suez Canal. As soon as anyone goes into hospital from here, they lose their stripes, but as you see, as soon as I returned to my unit, I had the stripe and the pay given back to me. So now it is alright again. Dai Thomas has just received his other stripe, so now he has three. Good luck to him for he deserves them long ago. When I returned from the Base, the Colonel told me that the first chance he had he would put me up another one, but I have not heard anything about it since. But don't say anything about it, because it is considered very bad form to anticipate anything like that. I haven't heard from Gib lately but I am expecting one from him any day now. I do not blame him for not wishing for any fuss made when he comes home for if I can help it, I shall not let anybody know the exact day I shall be coming, for I hate a fuss like that like poison. I shall sneak home either through Heol Gerrig or through Cwm Pengwern.[12] Our Dan is allowing enough time to answer my note, for according to Auntie Charlotte he was going to write in a fortnight's time. I suppose he would have enough to tell by then. I'm very glad to hear that Dan is getting on so well with Mr Higgs and I hope he won't get as many hidings as I had with him. Ha! Ha!

Well mother things are going alright with me at present, having just come back to the base, after having been out about fifteen miles, with a little party of men on out-post duty. I was out there for about three weeks and had rather a quiet time there, except for aeroplanes who came over there every day in batches ranging from four to ten. But now I am back with Dai and the other boys. We had to do our own cooking out there, so we lived well, having learnt to cook all manner of food, from stew and roast dinner to puddings and pastry. Not only that, we had to make our own oven before we could start cooking but that didn't take me long once I had the tin and other stuff. There are quite a number of R.A.M.C. men being transferred from here to the infantry but I don't think I shall be sent for some time, if I shall be sent at all. It was rather hard lines on Johnny Phillips after transferring, not to be put into the same lot as his brother Dai.[13] I had a letter from him a short time ago saying that he had been slightly gassed in France there somewhere, but that he would be quite alright in a week or two. Don't be surprised if someone calls on you at home there, for two pals of mine were wounded here a short time ago, one from Llansamlet, having had his foot off, by the name of Jack Thomas, and the other having had his arm severely smashed; his name is Jack Howell and lives at the Hafod. They have been sent home and asked me for the address before they went. So make them as comfortable as you can. I have no more to tell you at this time so I close

with Love to all from

Dick

Am enclosing Trevor James's photo. He gave it to me a few days ago.

By this time, with Richard approaching four years of full-time service with the 3rd WFA it is notable how serious injuries are treated with nonchalance. Even if we take into account that Richard was writing with the intent not to worry his mother, it is striking to read the phrase 'slightly gassed', with the rather blasé assumption that his friend will soon be fighting fit. We have no further information on Jack Thomas nor Jack Howell, but it is fair to assume that they were disabled for life. We do not know whether either of them called at Pengwern Road, but if they did we can be sure that it helped the family there to understand better what the soldiers of the EEF had experienced, and what the risks were. Such a visit would also be, in a very minor way perhaps, a substitute for Richard's presence. There was a void in the family home – three gaps around the family's dinner table, as it were – and if the mother could not have her eldest son home for the present, to be able to welcome someone who had recently been with him, who had seen the same sights and undergone many of the same experiences, might help to assuage her anxiety.

Notes

1. RE1918-05-12; RE1918-02-20, both below.
2. Presumably Mary Eustis's sister.
3. This is Thomas J. Mathews, a member of Mynyddbach chapel. The welcome home referred to is most probably linked to the presentation of medals at Treboeth Public Hall to him and three other soldiers on 15 February 1918: see 'Treboeth', *CDL*, 16 February 1918, 3.
4. See Appendix 2.
5. Grandfather: Rees Rees.
6. See Appendix 3.
7. Miss Walters might refer to the teacher in Tirdeunaw School. See also RE1918-06-03a, below, and RE1918-09-30b (ch. 11).
8. Comb out: conscripting working miners (who had previously been exempt) for the armed forces.
9. See Appendix 2.
10. John Higgs, master at Tirdeunaw School. See also RE1918-06-25, below, and RE1918-09-30b (ch. 11).
11. A hill with a picturesque view to the north of Morriston.
12. That is, to take the back roads home rather than to come along the main road.
13. Johnny Phillips was mentioned in the first surviving letter from Richard: RE1914-09-19 (ch. 2). For Dai Phillips, see Appendix 2.

9

Ivor Eustis on the Western Front, December 1917–September 1918

Ivor arrived in France in December 1917 and the series of sixteen letters in the collection which he sent over the next ten months give information about his activities and his state of mind. After his many months of training – and over three years of imagining what the war would be like – he was to experience the 'real war', in the trenches on the Western Front.

Following a brief period in Le Havre and Rouen he was posted to his new unit, the 17th Battalion of the Royal Welsh Fusiliers. His letters henceforward are vague regarding his location, just giving 'France' and very little further information, though it is possible to track the battalion's movements using the unit's war diaries.[1] These diaries rarely give any details on the activities of individual men, except for a few mentions of awards for bravery: although Ivor did receive the Military Medal in this period he is not one of those named.

The letters give very little information on any of the dangerous and unpleasant tasks that a soldier on the front line had to carry out, such as trench raids and scouting expeditions at night to no man's land.[2] Of course, when writing to his mother, he more often adopts a reassuring tone, playing down the risks and emphasising some of the lighter aspects of his duty. There is much discussion, as in previous letters, of developments back home, and Ivor's response to his sister Lottie's success in the exam speaks volumes for his affection both for learning and for her. The first letter Ivor wrote from France gives a revealing insight into his feelings for another sister, as he worries that Hannah might get tempted to volunteer for service in the Women's Army Auxiliary Corps. This letter was written on YMCA paper on

12 December 1917 and posted the following day. As with most of
the envelopes to have survived from Ivor's time in France, there is a
stamp to confirm that it has been passed by the censor.

IE1917-12-12

Dear Mother,

Just a line to let you know that I am all right and
in a fair state of health at present. It is the first decent
opportunity I have had of writing since I left home as I have
been on the move continually, or at least, if not actually
moving I have been kept under orders to do so all the time.
I was at Le Havre for some days expecting to leave every
minute, so I did not consider it the best plan to write from
there. I have been here since Monday [10 December] and
again I expect to go away at any time, but I was put on
guard this morning, and so I am utilising this opportunity of
relieving the suspense there must still exist at home. While
we were at Southampton, we went for some tea and having to
wait some time before the thing was ready, I thought I would
scribble you a post card to say that I had arrived safely there.

This I did and after addressing and stamping it I put
it on the table beside me. However, when I finished my tea
I marched out again leaving the post card still on the table.
I have been wondering ever since whether the waiter had
the common sense to post the card, which was not much
considering that it was stamped and addressed ready.

Well, so far, I have managed pretty well for myself. Of
course the conditions are not what they were at Kinmel but
nevertheless they have not been so bad that I have been unable
to put up with them. I had a bit of a cold in travelling from
Rouen to here but that cleared off nicely in two days. While
there we slept in a large hut, which resembled a poultry shed
as much as possible. We slept on square frames covered with
netting wire, with 3 blankets to keep us warm. Here we are
billeted in tents, with a waterproof sheet and some blankets
for a bed. So you see, things are not half as bad as one would
imagine. The food is all right consisting of about ¾ bully beef
and biscuits and I am rapidly growing fat on it. There is a decent

Sergeants' Mess here, and of course while we go there we get the ordinary food, dinner, tea etc. just like home, with no bully beef or biscuits but we are only here for the time being, so that we shall miss that again when next we get a move on.

So far I have found myself stranded as regards friends, in fact since I left home I have seen nobody I know, not a single soul. The fellow who came from Limerick with me is a bit of a 'boozer' in other words he is too fond of the beer, so I have very little to do with him. I did not know him before we got put in this draft together, and I don't want to know him when I get back neither.

I should like to know whether you have been able to draw any of that allowance yet. They pay us here in French money, in Francs and cents and I can tell you we have to be careful or we are easily 'done down' as the phrase goes. They have a coin called a franc which is very much like a shilling, but its value is 10 pence, so if you are not wide awake they do you out of twopence here. The same applies to a 5 cent piece which is very much like a sixpence but its value is 5 pence, and you can guess that a penny to a soldier is like a shilling to a chap at home. What is more, the French people are very apt to make these mistakes, accidentally of course, we All know that.

I am very anxious also about Hannah. Where she had that idea of the Auxiliary Corps from, I don't know, but I sincerely hope she will not join anything of the kind. There has been enough 'joining' and 'enlisting' in our family all ready. I should, indeed, be very much relieved to know that she has made up her mind to stay at home till we boys return.

I had been expecting to hear from Dick for some time before I left Kinmel Park, and if any thing came there after I left, a friend of mine would have sent it home. Will you keep anything that comes, safely till I send for it? It is advisable that you don't write to me to this address because I might leave here any minute, and if anything arrived here for me, it would probably get lost. So don't send anything on till I settle down in my proper battalion.

There is no more just now except that there is nothing to worry about as regards health etc of yours affectionately
Ivor

At some point over the following three weeks, Ivor joined A Company of the 17th Battalion of the RWF. It is possible that he joined the unit on 18 December, when they were on the front line at Houplines: the war diary notes '3 OR joined the Battalion'. Alternatively, he might have joined them later when they were stationed at Estaires: on 22 December (when four OR joined the unit) or 27 December (when three joined).

The 17th (Service) Battalion (2nd North Wales) RWF was originally raised in Llandudno and Blaenau Ffestiniog in February 1915. They were posted to France in December 1915 and formed part of the 38th (Welsh) Division, being attached to 115 Brigade. After a period of training in the trenches at Laventie they were put in the front line for the first time in January 1916. After a few months in the vicinity of Festubert, in June 1916 the battalion was moved south, along with the whole of the 38th (Welsh) Division towards the Somme battlefield. The battalion was heavily involved in the Battle of Mametz Wood, suffering 180 casualties (killed, wounded and missing) on 10 July 1916. The survivors returned north in August, to the Ypres sector. The next sustained action of the battalion was in the Battle of Pilckem Ridge (31 July 1917, at the start of the Passchendaele campaign), when there were 340 casualties. After this the battalion was engaged in routine trench duty for the rest of the year.

Ivor started the New Year with a letter to his mother. At the top he wrote 'Blwyddyn newydd dda i chwi, pob un trwy'r tu' [*Happy New Year to you, all that are in the house*], and then the address: '"A" Company, 17ᵗʰ R.W.F., B.E.F., France'. This letter, like most of the following letters he wrote from the Western Front, is on small lined paper (approximately 7 in. by 5 in.).

IE1918-01-01

Dear Mother,

Just a line on New Year's day to let you know that I am all right as regards health and contentment. Naturally, the new year was not welcomed in the same way here as it probably was at home – there was nobody to wake us up with carrols [*sic*] at the door, for the simple reason that we have no doors here, only entrances; we were, however, kept awake for some time last night, by some 'carrols' of an entirely different kind.

I have found my feet all right in this battalion now, and I know what I have to deal with, and once one knows this, it is his own fault if he cannot make himself comfortable. The weather is still exceedingly cold and frosty although the snow has practically cleared away, and if it does not get any worse than it is now, I shall do very well. You need have no worry about my being well fed, because we do very well here, though it is a very rough and ready way we have of eating, for instance, in the morning everyone here is seen sitting on the floor with some bacon between his finger and thumb, or chasing pickled onions about a bottle with a pencil, and a hundred others which are passed by by all the Tommies, but which would cause some amazement to any newcomer. What you appear to be short of at home, we are well off with, here; such as tea, bacon, margarine etc. I always think of the people at home when dishing out the margarine in the morning, and wishing I could send some of it home, as I know it would be very acceptable, and that fresh butter even at home is entirely out of the question.

The communication lines between France and England seem to be interrupted still, for I have only received two letters since I have been in France, one of which was dated Dec 10th & the other Dec 15th, and I can tell you they had travelled 'some', having been to Kinmel Park, Limerick, Le Havre, Rouen and finally arriving here, beyond recognition. There is no more at present so I'll tewi sôn [*be quiet*] for a bit.

With love to all,
Ivor

The battalion was out of the front line for much of January, and the war diary has many reports of boxing contests, cross-country races and shooting competitions. The next letter to have survived in the collection was written from 'Somewhere', France, on 6 February 1918 to sister Lottie, with the principal purpose of encouraging her in her scholastic pursuits. It is also one of the most direct statements in the collection of letters as to what the war is being fought for.

IE1918-02-06

Dear Lottie,

    I have heard that you intend to try the Scholarship
Examination at Gowerton next July and I must say that I
am very glad to hear that. You know quite well that all your
elder brothers and sisters have all had a trial at the same
thing and a few of us have been fortunate enough to succeed.
Others have been very unlucky, and though they were clever
enough for anything (I suppose that you know that Gib &
Dick, Hannah & Bess & Grace are all very smart and clever
at their work) yet there was one little thing wrong in each
case – in some cases only a little slip, yet it cost them the
scholarship.

    Now I want you to remember that Britain is fighting
against her enemies for fair play to little nations such as
Belgium who did her duty in trying to drive the enemy back.
Now in this great war, every [*two or three words illegible*]
must do something to help, some have a lot to do and others
a little bit. Now Dick and Gib are doing a very big 'bit', as
big a 'bit' as anybody is doing, and the people at home are all
doing their bit. Your little bit will be to do your bit to win
the Scholarship, so that you will be able to go to Gowerton
the same as Bess and Grace, so let us see if you can do your
duty to Britain and to Mother and Father, in the same way as
Belgium did her duty.

    Now if you win, you will go to Gowerton till you will
be big enough to go to College, and after about 4 years in
college you will be a Lady like Miss Gregory; but if you lose
you won't go to Gowerton & you won't go to College. So do
your best.

    Your affectionate Bro. <u>Ivor</u>

In the following letter (sent from 'France'), written on
12 February, Ivor does not give the name of the town where they
were stationed, Estaires. The battalion's war diary confirms Ivor's
statement that this was a relaxed period: on 8 February the officers
of the 17th RWF played the officers of the 10th SWB at football,
winning 5-1.

IE1918-02-12

Dear Mother,

Just a line to let you know that both your and A C's [Aunt Charlotte's] letters arrived safely today. I appreciate Grace's effort very much, thanks very much to her, a little news of Gowerton is always interesting, for it seems as if it were only yesterday that I left the old school.

Well, I really couldn't help laughing at the adventures you go through at home in quest of [*word illegible*] and having been in the Army a few [years?] I can quite understand what a discomfort is caused when a good meal cannot be enjoyed owing to the absence of sugar or such like. But after a while you all come to laugh at your misfortunes, instead of worrying over them.

Soldiers have long ago realised that things will get no better by worrying over them and that the best way to do is always to turn bad luck into a joke. We read very much about looking at the bright side of things, but I prefer to look at the humorous side of everything however bad it may be. Sometimes when our rations come up, instead of bread we get biscuits some specimens of modern cookery akin to what we used to feed Joe on.[3] As soon as these are shared out, somebody starts barking another will howl and this is taken up by the remainder, so that in a few seconds they all set up a horrible row enough to make a cat laugh.

Well, Mother, we have been having a ripping time of it this last week. We came out of the line to a town called ———— about 6 miles from the trenches and I must say we have enjoyed ourselves all right. It is generally the case that when we come out for what they call a 'rest' we have to work harder than we would in the line; but this time it has been different, for after doing some digging in the morning we had the afternoon off every time, and being billeted in a town we could enjoy such luxuries as nuts, buns and chocolates, and without having to carry our SBR's about like 'bibs' with us.[4]

Do you know what part of the line we are at now? Well, I am sorry I cannot state the name of the place in a letter but perhaps you know, or at least you may have a very good idea.

As regards Dick, I wrote to him when I was at
Le Havre to say that I was in France and asked him what he
thought of it, and I am waiting to hear what he says before I
write again. I have intended writing to Gib too this last week
or so but I have kept putting it off all the time. I will do so
as soon as I get time to sort myself out. I am posting the big
photo to you today let me know when it arrives. It shows the
remainder of the NCO's in our company and the officers.

The boys are roaring just now. One of the boys a
chap from Neath had his photograph taken the other day in
a French man's clothes and straw hat, and he is showing the
photo round now – hence the mirth.

How is Uncle Sam getting on these days. I sincerely
hope he is well again and that his progress was not much
impaired by the winter months.

Well ta! ta! for the present, the next you will hear of
us will be in 'Official News' where you will probably hear of
what we have done. With love to all. Ivor

Two days after he wrote this letter, the 17th RWF were moved
back to the front line. The war diary for 15 February notes 'the
usual work of maintenance of Trenches, Wiring & other work'.
The following day, '1 OR accidentally wounded whilst cleaning his
rifle. 1 OR accidentally killed by a comrade, the latter cleaning his
revolver.'[5] After a period out of the line, the battalion returned to
the front-line trenches on 1 March, and the war diary records their
action on 2–3 March:

> A Raiding Party of our 'A' Coy of 3 officers and 86 OR's raided
> a portion of the enemy's line ... Raiders moved from EVELYN
> POST to their place of assembly at 11.35pm. Zero hour was at
> 11.50pm. The raid was preceded by a well supported artillery
> bombardment. The result of raid was one prisoner captured.
> Identifications three. Killed four. Our casualties were thirteen
> wounded – two subsequently dying from wounds.[6]

Two men were subsequently awarded the Military Medal for their
'gallantry and devotion to duty' in this raid. Ivor gives no details
of this action in his next letter, written on 7 March, though this one
does give his mother some idea of their routine in the trenches.

IE1918-03-07

Dear Mother,

      Thanks very much for the cigarettes and the letter, which arrived safely yesterday. I don't think there was much room to spare in that tin and it is evident that you made an 'ymdrech deg' [*fair effort*] to let me have a good issue. These field cards that we are provided with are very handy, I must say, when we are too busy to write letters. When we go into the line, we have hardly any time to spare, and in fact it is very little sleep we get, while every odd five minutes we make the most of by getting to sleep in order to be a bit fresher in the [~~da~~] night. During the day we can only do odd jobs which can be done without the Germans seeing us, while we have still to keep some men standing by in case they attempt to pay us a visit. Then in the night there are a hundred and one things to be done under the cover of darkness which we would not dare attempt in daylight, such as setting up wire entanglements in front of our line. Also during the night there is no one allowed to go to a dugout, so that even if there is no work to be done, we still have to stand to. Of course after a certain period in the line we have a rest about 2 miles behind, and some other battalion comes instead of us.

      So you can expect but few letters while we are in line, and you should not worry if you do not hear from me for about a week or so.

      I wonder could you help me out of a difficulty. The food here is nothing to grumble about when one considers the circumstances, but we get no vegetables at all, with the result, so I am told, that, in my case, my blood has become overheated. Consequently, I find nasty things like boils setting up on my face and sores on my hands and legs; something of the same nature as what we used to call a 'cornwyd' [*abscess*] only smaller. They are not painful but they are a great nuisance, for it takes me about half a day to shave myself, while the thought of washing my hands and face in the morning almost breaks my heart. I have been wondering whether your old recipe 'treacle a brimstone' would do me any good. If I were at home I know you would

recommend the old 'cure-all', namely 'tê senna' [*senna tea*]
but thank goodness I am out of reach of that at present. Will
'treacle a brimstone' keep for about a fortnight? and do you
think it worth while trying?

    Will write again soon.

            with love to all <u>Ivor</u>

There is a gap in the surviving collection of letters, with nothing
extant from the subsequent eleven weeks, save for a field postcard
which Ivor wrote on 3 April. This stated that he was 'quite well
and am going on well' (with 'quite' underlined); 'Letter follows at
first opportunity' and 'I have received no letter from you for a long
time'. A letter from Gabriel in late April suggests that Ivor suffered
a minor wound at this time, but we have no further information.[7]
The war diary indicates that the attrition continued, with many
reports of ORs wounded, gassed or killed. Reinforcements arrived,
including a contingent of 44 ORs on 24 March. The battalion moved
south to the Somme district in April, being posted to the line in the
Bouzincourt sector on 25 March. Here the battalion attempted to
attack the German trenches on 1 May, but were repulsed by machine
gun fire. The casualties were 8 ORs killed, 21 ORs wounded and
7 ORs missing; a sergeant was awarded the DCM and a corporal the
MM for their 'gallantry and devotion to duty'. As the battalion were
being relieved of their front-line duties on 20 May, the Germans
launched a heavy bombardment with gas shells: 17 ORs were gassed.
Then they were billeted in Herissart, though the letter that Ivor
wrote on 28 May just gave his address as 'France'.

                         IE1918-05-28

Dear Mother,

    I received your letter tonight and as there is no excuse
for me not writing now, I will answer it straight away.

    Well, to begin with, I am in splendid health still, and
just beginning to feel the benefit of being out of the line.
We have been out nearly a week now and I thing [*sic*] I have
eaten more food during this week and paid more for it than
I ever did in a month before. And all the other boys are the
same. When we were in the line, we had good food except at

times, but it was the same thing day after day and after we had been in for some time we could do with a change. So you can imagine how much respect we give such things as eggs, milk, salmon, pears, tomatoes, oranges.

When we came out of the line, we were paid a big pay (we had been without any for a long time) and as they sold eggs and milk in almost every house, we began to live in style. We have been having eggs for breakfast, eggs for tea, & eggs between meals, eggs before going to bed, and eggs before parade. Boiled, fried, poached, & raw, and it is a wonder how they can keep up the supply. The Froggies charge us 5d apiece for them, or two eggs for a franc, and though we admit this to be a very high price, we are quite willing to pay anything for them as long as we can get them, for we haven't had the chance for some months past and it is not likely that we'll see them again when next we get in the line. I have written Dick a letter and I include it with this. I want you to post it, in the hope that it will get better luck than the ones I have written & posted from France. I think the address is correct but if it is not, you better readdress another envelope & put in my letter as it is. I have written to Gib also but it is too early for a reply yet. Everything is going smoothly now – plenty of hard work out in the boiling sun, but that is nothing. I am including some money to cover cost of repairing the watch. I think Hannah can change it for you. Also, I am trying to get some souvenirs home too.

No more this time
with love to all, Ivor

The next letter in the collection was written a few days later, on 2 June, when the 17th RWF was still stationed at Herissart. Presumably the aunt to whom it is addressed is Charlotte. The battalion's war diary gives details of all the competitions mentioned by Ivor in the letter.

IE1918-06-02

Dear Auntie & all,
I have come to the end of our all-too-brief holiday and we are on the point of going back to the line again. We have

been out exactly a fortnight and during that time we have had excellent weather, and though there has been plenty of work awaiting us at all times, I personally have enjoyed myself, though there has been little else to enjoy but eggs, tinned fruit and fresh air, not forgetting sleep <u>at night</u> (not during the day as is the case in the line). All we have had to worry us is air raids, of which we have had a very full issue, considering that Jerry has been over in his planes almost every night dropping bombs here there and everywhere. Still that was quite a minor detail and none of us ever worried about that.

We have been carrying on competitions here in various parts of the work, such as shooting, bayonet-fighting etc and the final for the whole Division occurred on Saturday, when there were a large number of 'Brass Hats' visiting us. Also, some time ago, during a big inspection by the Corps Commander, we were complimented as a battalion on our smart turn out.

The weather is exceedingly warm here and everything is as dry as a bone. Even our bread ration although kept under cover, gets very dry even during the night. Butter of course, disappears like greased lightning – the army substitute was not very famous for stability before, but now it requires a sentry over it.

By the time you receive this, I suppose everything will be working under full pressure for the coming examinations. I have the utmost confidence in both Bess & Lottie to get through, more so in the case of Lottie. She will get through all right but I think Bess will have to roll her sleeves up for honours.

How is O.C. Std 1 getting along. I presume he is what can be termed 'an old soldier' now and up to all the dodges.[8] Ha! Ha! I'm thinking of 'The Village Blacksmith'
'--------------- a mighty man is he'[9]
Well I expect to see Lottie's name at the head of the list of successes anyway, although it's only a 'practice run'.

No more, with love to all, Ivor

On the rear of this letter Ivor has written 'Photos for Dan', but there is no indication of what they were. Two days after writing this letter Ivor and his comrades were at the Divisional Reserve base where they received training, before moving on 7 June to the support trenches near Engle-Belmer. There was a few days' working to improve shelters and look-out posts before the battalion again moved to the front line for two days, after which they were sent to the Divisional Reserve area in Forceville for more training and manual labour. On 22 June, the day they returned to the front line (Mesnil left sector), one officer and ten ORs were killed, and eight ORs wounded. The battalion remained on the front line for eight days, with further casualties (one OR killed, five OR wounded) noted on 29 June.

The next letter in the collection was written to Hannah on 1 July 1918. It is on YMCA paper bearing the words 'On Active Service with the British Expeditionary Force'.

IE1918-07-01

My dear Nance,

Just a scribble to let you know that I have received both parcels quite safely and of course incidentally I did full justice to them.

Do you remember a few weeks ago Mother sent me back the watch in a registered envelope? She included a letter in it too, which of course I read straight away. Then I put the envelope in my pocket and thought no more of it, until a couple of days ago when I happened to be clearing away some old correspondence I came across this R Envelope and imagine my surprise when I found inside a letter from Dick! That nearly lost it eh! It is the first I have had from him in this country and even <u>it</u> was dated last April.

Don't you think I'm a careless bounder?

I read in the papers that you have had a dose of this mysterious illness in Blighty. We've had ours too, & in fact, we are still having it. It got me for 3 days a week ago. Alright now though!

Ivor

The 'mysterious illness' referred to is what was known as the 'Spanish Flu'. The first wave of mortalities in Britain were reported in late June 1918, then after a lull the death rate from the disease hit its peak in the autumn of 1918, as the virus mutated to a most aggressive and deadly strain. Ivor describes his symptoms in the following letter from 4 July 1918:

IE1918-07-04

Dear Mother

Just a line again hoping it will find everyone at home in the pink, and that this mysterious illness has not affected anyone at Mynydd Bach. I read in the papers that it is as common in England as it is in France. It is a very unpleasant complaint but not at all a serious one. Anyway, I have had my issue and I am not sorry neither. The last time we were out we were doing fatigues digging trenches and about 3 days before we went up to the line, I had to report sick with a rotten headache and a kind of rheumatism all over the body. The doctor took my temperature and found it to be 103 and after asking all sorts of funny questions he gave me a few pills and marked me 'Excused Duty'. I had Excused Duty for the next day and the one following but we were due to go up the line on the fourth and as my temperature had gone down a bit I was given Light Duty which meant that I had to go up the line as usual. Well, I got better day by day until when we got out I was well away and felt like a hungry bull. It was not painful at all during the 3 days it lasted but the worst of it is that it left me as weak as a chicken.

I got the two parcels all right and as you can imagine I did full justice to them. The tomatoes might have kept a bit better but I ate them and enjoyed them as they were, and beyond about 10 minutes 'bola tost' [*stomach ache*] I was none the worse for it.

Gib wrote me that Lottie had passed the first part of the Gowerton Exam, but I have heard nothing further to confirm it, but I am now waiting for the newspaper cutting to reach me with the list of successes, with Lottie among them.

According to the first arrangement we should have been in the back areas now having a rest, but things did not pan out as they were supposed to. We should have done 24 days in and

then go out but when we completed our time the division that
was to relieve us had to go elsewhere and we had to carry on.
Anyway we hope to go back at a very early date. It was only
a few days ago that I found the letter from Dick that you had
posted with the watch. Very careless of me to do that.

No more with love to all

Ivor

On this occasion, there is a discrepancy between Ivor's statement that
he was still in the line and the information given in the battalion war
diary, which states that the battalion was relieved and moved to the
Forceville reserve area on 1 July for rest, training and manual labour.
According to the diary the unit returned to the line (Mesnel left sector, to the left of Aveloy Wood) on 9 July. Here, fifty-three ORs were
gassed following an attack on 15 July. However, Ivor reported in a
letter to Gabriel on 11 July that he was serving as orderly sergeant
at company headquarters, so presumably he was away from that
particular danger.[10] No concrete details of his activities are given in
Ivor's next three letters home, but instead they are dominated by
good news of his sister Lottie's exam results. He wrote on 15 July:

IE1918-07-15

Dear Mother,

I received a letter a few nights ago from Auntie
Charlotte, in which she says it was quite true that Lottie
had got through the first part of the Gowerton Scholarship.
Well, you don't know how pleased I was to hear this, though
I had great confidence in 'Charlotte Fach' all along, but the
one thing I feared was her inexperience as she is so young.
Fancy the other poor children trying for the 2nd time and
failing, while a youngster like Lottie gets through on the first
attempt. I always said she was the smartest of the lot of us,
and with a little looking after, she will do great things.

However, she only wants a little bit of luck now and
she will be right.

I am wondering whether Gib has returned yet, for the
last I heard of him was that he had had another extension.
I thought before that, that he had long ago returned to his

ship, as someone told me that there was to be no extensions this time.

There is no special news this time again so I concluded with love to all at home

from Ivor

In the next two letters, both written on 27 July, there is further reaction to the news of his sisters' exams. In the letter to his mother, Ivor also gives an indication of what the troops on the front line thought of the higher command in the rear.

IE1918-07-27a

Dear Mother,

Just a few lines to let you know that I received your letter a few days ago and that I am delighted to hear that Lottie got the Scholarship she so well earned. I said all along from the beginning that she was right for it and now she has shown that I was right.

I should like to know when she starts and all that so that I can do what I can to make things easy for her and you, and to get things to run smoothly.

I promised to make her a present of some kind or other if she succeeded and I am quite prepared to keep my promise, and what is more, the more she wins the more she gets.

It was very hard lines for Bessie – very unlucky I must say, but still that will not cause as much of a drawback as it would if she had been taken ill some months before the exam and had been unable to carry on her studies. As it is she has done all the work and will be none the worse for not having tried the examination. Still there is the loss of the certificate to consider and also the experience she would have had in the examination itself.

But she will be able to go on the next step and I should like to see her having a shot at the Senior Certificate next year instead of waiting, as I did, till she gets to Form 6. All is going well in that line just now, and I hope they will last so.

With me, they are just the same as usual, as busy as ever. We have been out now about a week, and we have done

nothing but polishing and quick marching ever since. When
we are not in the line we are expected to have everything
shining like glass, but when we go into the line again, the
gentlemen who enforce all this cleaning are miles on rear
and never come anywhere near shell fire, whereas we poor
beggars will be up to our eye brows in mud as soon as the
first shower is over. A fat lot we think of polish then, Ha!
Ha! We don't wash or shave for about a week on end while
we get a clean shirt regularly every 5 months.

No more

with love to all.

Ivor

IE1918-07-27b

Dear Lottie,

Hearty congratulations on winning that Scholarship;
I must say you have done remarkably well and scored an
immense success which we all think a great deal of. I said
long ago that you would get it and you have fully justified
the confidence I had in you. I am really proud to think that I
have such a clever little sister.

I promised to reward you for your energies if you
succeeded and I am quite prepared to fulfil my promise.
Write and let me know what you would like to have and I
shall see that you get it. Of course, we have no penny bazaars
in the trenches but even if I cannot get it myself, I'll see that
you get it all right by some means or other. So don't forget to
let me know when you start the term.

Once again – Well done Lottie Fach!

Yours affectionately

Ivor

It is likely that these two letters were written from Herrisart, where
the battalion had arrived on 19 July. Here there was further training and some relaxation. The divisional band entertained the men
on 24 July, and on 29 July, 'In the morning Battalion paraded full
marching order for inspection by the Commanding Officer. Brigade
Sports held in the afternoon.' The following day the battalion moved

to Acheux, where training continued for four days. It must have been from here that Ivor wrote his letter home on 3 August.

IE1918-08-03

Dear Mother,
    Just a few lines to let you know that I am all right and in good health and spirits though things are a wee bit uncomfortable owing to the weather having taken a turn for the worse.
    We left the place we were in last week and moved forward again as far as here (about 2 miles behind the line) and we have been very unfortunate ever since. On the day of the march, it was boiling hot and the roads as dry as a bone; besides this we had 'full marching order' to carry, that is, pack and parcel everything we've got. The whole journey was about 15 miles, and long before we reached the end of it, the boys were falling out by the dozen. One poor fellow died before they could get him to hospital; he must have strained himself or something. However I managed to stick it somehow or other and I was not sorry when we reached our destination neither.
    Our new homes consisted of the usual bivouacs but as the place was rather crowded some of us slept out in the open, as the weather was all right. Well, the following day it started raining and it has been raining off and on ever since, with the result that the whole place is nothing but a mass of sticky mud from one end to the other. The bivouacs sheets (that is the roof part) stood all right for a while but as it continued to rain, they gradually let the rain in drop by drop.
    I received a letter from Dick dated June 3rd yesterday and I was quite pleased to find myself in communication with him again, after being so long hanging about. It was a splendid letter, just as he used to send me when I was at Kinmel Park, stating exactly what it is like with him. He seems to think that I am in a worse place than he, and he would rather see me in Egypt than in France, but I think he is making a mistake there, for in my opinion, taking it all round, they get a rougher time of it in Palestine than we do in France. No doubt we have more shells to put up with, but

then we have not so much marching to do; besides this we
have a better climate and good roads.

    Will you ask Bess Ann to hunt up and find me a
little book called 'Platoon and Company Drill'. It is about
6 inches long by about 4 broad, with a yellow cloth cover. I
think she will find it amongst the odds and ends in the spare
bookcase. I should like this to be sent me as soon as possible.

    There is no further news at present so I'll wind up with
        Love to all
          from Ivor

After this letter there is a five-week gap in the collection. For
much of this time, the 17th RWF was involved in operations on the
front line, as the tide turned on the Western Front and the Allies
moved to the offensive. The 'Hundred Days' campaign that was to
send the German army reeling began on 8 August (a day noted by
the German commander Ludendorff as 'the black day of the German
Army'), and from then until the Armistice the Allied armies launched
a series of attacks at a variety of points along the line. It seems that
the 17th RWF, stationed in the Bouzincourt sector, was not involved
in the early stages of this offensive, but the war diary has a report of
an action by the 17th RWF near Bouzincourt on 24 August 1918.

At 1 a.m. under a heavy artillery barrage, the battalion
in conjunction with the 2nd R.W.F. on the left and the
113th Brigade on the right attacked the enemy line.

    The Battalion attacked on a frontage of about 500 yards
with 'B' Coy. left front, and was then held up by heavy M. G.
[machine gun] fire. The Battalion captured 200 prisoners and
a number of M. Guns. 'A' & 'B' Coys advanced into a post of
M. Guns, and were almost surrounded but fought their way
through, Casualties 6 Officers and about 100 O R's[11]

At this stage in the war diary, the details of casualties are often
sketchy, but according to the database of the Commonwealth War
Graves Commission (CWGC), three soldiers of the 17th RWF died
on 25 August, two on 26 August and one the following day.[12] On
25 August the battalion made their way to territory that would
have been familiar to some of the men from two years earlier,

1,000 yards north-west of Mametz Wood. The following day the battalion took High Wood (another name that resonates with those familiar with the exploits of the Welsh in the Battle of the Somme). The toll continued to rise: the CWGC database lists four men of the 17th RWF who died on 29 August; sixteen for 30 August; two for 31 August; fourteen for 1 September; seven for 2 September and ten for 3 September. According to the war diary, the unit was involved in an attack on Sailly-Saillisel on 1 September but despite their success the unit that was supposed to support them on their right did not materialise, leading to a German counter-attack which outflanked them and forced a retreat. However, the enemy withdrew on the morning of 3 September, allowing the 17th RWF to advance to St Martin's Wood.[13] Ivor sent home a field postcard on 4 September, saying that he was quite well and had received the letter dated 29 August. The battalion was relieved on 5 September, retiring to a bivouac area between Les Boeufs and Morval.

On 9 September Ivor wrote a letter to his mother from France, but unfortunately the top left-hand quarter of the first page has weathered to render large parts illegible. In this Ivor reports that he has not received the watch which he had sent back home for repair, although he had been told in a letter to expect it. He continues:

IE1918-09-09

I did not think it would cost as [much?] as it did and so I am glad I sent some money to cover it. You did not say in your letter whether you had it or not. I hope it got back all right and that you were able to change it.

Well I have not heard from Dick yet. I was told the other day that a Welsh Division was coming from Dick's place to France and that the biggest part had already arrived. I was beginning to think it might be the one Dick was in, but I soon learnt that it was not, for the numbers did not correspond. I don't think it is likely that he will come over here for from what I here [sic] the RAMC have as much as they can do over there already. That reminds me – when I was at -------- on rest I just managed to catch a glimpse of Bryn Thomas again.[14] I saw him when we were coming out and again when we were returning to the line. Sorry I did not have the opportunity of spending an evening with him. I have not seen T. J. Cole this long time. Being in the same Brigade as myself, he was out for a rest as well, but not in the same village.

I wonder if Gib has managed to get his leave yet. I am hoping he has and I am writing him a letter, addressing it home; if he has not arrived by the time the letter comes keep it for him till he comes. I don't suppose he will be lucky enough to get a few months this time as he did last time.

Have you received that souvenir testament I sent you? What do you think of it.

No more this time
with love to all.
Ivor

The day after writing this letter, Ivor's battalion moved to Léchelle, and back into the action. On 12 September, they provided support for an attack by the New Zealand Division and the SWB, which began at 5.25 a.m. The role of the 17th RWF was 'to push out patrols to ascertain if enemy front line is held or not': in this operation three ORs were killed and fifteen wounded. There was a German counter-attack the following morning ('Raid repulsed leaving one dead Hun in our lines') which led to nineteen casualties among the ORs.[15] Although the following three days are described in the war diary as 'quiet' there were still casualties, with five ORs suffering from gas on 15 September.

On 16 September the battalion was posted to Brigade Reserve and according to a letter Ivor wrote to Gabriel on 18 September he was 'well behind lines' on a 'soft job'.[16] The war diary states that the battalion returned to Léchelle on 20 September for rest, reorganisation and cleaning up. After more training they moved on to Sorel-le-Grand on 28 September, where they were to remain for a further week.

Ivor wrote the following letter on 19 September, which includes some enlightening and entertaining insights into his role as an interpreter of army routine to one who was at sea in the British Army. Sadly, the letter from Morris referred to in this letter has not been kept in the collection. Ivor's letter also reveals that he has been awarded the Military Medal: clearly the details of this news had already been conveyed to Mynyddbach in another letter, now lost. It is possible that Ivor gained this medal for his contribution to the

actions on 24 August or 1 September, though no further evidence
has come to light to resolve the question.[17]

IE1918-09-19

Dear Mother, and all,
        Your letter of the 13th inst arrived today after being
on two or three buckshee journeys down to Battle Surplus
and up to the line to the Battalion and so on.[18] Having been
moving about so much lately, I have not been able to get any
mail, so that when I finally got my issue today, there was
quite a good lot awaiting me, including one from Auntie
Charlotte, one from 'Somewhere else' Ha! Ha! and one
from an old soldier who used to be with us, but who has
now been admitted into hospital. I include that one for your
perusal – don't destroy it but keep it for me. I have read it
about 50 times already and each time I find something new to
laugh at. Poor old fellow, he was undeniably not much of an
Englishman, though he was a decent little Welshman.
        There is quite a story to be told about this interesting
specimen of humanity. He is a small little man; thin and very
old as far as the military standard goes, being about 45 years
of age. To look at him you would say he was probably
a hundred & 45, for what with his bald head and heavy
moustache, to see him on the battle field gave the idea that
the man power of the British was almost exhausted and that
we were fetching up our great grandfathers. Still he had his
good points, and they were many.
        Having been in all other platoons he finally landed
in mine, No 3, where he stuck. On account of his age and
infirmities that means to say he was not so agile as us youngsters,
I always gave him the easiest jobs, while bestowing the heavier
tasks on chaps like myself, in a fit state to do them. The reason
I took him under my wing was twofold, firstly his age etc,
and secondly the fact that being a poor orator in the English
language, he could neither explain himself when in difficulty nor
could he argue the point with the English boys and so claim his
rights and dues. Also, as he hailed from North Wales, it took
him as long to understand my Welsh as it took me to understand

his English, and you can imagine what a fix we were in at times, especially if either of us got the least excited about it.

However, though other N.C.O's could do nothing with him, Old Morris would do absolutely anything for me. Even at the end of a long march when everyone was done up completely, and I would have to fix a [~~guard~~] sentry for the platoon, where I would have a lot of grumbling from younger fellows, I would only have to say 'Morris! you are on Gas Guard tonight' and he would reply 'Very good, Corpol' that was the way he pronounced it. Then would follow minor questions such as 'Corpol! what amser [*time*] we be start?' or 'Ble do gaurd sefyll, Corpol?' [*Where does the guard stand, Corpol?*] No doubt you will find some difficulty with his letter, especially the tit-bit that I have underlined; what he means to say is this:- that 'it would have been better for him if he had taken my advice and gone down to see the doctor that morning with the Ration Party.' Anyway I am glad that he is in dock (Hospital), as I told him in my reply, the line is no place for him.

I am enclosing a letter for Will Simon John, but I don't know whether the address is correct or not. Could someone find out and if it is not, put the letter in an envelope and address it to the proper destination.

I see Mynydd Bach is getting noted for Military Medals just now – what with Eddie Morgan's, Will Simon's and mine, I think the district is costing the Government a lot in tin, or iron, or what the dickens they are made of.[19]

I am still having a comfortable time of it, doing nothing but stroll around the place like a spare insurance agent 'ar y plwyf' [*on the parish*]. One can appreciate a job like this after spending a few weeks in shell holes, wet and hungry, etc. etc. However, as long as the job lasts, I'm simply laughing.

> Dim rhagor heno,
> gyda chariad oddiwrth Ivor
> [*No more tonight*
> *with love from Ivor*]

The final letter from Ivor from his time on active service in France was written on 27 September 1918. It begins with an appeal to British patriotism: the only such explicit statement in his letters. It is clear that he has an inkling of the tough and dangerous task that lies ahead, but which cannot be shirked. There is a lighter side also, as he is still able to envisage going home on leave, although he knows that such a possibility is not imminent. There is also mention of something that was to become a sore issue in future letters, that of his rank.

IE1918-09-27

Dear Mother

Here we are again at the end of a good time and ready for a bit more good work for our dear old country, and the more I look around me the more consolation I find [out] in the knowledge that what we are about to endure is for the sake of our country – 'Blighty' as we call it. The place we are in now was probably a prosperous town of considerable size before the war, but now there only remains a wall here and there with perhaps a chimney balancing itself like an acrobat on the end of a brick while behind us there is not a house standing, not even a wall, for a distance of about 30 miles, with a heap of bricks to denote where villages once stood.

You have probably read the letters which I wrote Auntie Charlotte a couple of days ago and I hope it will not depress you too much. I know it is really very sad, still what's got to be – got to be, as the boys put it, and we are powerless to alter it.

I had a postcard from Dick yesterday and with it the good news that he is still all right. It was dated Sept 5th and he said that he had not heard from me for some time, but he had probably done so since. I have heard nothing from Gib but I am looking forward to a line every day. I have sent to ask him when he is expecting leave next so that if it is possible we shall do our best to come together. I am afraid you are over anxious to see me home, because I notice that everyone is expecting me home any day – but you must be patient, Mam fach, there are a few to go before me yet.

Well, I've got that third stripe up again, how long it is going to remain there I don't exactly know – I expect I'll lose it for something or other again soon, and carry on with the old 'brace of dogs legs'. It's funny, but I can keep two alright, but I'm blowed if I can keep three. Still, it makes no difference – it's the same work I do whether I have two or three so that it makes little difference out here.

'Does dim rhagor o newydd rwan, felly rwyf am ddiweddi gyda chariad i bawb gartre'. Yr eiddoch yn gynes, [*I have no more news now, so I will end with love to everyone at home. Yours, with warmth,*]

Ivor

The short piece in Welsh at the end of this letter is the only time that Ivor writes two complete sentences in his family language in the entire collection.

On 3 October the 17th RWF marched to Lempire, moving into the front line at Le Catelet the following morning. On 5 October they advanced to a line near Aubencheul-aux-Bois, with no casualties. At 1 a.m. on 8 October they attacked: 'Objective BEAUREVOIR LINE and high ground in front of VILLERS OUTREAUX. All objectives taken. About 50 prisoners were taken. Casualties 10 Officers – 120 OR.'[20] In the database of the CWGC, there are 140 men of the RWF who died in France on 8 October 1918. Forty-two of them were serving with the 17th Battalion, of whom twenty-five are buried at Prospect Hill Cemetery, Gouy, and twelve have no known grave, being commemorated at the Vis-en-Artois memorial. One who is buried at Prospect Hill is Lance-Corporal Oswald Williams of Varteg, near Ystradgynlais.[21] The story his family received about his death was that 'He was in charge of a party that volunteered to rush a dangerous position, when eight of their number, including Williams, were killed by a "whizz-bang."'[22]

We have no details of what exactly happened to Ivor that day, save what his subsequent letters tell us: that he received a wound to his temple from shrapnel from a British shell.

Notes

1. These diaries, kept in the National Archives, have the reference WO 95/2561/2. They have been digitised and are available to browse via *www.ancestry.co.uk* (accessed July 2017). All references to the war diaries in this chapter are taken from this source.

2. For eyewitness accounts of the activities of the 2nd RWF (which served alongside the 17th RWF in the 115th Brigade from January 1918 onwards), see J. Churchill Dunn, *The War the Infantry Knew 1914–1919: A Chronicle of Service in France and Belgium* (London: P. S. King, 1938).

3. The family's dog.

4. SBR: small box respirator.

5. The CWGC records no casualties for the 17th RWF on 16 February 1918, but Pte J. W. Kerry is recorded as dying on 15 February, and is buried at Erquinghem-Lys Churchyard Extension: *http://www.cwgc.org/find-war-dead/casualty/192674/KERRY,%20J%20W* (accessed January 2018).

6. It is possible that these two dead were Pte R. Morris and Pte J. H. Morgan, both buried at Erquinghem-Lys Churchyard Extension: *http://www.cwgc.org/find-war-dead/casualty/192741/MORRIS,%20R* and *http://www.cwgc.org/find-war-dead/casualty/192740/MORGAN,%20J%20H* (accessed January 2018). However, there are four other men from the 17th RWF who died in the week after this raid buried in this graveyard.

7. GE1918-04-24 (ch. 10).

8. Ivor here is referring to his little brother Daniel (three months short of his seventh birthday) as 'Officer Commanding, Standard 1', that is, his class at school.

9. From the poem 'The Village Blacksmith' by Henry Longfellow.

10. GE1918-07-27 (ch. 10).

11. Ivor was in A Company.

12. The CWGC database lists the known details of the vast majority of the British (and Imperial) servicemen who died in the First World War, with over a million records.

13. An account of the 2nd RWF's activities from 1 to 3 September can be found in Dunn, *The War the Infantry Knew*, pp. 523–35. The actions of the 115th Brigade (which included the 2nd and 17th RWF) on these dates are described in C. H. Dudley Ward, *Regimental Records of the Royal Welch Fusiliers, Vol. III 1914–1918 France and Flanders* (London: Forster Groom, 1928), pp. 462–8.

14. Although this could conceivably refer to Bryn Thomas of Vicarage Road (see Appendix 3), it is more likely to be Brynley Thomas of Mynyddcadle, who, like Richard Eustis, worked at Mynydd Newydd colliery and joined the 3rd Welsh Field Ambulance on 1 July 1913. However, whereas Richard was with the 1/3rd WFA who went to Gallipoli and then to Egypt, Brynley was with the 2/3rd WFA, and he was stationed in Britain until sent to France in November 1916. His unit, 131 Field Ambulance, was attached to the 38th (Welsh) Division.

15. One of those casualties was Percy Edwards, who died of his wounds fifteen days later. See Peter Doyle, *Percy: A Story of 1918* (London: Unicorn Press, 2018), pp. 90–101.
16. GE1918-09-a (ch. 10).
17. When confirmation of Ivor's Military Medal was published in the *London Gazette*, it was in the edition of 11 February 1919 (Supplement, 2107), which dealt with medals awarded for bravery in the period 8 August to 6 September 1918. News of the award can also be found in 'Treboeth', *CDL*, 9 October 1918, 4.
18. Inst is an abbreviation of 'instant', meaning 'of the present month'. For 'buckshee' see ch. 1.
19. See Appendix 2.
20. A little more information on the activities of the 17th RWF can be found in Dudley Ward, *Regimental Records, Vol. III*, p. 480. A vivid account of the involvement of the 2nd RWF on this day can be found in Dunn, *The War the Infantry Knew*, pp. 550–6.
21. *http://www.cwgc.org/find-war-dead/casualty/182506/WILLIAMS,%20 L%20O* (accessed January 2018).
22. 'Ystradgynlais Notes', *Llais Llafur*, 26 October 1918, 1.

10

Gabriel Eustis aboard *HMT Saxon*, November 1917–October 1918

The most extensive source of information regarding Gabriel's war experience comes from the letters he wrote in the final year of the war. There are sixteen letters extant which he wrote between November 1917 and October 1918. As in his previous letters, he gives few details of his day-to-day activities, and of the action that the *Saxon* saw in this period. The letters focus instead more on family matters and the news he has received from his brothers and other friends and relatives. One immediate concern that is evident in numerous letters is the financial situation of the family back home. The first letter mentions a cheque being sent home and the second states that Gabriel is now sending an extra 3/6 to his parents: this ties in with Richard's comment that the family's finances were running low following Gabriel's extended leave.[1] However, Gabriel's tone overall is optimistic, as he seeks to cope with the situation rather than complain. There are also some thoughts about the future, and what it has in store now that the war's end is in sight.

Through the beginning of this period, the *Saxon* was involved in the same kind of patrol work in the north Atlantic as previously, but Gabriel noted in a (lost) letter home in early 1918 that the ship had been moved to convoy duty.[2] One action about which there is information is the rescue of the crew from *HMS Chagford*, one of the 'Q-ships' that had been equipped to hunt German U-boats. Sailing about 120 miles north-west of Ireland on 5 August 1917, the *Chagford* was hit by a torpedo. The crew took to a small boat as their ship slowly sank and German U-boats were occasionally sighted. The following morning the crew were saved when the *Saxon* appeared. They searched in vain for U-boats in the area and then attempted to tow the stricken *Chagford* into port but were defeated by poor weather and heavy seas. However, the surviving crew members were landed safely at Oban on 8 August.[3] Gabriel would have had the opportunity to tell his family about this and other adventures directly, for he had extended home leave in September 1917 (which Richard's letter suggests lasted for five weeks).[4]

The sequence of letters begins with one that Gabriel wrote from the *Saxon* on 20 November 1917.

GE1917-11-20

Dear Mother & All,

Just a few lines in a hurry & a <u>cheque</u> to help win the war. I received your letter when we came in on Sunday after about 18 or 20 days at sea. We should have been in on the 14th but circumstances alter cases & we were glad enough to come in any time for we've been tossed about a bit this last trip. We had rotten weather from the time we left here till we came in again. We kept running from one little puff to another all the time, & it caused some sport too in the mess deck. You should have seen us at meal times, each one hanging on to his plate with one hand & on to his seat with the other & snatching a bite & a sup in between times. I don't think my sub eat [*sic*] a dozen meals for the first fortnight. I wasn't extra chirpy myself at times but he was 'dead-o' most of the time. He used to be sitting down with his head in his hands moping day & night like a little child not a great big lad of nearly my own age.

Well Mother, I was very glad to hear that Ivor had been home for a few days & I hope he thoroughly enjoyed himself. I understand now why he failed to meet me at Chester. I haven't had a letter from Dick this time but I expect to get one 'fore the end of the week. I've had two from him since I was home so I can't grumble. Sorry to hear that Dad lost two turns through his firemen striking, it's a pity they have nothing better to do.[5] How is Eustis Bach & the rest of them getting on down there now & how is Uncle

Sam improving? I had a letter from Aunt C dated Oct 30th
& Nov 5th & she said she was going to write again so I shall
wait a day or two before answering.

I've been pretty busy today. I've been before the
commander here for my 3 year stripe & got it so I'll have 3d
a day more. I lost my old Pal Bunty yesterday, went away to
another ship but I expect he will be back in a month or so.

No more this trip

Love to All,

Gib.

The following letter was written on New Year's Day 1918. The
sinking ship Gabriel refers to was *HMS Grive*, which had earlier
been torpedoed off Shetland and, after repairs, left Lerwick under
tow on 23 December. In foul weather she started to leak and settle,
and *Saxon* took the crew off before she sank.[6]

GE1918-01-01

Dear Mother,

I was very glad to read your letter of the 26th that
Dad had received what I sent, for I was beginning to think
that it had gone adrift somewhere. So many parcels posted
nowadays never reach their destination. So Christmas Day
was very quiet down there as everywhere else, but it's only
what's to be expected the fourth wartime Christmas.

I had a better time at Christmas myself than what I
had expected. We left port on Xmas Eve & should have been
at sea on Christmas Day, but we took off the crew from a
sinking ship late on Xmas Eve & brought them into port the
following day. It was very rough on the 24th but it was nice
& fine Xmas Day & after dinner, (a plateful of 'scouse') the
other sparker & I went ashore for a stroll and had a good
tea of bacon, eggs & chips ending up with an evening at the
pictures. It was quite enjoyable especially when we should
have been punching about at sea. We had a far better dinner
Boxing Day than we had Christmas Day. Our Xmas dinner
was stew made with spuds, carrots & meat that had been
hung up for a fortnight or so, so you can guess there was

quite a distinct flavour about it. We had about 40 survivors to feed Xmas morning beside ourselves, so the cook filled up a big 6 gallon boiler with stew. You would have laughed to see us. There were not nearly enough plates to go round, so all sorts of vessels were requisitioned. The table was full up & all round the mess deck were men standing mopping 'scouse' from plates, basins, tin mugs, one had a small pie dish & another had a small oxo pot. However the survivors said it was 'the best drop of soup they had ever tasted since joining the service.' On Boxing Day we had a slap-up spread of roast beef (<u>fresh</u>), 'potch tatto' [*mashed potato*] etc followed by plum pudding with custard. The officer gave us the puddings & they were great. We boiled three in our mess, which ran to one between three, so I needn't tell you that I could hardly get up from the table. I was like the little girl who had been to the tea-party & when told to go to the nursery replied 'Oh Aunty, I can't go myself, please carry me <u>but don't bend me</u>.'

We left for sea that night but got into port again the following night. The best of this job is that although we are kept very busy we are never out more than 3 or 4 days. We did not accompany Dai Harris' ship, although we were to have gone over, but our orders were altered at the last moment. I did not see Dai's ship but I expect she was with the crowd. I had a letter from him on the 27th saying he was coming here, but I expect he had come & gone before we got back as he expected to leave the day before Xmas.

So Ivor Humphreys was home for Christmas, eh? the lucky dog. I wish I had been home too. I hope if he is going to be shifted he comes around this part of the world. I had a letter from Dick on the 27th, but there is no special news, except that he is still in hopes of leave 'before the war is over.' Of course I haven't had a letter from Ivor since he was on leave, & I don't expect any till he has settled down & can send me his address. Excuse my using a pencil Mother but the ink-pot has gone on strike.

With best Love & Wishes to All

Gib

P.S. Have you started drawing the extra 3/6 a week allotment yet?

There is further mention of Dai Harris in the next two letters from Gabriel. These were written from *HMT Saxon*, stationed at Inverness: the envelope of the first of these confirms that the aunt he wrote to was Charlotte.

GE1918-01-19

Dear Aunty,

I'm trying to rush off a few lines on the chance of being able to post before we go to sea. I received your letter of January 1st about 9 or 10 days ago, but I've been too busy to answer before. As I told Mother, we get very little time to ourselves when in port here & I've been unable to do any writing lately on account of the bad weather we've been having every time out this month. It's been pretty cold up here lately too, but the weather is getting a bit better now. We generally do 3 or 4 days out from here & reckon ourselves lucky if we get 24 hours in between each trip. We accompany ships bound for the same destination as Dai Harris's ship, but I have not met him up this way yet. It's a pretty rotten job after the Oban stunt, but there are strong rumours that we are going to be taken off this particular duty soon. I hope it's true, we might have a little more time in then, so the sooner the better I say.

Well Aunty, I was glad to hear that Ivor is sticking to his blue ribbon & I hope he keeps on, drink is no use to anyone & it has been the ruin of thousands during this war.[7] I haven't had a letter from Ivor since he was on leave but then I have only written to him once. I'm on the look-out for one from him with every mail. I'm expecting one from Dick shortly too, for I haven't heard from him for some time. I had a nice letter from Mrs Whyatt (Louise) in answer to the one I had written to Mrs Williams in Dec. I see that Mr Whyatt has been laid up for a bit with a bad cold or something. Did I tell you that I had received the parcel from Mynydd Bach? I also had a parcel from Swansea from the Mayor's War Fund but I haven't acknowledged either yet. The Mayor's parcel contained a shirt, two pairs of socks & 50 cigarettes.

Old Bunty is still in Chatham or was rather when he wrote me on the 5ᵗʰ of Jan. but he still hopes to return to the old Saxon. I had a letter from Watkins, my Dundee chum, a couple of weeks ago. He is still in Malta & hopes to get home on leave shortly.

How is Danny now, is he quite alright again & how are Grandad, Grandma & Grace. I heard from mother that Uriel had been home on leave & that he had improved a bit since donning Khaki. Do you know Aunty, I haven't had a line from him since he joined up though he used to drop me a few lines now & then when he was home. Glad to hear that the Eisteddfod & Concert went off so well. No wonder the flags went so well with the verse on the back. I see Uncle Sam did alright out of that raffle. How is he improving now? How did Daniel Jones' drawing go off?

No more this time,
        With Best Love to All
            Gib

The reference to the eisteddfod and concert is to an event held in Mynyddbach on 29 December in aid of the chapel's Soldiers' and Sailors' Fund. The event raised over £55, which included £3 7s. 7d from the sale of flags.[8]

In the next letter to his mother Gabriel strikes a patriotic note as he encourages her to persevere despite the current hardship. The word 'that' in the fifth line is written large and underlined twice.

GE1918-02-01

Dear Mother,
      I received your letter of Jan 20th last mail day (Thursday) having been posted on from Oban as you had addressed it c/o A.M.O. Oban instead of Inverness. Sorry to hear you are put to a bit of inconvenience over the feeding down there. It's a bit awkward but depend on it, the Germans are a sight worse off than us. What does it matter anyhow as long as we win the war & **that** we will do, if it takes us ever so long. We struck a bad patch up here early

in the month as regards grub. For 3 weeks we had no fresh
meat, no butter, cheese, very little flour or spuds, practically
all we had was burgo (porridge), corned beef & bread. That
was because the weather had been too bad for the store ships
to come up, but things are far better now. Of course the
price of foodstuffs is pretty high here as at every other place
but we get 3d a day more victualling money now you know
making 1/8 a day so it's not so bad.

Well Mother, I'm glad to hear that Ivor is alright. I
haven't had a letter from him yet, but I suppose he hasn't
the same facilities for writing now as he had in Kinmel Park.
The last letter I had from Dick was the week after Christmas
dated Dec 3rd so I expect another shortly unless his letters
were lost with that last mail.

As for me, things are easing up a bit here lately &
we are not half so busy, in fact we haven't been more than
80 miles from here for the last fortnight. The last long trip
we made, we returned in company with Dai Harris' ship
& we had only got in an hour or so when she 'went west'.
It seems that Dai was aboard the depôt ship for a few days
after & I did not know it else I could have gone to see him,
as we were in for a couple of days after. One of my old
shipmates was invalided out and was sent to barracks for
his discharge & he had written to another chap here saying,
'Tell Eustis that his cousin Harris has been blown up with
that last convoy and is proceeding to barracks' so I presume
they must have met on the depôt ship or else travelled down
together.[9]

Old Bunty is still in Chatham but is not coming back
here, according to his last letter. I'm sorry to part from him
for he was a cheery old soul & we had been pals for over two
years. I'm sending you a little splosh again, to help things
along.

> No more this time Mam
> Love to All,
> Gib

The next letter is the only one from Gabriel to his sister Lottie
to have survived in the collection.

GE1918-02-15

Dear Lottie,

Here goes a few lines in answer to your delightful
letter of Jan 29th which I received some time ago. Sorry I
have not answered it earlier but I've been pretty busy of late
& have not had much time for letter writing. Do you know
I have ten letters to answer already & there will be another
mail in a day or two. I think I will have to engage a typist or
a private secretary, for I have lots of writing to do besides
answering letters every time we come into port.

Well I am very pleased to hear you are going in for
the Gowerton scholarship, & I would advise you to try your
very best, for if you don't, you will surely regret it later on.
How I wish I had made more of the chances I had. I have the
greatest confidence in your abilities & if you only put your
mind to it you will pass like a shot. Do your best & show
them what the Eustises can do if they try. I'll make you an
offer something similar to what I made Grace. If you pass I'll
make you a present of 10/- & if you come out first, second or
third, I will increase it to 15/-. Now pull in your slacks & go
in & win & make us all proud of you.

Glad to hear you enjoyed the Caersalem concert, it's
very few concerts we get up this way. We had one here a few
weeks ago, in which the artistes were all sailors & it was one
of the best of its kind I've seen for a long while. Three of
them were dressed up as ladies & we never knew until they
took off their wigs at the conclusion.

Well I must close now, sis, as I am going ashore for a
few hours & if I don't hurry up the duty boat which takes us
ashore will be alongside before I am ready then I'll have to
stop aboard. Let me know how you get on with your lessons,
what subjects you get etc.

No more this trip,
Best love,
Gib

The next letter is dated 'Sat 23rd' which means it could be
from March 1918, but the fact that it is stored in the same

envelope as the previous letter suggests that it is more probably from February.

GE1918-02-23

Dear Mother

Just a line or two as we expect to go to sea this afternoon. I received your letter of the 14th on Thursday & was very pleased to hear all are in the pink at home as this leaves me at present. We are having quite a decent time of it up here now, having plenty of time in port between each trip. I can get shore leave almost every night in harbour & I've been ashore every night this week, so you see I'm having a nice time of it. We have plenty of grub, having meat every day for dinner (unless we get a bit of fish) & often get a bit of bacon or steak for breakfast or tea. There is no lack of spuds here & we get plenty of tea, sugar, margarine etc. so with plenty of grub, smokes, shore leave every night & a few bob in his pocket, what more does a fellow want? Besides, we get a little recreation in the way of a game of football every now & then, & as you know, I was always fond of football.

According to the tone of letters I've had from home lately, you all seem to be expecting me home on leave any moment now. No such luck though, I'm afraid you'll have to 'bide awhile' for we don't expect to dock till about the end of May. Our time is up for refitting in April, but there are several ships waiting to go before us, some of which are two months overdue already. With a little bit of luck I might be home for Whitsun; it would suit me alright for there's a better chance of fine weather then. Although I've been home so often since I donned 'baggy trousers', I've only been home once in summer time, that was in 1915 when I got leave from Chatham.

Well Mother, I think I told you I had letters from Dick & Ivor lately. I've answered both & I intend to write to them again next week instead of waiting for an answer first. Of course Ivor hasn't so much spare time now as he used to have at K.P. so I can't expect a letter from him by every mail. I got a nice parcel from Treboeth Ladies' Comforts Guild last week.

Poor old Bunty is still in hospital in Chatham, still in bed. The doctor let him get up one day, but he says he was in such pain he had to be put back at once. He says he was operated on, the day he got my last letter. He's as cheery as a bird through it all. He wants to know when I am going on leave for he means to be in London to meet me 'by hook or by crook' as he says. He longs to be back on 'the old lifeboat'. Yes Mother, Dick always was very good at choosing presents. Aunt Charlotte must be very proud of that Bible. Tell Eustis Bach, I'm very pleased he is helping you all he can & I won't forget when I come on leave again.

No more in this bucket,

Love to all, Gaboose

The next surviving letter from Gabriel was written from *Saxon* to Aunt Charlotte on 24 April 1918. The mention of Armentières refers to the second phase of the German Spring Offensive on the Western Front, launched on 9 April 1918.[10]

GE1918-04-24

Dear Aunty,

Yours of the 15th & Mam's of 15th & 16th arrived last Monday so I'm killing three birds with one stone, in other words, skimping work as usual. You know I never was frantically in love with work before the war & I know I'm worse now, in fact I've been told more than once that the hardest work I do is dodging it, if you can understand such a phrase. I haven't done what could be called hard manual labour for some time now & I don't want to, a good dose of it would kill me just now. Not that I'm doing nothing for 'Uncle George' or the old country all the same. We are having a busy time of it up here lately, having only had one night in port since Monday week. We came in last Saturday about 5.0 pm but out we had to go again at 7.0 pm. We've had a little sport & excitement lately, nothing much, just enough to keep us awake.

Well Aunty, I was very glad to hear that Ivor's wound, whatever it is, is not much & I hope he is again in the best of health & spirits. I sincerely hope it kept him out of the recent heavy fighting around Armentierres & that he is soon back in Blighty again following his purpose. I expect you know now what his intentions were when he left K.P. I haven't had a letter from either him or Dick recently, but I'm looking forward to something with the next few mails. What about that 'leave for the band-boys' rumour now, anything definite known yet? I've had several enquiries as to when I'm coming home now, but I can only tell them to 'expect me when they see me.' The nearest I can say is 'sometime during the next month or two' or just as soon as Dai Beatty has two super dreadnoughts to take our place for a few weeks. However I'll try & let you know what <u>week</u> I expect to get home as soon as we arrive in dock.

I was surprised to hear Uriel had landed in France, I expect he & the other 'Bantams' are only over to release bigger chaps from the bases or to 'berwi tê i'r dynon' [*boil tea for the men*] as Dick used to do with 'Williamsamort'. Joking aside though, the Bantams have played their part in this war & I'm sure Uriel will 'be there when he's wanted.' What is his address now? I want to answer the letter he wrote me some time 'fore he left England. I'm glad to hear some of the local 'knuts' are being combed out, there's hundreds more of them skulking in the munitions works.

While I remember, I must thank you for the Thompsons which I get almost every week, in fact, I get them so regularly, I look upon them as a matter of course & don't think of thanking you for them, you see what an ingrate I am.[11]

Had a letter from Ivor Humphreys last week saying he was about to go on leave, so I expect he's enjoying himself at home just now. Bunty has also been home for 14 days from Chatham Barracks having been discharged from hospital a few weeks ago.

Well I must dry up now Aunty as my watch is nearly over for the night & I must 'prepare the feathers' for a wee nap before I'm called out again.

Best Love to All

Gib

PS How do you address Ivor's letters now?

There is a gap in the letters for the months of May and June, but a newspaper report tells us that Gabriel had another period of home leave, for he was presented with a medal and Treasury note by the Treboeth and District Succour Fund on 24 June. Among those that made speeches at the event was the Rev. James Davies, minister of Mynyddbach chapel.[12] Gabriel was back aboard the *Saxon*, stationed in Inverness, when he wrote home on 27 July 1918.

GE1918-07-27

Dear Mother

I was delighted to receive your two letters of July 16ᵗʰ & 19ᵗʰ & the one from Ivor which you sent on. Sorry to hear that Bessie has been down with the Flu & I hope she has recovered completely by now and is back at school again. I was delighted to hear Lottie had passed, I knew she would do it if she only tried, & put a little heart in her work. I have the greatest confidence in her making a very good show at Gowerton & if she does her best she will go far in it. What place did she hold on the list Mam? If I remember rightly I told her that if she passed I would give her 10/- & if she was in the first three she would get 15/- wasn't that it? I suppose Danny has already had his orders to buck up & be ready as he is next. No wonder the Eustis-s (or rather the younger members) get a rub up so often.

Ivor tells me he is now at company headquarters as orderly sergeant & is rather busy at present & has been lately. His letter was dated July 11ᵗʰ & he said they were all expecting 'Jerry' (as he now calls the Germans) over any minute. Since then I've read in the papers that instead of them attacking in great strength, we are driving them back bit by bit & taking thousands of prisoners. I haven't seen a paper lately but I heard that they have taken another 25,500 prisoners according to today's news.

I haven't had a letter from Dick since the two I got before coming back here. What does he say in his last letter, same old story I suppose, not very busy & doing alright. Did you get the small packets I sent for him from ———— just before coming to sea & also what I sent for Dad?

Yes Mam, I am just settling down to trawler life again after the glorious holiday. We had splendid weather coming up here & a very good job too, for if it had been rough, I'm afraid a lot of us would have needed medical treatment. Even as it was most of us felt rather shaky the first couple of days & there wasn't much food eaten I can promise you. Everybody seemed to be as miserable & cross as wild bears for the first few days but they soon bucked up again. We've been rather busy since we came back & until tonight I had only been ashore one night, that was last Sunday. We got here on Sunday morning & Sunday afternoon I had my old chum Bunty aboard to tea & we were together for a few hours. His ship has been up here for about a month & he had been looking out for us every day. He was here this afternoon again & we went ashore together, but he had to return aboard at 7-0 while I had leave until 9.30 p.m. He only gets leave every third night while I can get ashore every night we're in harbour if I wish. Gill left me again on Thursday, going aboard another trawler to take the place of a sparker gone sick & I have had a new chap as 'number two.' This chap has never been to sea before & is rather new at the game, so I'll have the rôle of instructor again for a while. He has only been out with us once and although it was pretty calm he was as sick as a dog. He had my sympathy & of course I did all I could for him for which he was very grateful. He seems quite a decent chap & if he remains aboard here I think we'll get on alright together. It's an even chance whether Gill comes back or not, for there is a possibility of his going on another ship, if he is not kept where he is now.

No more this time Mother

Love to All,

Gib

P.S. Please tell Aunty Charlotte I will write in a day or two.

A month later he wrote from Inverness with news of his promotion. He also needed to apologise for neglecting to write to his mother although he had found time to write a letter (now lost) to sister Hannah.

GE1918-08-29

Dear Mother,
      Here I am back on the old trolley again after
having been away for a week. I left here last Thursday for
a place well to the southward which I reached on Friday
morning. All day Friday I was under examination by a
Lieutenant R.N. for the rating of leading telegraphist. It
was a pretty stiff test, both practical & theoretical & I felt
half inclined to chuck it up, but I stuck it out & I'm glad
to say I passed alright. I don't know whether I shall have
to appear before the Commander again. I don't think so, I
reckon I shall be rated from the day of the exam, possibly
dated back.[13] It will mean a rise of about sixpence a day to me
while I remain on trawlers. There is a possibility of my being
shifted to another ship now but I hope not; I would be losing
deal [*sic*] if I were drafted to a bigger vessel, as we get what
we call 'hard lying money' on trawlers which we don't get on
bigger ships. Anyway we'll wait & see.
      I was delighted to get your letter of Aug. 24th on my
return here this morning, although you jumped down my
throat at the very beginning ha ha. Now I'm very sorry
that I offended you Mam by sending that letter to Nance. I
admit it was not exactly the thing to do, although I did not
think you would be offended. I shan't try to explain but I'll
stand the racket for I'm too far away to have a 'côs brwsh'
[*brush handle*] laid across my back unless you put it down in
the family log by the time I come home again, ha ha. I also
apologise for only having written once to you since I came
back. Fact is, I thought it was all the same whether I wrote to
you or Aunty Charlotte & I never thought who I had written
to last. I wrote to Aunty while I was on the Impereuse
so you've probably given me another wigging for that.[14]
Honestly Mam, the reason why I did not write that to you
was that I intended sending you the enclosed photograph
which I received just before I left here last Thursday &
which I had left in my ditty box on board here as I only took
a small bag with towel & soap, brushes etc with me. I can
see your point in the matter & you are quite right & I shall

remedy the defect in future. Well Mother, I had a letter from
Dick along with yours today, in reply to one I wrote while
on leave (June 30th). He mentions nothing about fags so they
'went west' as we surmised. He complains that a lot of letters
to him have gone astray & wonders where they go to. He
does not say anything about his second stripe yet. What's the
news from Ivor lately? I haven't heard from him for some
time. Had a letter from Uriel last week which I must answer
first chance. Also one of about 18 lines from Nance in which
she told me she had had a week's holiday.

    No more this issue.

        Love to All.

           Gib

It seems that this letter did not arrive home promptly, as the next
letter shows that Gabriel had received another letter from his mother
scolding him for not writing. This one, written on 10 September, was
sent from the 'Same old show'.

                  GE1918-09-10

Dear Mother,

    I was very much surprised to see in your letter of
Sept 5th which I got last night, that you still get no letters
from me. Where do they get to? When I got your last & you
complained that you did not get letters from me I wrote
straightaway but it seems you have not had it. I'm very
sorry that you have cause to complain about the lack of
letters & I tried to explain a little in my last letter. I can quite
understand your feelings over the matter & I will do my best
to rectify the mistake in the future, it isn't exactly pleasant to
get 'told off' in every letter I get. I was thinking of starting a
complaining campaign myself for it's few letters I get from
anywhere nowadays, but your counter offensive on the same
line has just about put the ki-bosh on me. Anyway I hope
you have had my other letter by now & trust you will not
have a reason to complain in the future.

    Well Mother, I was very sorry to hear about the two
sad accidents at the Mynydd & Pentre. I knew both the chaps

fairly well.[15] I am also sorry to hear about young Andrews &
Bryn Thomas, Clyndu.[16] I had heard from Auntie Charlotte
about the latter. Is Hannah going to Rhyl? She told me she had
written to Ivor to ask whether she was to accept the invitation
or no & was awaiting a reply. So Tom Evans has a month's
leave & is getting married, eh?[17] Good luck to him I say.

I had a letter from Auntie Charlotte last Monday
week & she said a field card had arrived that day (29th) from
Ivor dated 25th August. I haven't had a line from him for
weeks now, but it doesn't matter as long as I get news of
him from you & Aunt C. I had a letter from Dick dated
July 28th nothing much only the old complaint about getting
no letters. I haven't written to him yet as it was only the day
before I had written to him, but I shall drop him another by
next mail day.

As for myself , I'm just rolling along as usual, come
day go day style. We are not having at all a bad time of it as
present, but the grub hasn't been so good the last few weeks
as it used to be, mainly on account of the meat not 'keeping'
very well although we haven't had much heat here this
summer. The fishing season is about done now too so our
supply from that source is about nil.

There has been no 'official' news about moving me
but there were a lot of rumours when I got the 'hook' first;
In fact, the first thing I heard when I returned was that I was
to be shifted to another ship 'down south' but nothing came
of it.

I don't want to be shifted myself, I'm quite content
where I am till the war is over. It's three years this month
since I joined this old raft & three years this week since I left
Archangel. Rather a long time isn't it. It's close on four years
since I joined up, (& I gave it eight months as the extreme
limit.) Never mind, I don't think we shall be very long now
before we are all back again for good.

Well I must dry up now Mother, tell Auntie Charlotte
I got her letter & papers alright & will write shortly
       No more in this bucket,
              Love to All,
                     Gib.

The letter Gabriel wrote to his sister Hannah on 13 September has survived. In keeping with the playful nature of some of his writings to his younger siblings, he gave his address as 'H.M.Super-Super-Dreadnought Saxon' in Inverness. The second sentence has been written in a script twice the size of the rest of the letter to make it stand out.

GE1918-09-13

Dear Nance,

  Just a line or two to give you the news you crave so anxiously. **I am still Aboard the Old North Atlantic Lifeboat** & doing fairly well thank you. Got your letter and the papers yesterday morning, thanks very much, I think I've read almost every line of each paper, adverts, birth marriages & deaths, maids & general servants wanted & who wants to buy or sell a grand piano or a couple of chicks. I've thought many a time of giving you one little tip & that is to just scribble a line or two of any news of importance to enclose with the papers when you haven't time for a proper letter, just, 'Got letter from Ivor, alright; went up home yesterday. Lloyd George at our place for tea. Cat got seven kittens. Peace declared. Germans landed at Llangyfelach' or any small items like that. You can give me a full account of these happenings in your letters.

  Glad to hear all's well at home & that you have had P.C.s from Dick from Alexandria. Apparently he has been to the latter place on leave & I hope he thoroughly enjoyed himself. I think I told you I had had a letter from him about a fortnight ago. Haven't heard from Ivor for some time either but I don't worry so long as I get news of him from 'headquarters.' Must write to both next mail. What's up with you all at home lately or what am I supposed to have done? I seem to get my neck screwed by every one of you in recent letters for something or other. If I've done any wrong it was unintentional & I apologise & grovel at your feet for pardon, (like the young '<u>men</u>' at home are doing for exemption from the army, the white-livered, chicken hearted, windy, white feathered, cold footed young cubs). Wouldn't I make a fine recruiting sergeant? ha ha.

Am having a fairish time of it just now. Was at a
supper & dance just over a week ago, but did not enjoy it so
well as I usually do, don't know why. Had a bit of a shake
up today, being out in a fierce nor-wester from 4.0 AM
to 5-30 PM the old raft didn't half bounce either. Pots
pans boots books etc seemed to have become exceedingly
energetic. Nearly half the lads sick, only two men ate a
proper dinner in our mess, only had a lump of duff myself, as
you can guess we had great sport I don't think.

One sentence in the letter is scrubbed out at this point, but it does
not seem to have been deleted by a censor.

Must dry up now nearly 11-30 PM. Tell Mr Whyatt
am writing this within two hundred yards of Ossy Davies'
(Ammanford) ship, have not seen him yet, might see him in
the morning.[18]
Toodle-oo-oo-oo-oo-oo-oo-oo-oo-oo-oo-oo-oo-oo
Best Love
Gaboose

The next letter in the sequence is dated simply 'Saxon, Monday',
but the content makes it clear it was written on either 23 or
30 September.

GE1918-09-a

Dear Mother,
This is only just a few lines to let you know I got
your letter of Sept 14th when we came in from sea Friday
morning. I was glad to hear you had got the photo alright
for I was so long without hearing that it had arrived, I was
beginning to think it had gone awandering or something.
Glad to hear all's well at home as it is here with me at
present. We are having a fairly easy time of it just now
though when we do go to sea we generally cop it a bit
rough for winter has set in here already. We had a bit of a
shake up last trip both going down & coming back as there
was a gale blowing from west > nor-west. Of course we can

expect bad weather about this time of the year. I thought I had got properly used to 'Jellicoe's Rocking Horses' as they call these trawlers, but no, even now, in bad weather I have no appetite for grub. We are outside doing a bit of fishing just now & will probably go in again about tea-time, when I hope to get a few letters as the mail boat has just passed us.

Last mail day, along with yours I got one each from Dick and Ivor and also one from my old pal Bunty. Ivor had written the letter on August 21ˢᵗ half an hour before an advance and posted it nearly a month after, presumably when they returned for a rest again in reserve. I was surprised to hear that Dick expected a move from Palestine as I thought they were fixed there now until [the] war was over. He said he had received one of the parcels I sent him, but told me not to trouble to send him any more as he could buy most things out there, (but at a high price) & the chances were that they would get lost on the way. Bunty is at present in Ireland & is going on leave in a week or two, as likely as not he is home on leave already.

So they are all getting 'spliced' down there, are they? Good luck to them, one and all. By the looks of things Ivor Humphreys & I will be the only two 'free' by the time this war is over ha ha. Catch us facing the parson with a skirt in tow ha ha. When is Hannah going to Rhyl now? I asked her to let me know when she was going but I've got no reply yet. Well if she is going, I hope she has a nice holiday & enjoys herself.

How is Dad's health now, is it improving & how is Dan getting on. Is he helping you to dig the spuds? How are all the folk at Granny's & how are the girls getting on at school. What about Uncle Sam, is he alright again & how are the folk at Pantlasse?[19]

Teatime Just had letter from Ivor dated 18ᵗʰ Sept. says he is well behind lines at present on a soft job. Also letter from Aunt Charlotte & papers from Nance.

Must dry up now or miss post,
Love to all
Gib

On 30 October Gabriel wrote the following letter home from aboard *Saxon* at Inverness.

GE1918-10-30

Dear Mother,

Just a line or two to let you know I received your letter of the 20th on our return here yesterday morning. I was very sorry to hear that Danny & Lottie were down with the 'flu', Danny being rather weak already, he will take a bit of time to recover properly again. I expect Lottie isn't overstrong either. However, Auntie Charlotte said in her last letter that they were a little better & I hope both will soon recover from it. There seems to be quite an epidemic of it 'down south' again.

I was very pleased to hear that Ivor got home on a bit of leave at last & that he was only slightly wounded. I understand he is to report back today (bar 'extensions') but where I don't know as no one mentioned where he came on leave from or where he was to return to. I hope that he will be kept in 'Blighty' now for a few months, I wish he was kept this side until peace was declared, I suppose there's no need to ask if he enjoyed his leave, who wouldn't after a spell in the line? I am looking forward to a few lines from him by tomorrow's mail. I hope my wire to him did not frighten you all, you must have thought it was a recall or something.[20]

I'm sorry to hear you never got the little parcel I sent you in August: another bit of 'Harry Free's' for someone. They must have gone astray somewhere in South Wales, for I believe they were posted right enough. I'm glad the other arrived in good time, had I known it would arrive just as Ivor got home I would have tried to make it a little bigger. I can only trust there were enough to carry him through his leave.

I had a letter last week from Dick dated Sept 25th in which he tells me about his unit being broken up & that he is now at the Base Depôt on the Suez Canal. It's a pity he has been separated from Dai. R. after having been together for so long. In one way, he is very lucky to have been with pals from the very beginning, in my four years service I haven't been shipmates with anybody I have known before the war. Of course a chap makes chums everywhere, but it's not exactly the same as having chums from the old place. Old Bunty has left here again so I suppose it will be another long while before I see him again. I spent one afternoon with him aboard his ship as he could not come ashore, his leave having been stopped for 42 days for being 36 hours late returning from home leave.

Things are just the same up here with me Mam, & I'm in the best of health & spirits. I believe we are going out again tonight on another two or three days' trip.

Will have to shut up now as I want to write a letter to Dick also before we go out.

Love to All,

Gib

This is the final letter to have survived from Gabriel's time on *HMT Saxon*. Even though it was written within two weeks of the Armistice it seems that he was not expecting the war to end quite so soon, as evidenced by his hope that Ivor would be kept in 'Blighty' for 'a few months'. Gabriel and his shipmates still had a job to do, as German U-boats were still active in the Atlantic. Yet throughout these letters Gabriel adopts a cheery manner that is sometimes jocular: the phrase 'ha ha' appears four times in these letters. He stated his firm belief in the letter of 1 February 1918 that 'we' would 'win the war', and that optimism seems never to have wavered.

The *Saxon* was returned to its pre-war owner in 1919 and then sold to a company that sailed her out of Fleetwood. In August 1930 the ship was lost in a storm off the island of Tiree in the Inner Hebrides, although the crew managed to reach the shore.

Notes

1. RE1917-11-20 (ch. 6).
2. Referred to in RE1918-03-20b (ch. 8).
3. Edward Keble Chatterton, *Q-ships and their story* (London: Sidgwick and Jackson, 1922), pp. 230–1.
4. See the references to this in IE1917-09-30 (ch. 7) and RE1917-11-20 (ch. 6).
5. Turn: a shift.

6. For more information, see National Archives ADM 137/3712.

7. The blue ribbon was a sign of the Temperance movement.

8. WGAS, Records of Mynydd-bach chapel, D/D Ind 24 50.

9. Cf. the comment in RE1918-03-20b (ch. 8) about Dai Harris being home on leave after being torpedoed. It is not clear whether Dai Harris was, in fact, a cousin of the Eustises.

10. Although none of the surviving letters mention him, the first member of Mynyddbach chapel to be killed in the war was a casualty of the first phase of the German Spring Offensive. Edgar Williams of Parkhill Road, Treboeth, was reported as 'missing' on 28 March 1918. His photograph can be seen in *CDL*, 17 May 1918, 3.

11. This could refer to Thompson's pills: see the advertisement for 'Thompson's Burdock Pills' and 'Thompson's Electric Life Drops', *HoW*, 2 May 1914, 11.

12. 'Treboeth', *CDL*, 25 June 1918, 4. The other serviceman honoured at this meeting was Lance-Corporal David N. Griffiths.

13. Gabriel's naval record has him as a leading telegraphist from (Friday) 23 August 1918, so he was indeed rated from the day of the exam.

14. *HMS Imperieuse* (formerly *HMS Audacious*) was a receiving ship stationed at Scapa Flow.

15. John Lewis (Mynydd Newydd colliery) and William John (Pentre Colliery) were killed in accidents on 2 and 3 September. 'Local Pit Fatalities', *CDL*, 3 September 1918, 3. See also RE1918-10-29 (ch. 11).

16. Andrews is most probably Captain Glyndwr Andrews of Fforestfach, killed in action on 21 August 1918. He had been educated at Gowerton School and it seems likely that Ivor knew him. See 'Scroll of Fame', *CDL*, 31 August 1918, 3; 'Fforestfach's Hero', *CDL*, 2 September 1918, 3 and *https://www.cwgc.org/find-war-dead/casualty/552528/andrews,-/* (accessed January 2018). 'Bryn Thomas, Clyndu' refers to the Bryn Thomas from Vicarage Road: see Appendix 3.

17. Sgt. Tom Evans (RAMC) was married at Mynyddbach chapel on 7 September: see 'Mynddbach', *CDL*, 9 September 1918, 3.

18. This might be Oswald Davies, who served in the Royal Navy as a signaller or wireless operator: see 'Ammanford', *HoW*, 17 March 1917, 2 and 'Ammanford', *Amman Valley Chronicle*, 26 December 1918, 3.

19. Pantlasau: 1.5 miles north-east of Mynyddbach.

20. Wire: telegram.

11

Richard Eustis in Egypt, July 1918–November 1918

As the course of the war changed in Europe over the summer of 1918, so too did the situation shift in the east, to favour the Allies. The EEF under General Allenby was marshalling its forces in preparation for an all-out offensive on the Turkish lines in Palestine. When this was eventually launched in September, it was a tremendous success, devastating the Ottoman forces and ensuring the collapse of their empire in the Middle East. However, by then Richard's unit, the 1/3rd WFA, had been broken up and the men dispersed to various locations. Richard was sent to a prisoner-of-war hospital in Egypt, not far from the Suez Canal, although he kept in touch with many of his old comrades.

There are extant seven letters Richard sent home during this period and two postcards. The principal causes for concern running through these letters are Ivor's situation and worries about what is going on back home. Richard himself was removed from the physical dangers of the war, although disease was still a threat, but he was aware that Ivor was in a perilous place. The first two of these letters discuss Mary Lizzie, as Richard fretted about what their lack of communication might mean.

Richard had expressed hope in his letters from Palestine in May and June 1918 that he might have leave in Egypt and that came about. He was in Alexandria on his twenty-fifth birthday, 18 July 1918, and he sent a postcard home showing the Nouzha Gardens.

RE1918-07-18 Postcard

Dear Mother
    Just a line hoping that all is well at home there.
Another birthday abroad, making the fourth away from
home. I sincerely hope I'll be home long before the next one
comes round.
            Dick

Another postcard was sent to his mother from Alexandria eight days
later, with a brief message to say that 'all is well here'. The next letter
to have survived was written from Palestine on 22 August.

RE1918-08-22

Dear Mother,
    I was very pleased to receive your letter today, also
the tin of fags you sent from Gib, so you see, although you
said in the letter that you had not yet packed them, I have
received them the same time as the letter. So you see how
much you can rely on the mails coming to time. But the
funny part about it is that although I receive the letters from
you everywhere pretty regular, I have only received two
from Mary Lizzie since February so what happens to them
I don't know. I received a box of fags that she sent, also two
birthday cards, yet I cannot get a letter from there.
    So Dai Evans is still at home eh? Well if he has been
classified as A.1. he had better make the most of his time
for they will surely 'yank' him out of it before long. Still
good luck to him if he can keep clear of them. As you say,
it is hardly fair to others that he is still at home, but even if
he was called up, it would not do us any good would it? So
good luck to him, I say.
    It was terribly hard lines on Bess Ann having to forego
the Exam after studying and thinking so much of it. But if you
had to send a doctor's certificate to show that she couldn't
attend, she may have a chance of sitting for it without waiting
another year. That would be hardly fair would it? I sincerely
hope that she will have the chance, anyhow.

Well Mam, the next time I remit money home, I may
be able to spare you the walk to Landore by directing it to
Tirdeunaw Post Office. That would be better, wouldn't it?
I'm sorry to hear about that first parcel that you sent me for
it must have cost you something. That is why I don't want
you to send me anything except what I ask for because the
chances are so great that they will be sunk on the way then it
is only a waste of money. I am very glad to learn that Lottie
has passed her Exam for Gowerton for it puts heart in a chap
to think they are doing so well. The 'arholiad' naturally took
some doing, but I'm afraid Mam, that they have more interest
in it than I have, sorry to say.[1] As you say if Lottie is the same
now as she used to be she is fit to go anywhere. I am also very
glad to hear that Sam Eustis has started to work again for
he has had a very long spell.[2] Does Dad go down to see him
sometimes? I daresay he does, so tell him to remember me
to him, and that I am still waiting for a letter from him. The
last I sent him, I haven't heard whether he received it or not.
I also sent him a photo. I had a letter from Auntie Charlotte
the other day saying that Hannah Jane Owen had been
buried. I am very sorry to hear that, for I was very friendly
with her and had known her for years. I fancy this Spanish
Flu is getting rather serious for there are scores of cases of it
out here, even my pal has had it in Alexandria.

Well Mother, according to rumour here we, as a unit,
are going to be broken up, and we are expecting to go down
to Egypt very, very soon. What is going to happen to us
afterwards, I don't know, but we'll hope for the best, and
that I will manage to be sent to a good job somewhere else.
I am looking forward to going down to Egypt, for after
being up here for so long, it will be quite a pleasant place to
pass the winter quite different to France or up here. Tommy
Thomas is down there now and from what I understand, he
has touched for a good job down there. All the village boys
are here and enjoying the best of health and spirits. I have no
more to say this time, except to thank you for the fags, and
for Ivor's address.

Love to all from
Dick

The next letter, from Palestine two days later, contains a passage that requires some conjecture to make sense of it. It is clear that Richard is very angry with a Daniel, but this is obviously not his little brother. The whole tirade comes as Richard's thoughts are full of anxiety vis-à-vis his relationship with Mary Lizzie. The phrase 'you will have to take her up home for she has no one to turn to' must surely refer to her. Given that, it is probable that the Dan who is courting is Daniel Morgan, Mary Lizzie's uncle with whom she was living at the time of the 1911 Census, in her grandmother's house. If so, then it seems that the domestic situation there had become rather difficult – and of course, being 2,500 miles away and only receiving incomplete reports three or four weeks after the events, Richard was painfully aware of his powerlessness to help.

RE1918-08-24

Dear Mother,
        I was very pleased to receive your letter dated
July 26th along with one from Bess Anne, the other day.
I am glad to hear that you are receiving the letters pretty
regularly now, for it encourages a fellow to write. Anyway
I get letters pretty fair here now except Morriston letters. I
haven't had one from Mary Lizzie for ages. Where they are
going to I don't know. About that letter I sent her I sent one
immediately after it, apologising for the sarcastic remarks I
made in it. But you can imagine what I felt like after being
waiting for weeks for a letter and not a sign of one in the
end. I was in a terrible stew, and I must say that I took up
the pencil in such a temper, and goodness only knows what
I wrote altogether. After I posted it, I was sorry, for I knew
quite well that it was not her fault, so I wrote another asking
her to excuse it because I was so wild at the time. I admit that
it was very unfair. Never mind, I daresay that she received
my other letters by now and that things are all right again.
But still I am waiting for a letter, so where can they be going
to? I have received the birthday cards, also one of the parcels
of cigarettes, but no letter.
        So Dan is courting, is he? Well if anything happens
there you will have to take her up home for she has no one to

turn to. Surely they won't keep us out here much longer now without giving us leave. If I could get leave, I would very soon square things up there and Dan could marry as soon as he liked after. I am relying on you to put some of that money by for me, to give me a start. As for Danny Bach don't take any notice of him, for he is beneath contempt. As for writing to him, not a line have I sent him since I'm away and what's more I don't intend to, for I know too well what he is. He is not worth talking about.

I heard that Lottie has passed the Gowerton Exam and I have told Bess Anne in her letter that I will remit them a £1 each, the next chance I get, Lottie, Grace, Dan & Bess Anne, as a present for doing so well with the Examinations and Arholiad. It is only about three days ago I sent you a letter, so I haven't much news to give you this time, so I close with

Love to all from

Dick

There is a gap of over a month before the next pair of letters in the collection, written on 30 September, by which time (as Richard explains) he was back at a base near the Suez Canal.

RE1918-09-30a

Dear Mother,

Just a few lines to let you know that I received your letter dated August 24th and am pleased to learn that all are well at home there. So Dan has been pretty busy during the holidays? Well it is only what one can expect, after a month away from school. Besides I would rather see him like that, than pining, and keeping[??] quiet for it shows that he is healthy enough and full of mischief. I have had a post-card from Auntie Charlotte, also one from Mary Lizzie saying that you all had a fine time at the Mumbles. I only wish I was there too. So you did not go with them to the National at Neath?[3] I daresay it was very crowded there.

I had a letter from Gab the other day, also one from Ivor. They seemed to be alright at the time of writing. That Gab has been a lucky bounder as regards leave, hasn't he? I have no hopes of leave from here until the war is over unless I get drafted to France, I might stand a chance then. Ivor says he is looking forward to having leave now. Good luck to him if he can get it. I have had a letter from Uriel, too, saying that he had a good job at the Base in France, how long he will keep it, I don't know. I have not received the cigarettes you sent me yet but I daresay they will turn up one of these days. I hope that by now you have seen that letter I sent to Auntie Charlotte saying of my change of address. The unit has been broken up, and most of us have been sent down to Egypt. Dai R. Thomas has remained up there with an Indian Fd Ambulance. I tried my utmost to stop with him, and succeeded for a few days, but I was recalled, hence I'm down here. Ivor Lewis also remained up there, but not with the same lot. I have lost my stripe and the fivepence a day I had with it so my address now is 368053 Pte R. Eustis, R.A.M.C., Base Depot, Egyptian Expeditionary Force. That will find me alright, and wherever I shall be sent from here my letters will follow I don't know what will happen to me now. I may be sent to any other unit as reinforcements, maybe sent to France, and <u>may</u> be turned into infantry, but I don't care what happens for I think I can hold my own anywhere after 3½ years active service. So don't worry, you know that I am well able to look after myself wherever I go. I never expected the old unit to finish up like that, for after being so long together, I thought that we would remain till the final [*sic*].

I sent Aunt Charlotte a letter the other day, also one to Gabe & Ivor. At present I am on the banks of the Suez Canal again having a good time. I have nothing to grumble about for we have plenty of food and very little work. It is quite a pleasant change after having been in the line for three years. Don't send me anything unless I ask for it, for down here, I can buy almost anything I want. Of the village boys, only Sammy Rees & myself are down here. We have met Tommy Thomas a few times but he is in the Infantry and not in the same camp as we are. I have no more to tell you this time except that I enclose a note for Dan so I conclude with love to all from

Dick

The note to Dan is written half in Welsh, half in English.

RE1918-09-30b

Dear Dan,

R'Oedd yn dda gennyf gael dy lythyr di yr wythnos ddiwethaf ag rwyf yn falch i glywed dy fod wedi cael amser go dda dros yr holidays. Oedd mam yn gweyd yn ei llythyr, bod ti wedi torri dy ddyllad yn ribane, a bod hi yn gorffod mynd i'r dre i byrni rig-out newydd i ti. Wel beth wyt ti mynd i wneud ar ol i ti adael ysgol. A wyt ti mynd i Gowerton, ne wyt ti mynd i weithio. Fydd llawer yn well i ti wneuther dy orau i basso i Gowerton, i ti gael mynd i'r College. Nawr mae Bess Anne, Grace a Lottie wedi gwneuther yn dda, gad i ni weld os gallu di wneuther yr un peth. Oet ti am i fi ala tricycle i ti oddiyma, wel Dan, mae yn flin gennyf weyd nag oes dim tricycles maes yma am fod y tywydd ri dwym i rido nhw. Wel Dan, dyma dipyn o Gymraeg i ti, nawr am dipyn o Saesneg.

[*I was pleased to receive your letter last week and I am glad to hear that you had a good time over the holidays. Mam said in her letter that you had torn your clothes to ribbons, and that she had to go to the town to buy you a new rig-out. Well, what are you going to do after leaving school? Are you going to go to Gowerton, or are you going to work? It would be much better for you to do your best to pass to go to Gowerton, so that you can go to College. Now, Bess Anne, Grace and Lottie have done well, let's see if you can do the same. You wanted me to send you a tricycle from out here, well Dan, I am sorry to say that there are no tricycles out here, because the weather is too hot to ride them. Well Dan, there's some Welsh for you, now for a little English.*]

Well Dan, how are you getting on at school? What sort of friends are you and Mr Higgs, does he give you the cane now and again? Who is your teacher, is it Miss Walters? And does she give you the cane? There are no schools for the little boys out here, especially those that live out in the desert miles from any town. Little boys here have to sell oranges,

figs, nuts and tomatoes out here, for they have no schools.
And they have no good clothes like you have at home, for
they have clothes made of old sacks. They have no houses
like we have, but little huts built of mud, and they live and
sleep in the same room.

Well Dan bach, I have no more to tell you this time so
I close hoping that you will write again soon

Yours,

Dick

There is another gap in the collection at this point, as the next
extant letter from Richard was written from Egypt on 20 October,
to his sister Hannah.

RE1918-10-20

Dear Nance,

Just a few lines to let you know that all is well with
me at present hoping that things are likewise with you. Well,
as you know, I have come down from the line a few weeks
ago, and at the time there was a great deal of speculation as
to what was going to happen to us as a unit. There were so
many stories going about at the time about transferring us to
the Infantry and this that and the other, that we didn't know
really what was going to happen to us. Well, we came down
from the line to Egypt and after being at the Base Depot for
about a week or so, we were sent practically all together to a
Prisoner of War hospital. So you see, at last, I have touched
for a base job, the first since I came out in 1915. Being a
new hospital we have been rather busy lately, getting things
straight here, but I expect we shall be comfortable enough
as soon as we get the hospital going. We are at Tel-el-Kebir
the famous battle-ground but you need not mention that in
the addressing of my letters.[4] My address is Pte (I have lost
my stripes) Eustis 268053 No 7 Prisoners of War Hospital,
Egyptian Expeditionary Force. That will find me alright,
and possibly I shall get my letters a little more regular than

when I was up in the line. You talk about leave. There is no possible chance of leave from here but things seem to be moving pretty fast now, and I hope it will soon be all over and that we shall soon come home for good. I was very pleased to hear that Gabe has passed leading telegraphist, but I am sorry to hear that he will probably have to leave his ship, for he has been on it for such a long time. He has got on much better than I have, for after holding a stripe for three+ a half years instead of having another, I have lost it, but it was through no fault of mine, and if I tried to explain to you, you wouldn't be able to understand.

Well Nance, I am enclosing an address for you in Swansea that I want you to call at. A pal of mine out here (we have slept together for three years) would like you to call at his home to see his only sister. He has written to tell her to expect you and their home is at 49 Carlton Terrace. (Miss Nellie Williams) So I would be most obliged if you called to see her. You must have seen a photograph of her brother at home, for I have sent a few photos of him home. He was with me at Alexandria when I went there on leave. I wonder how things are going with Ivor in France. I expect he is in the thick of this last offensive. I heard from home that he was alright early in September but I haven't heard anything of him since so I hope he is still alright. Well I have no more to tell you this time so I close with

Love from Bro
Dick

The soldier whose sister Richard asked Hannah to visit was George Morris Williams.[5] Just as there are previous examples of Richard facilitating meetings between the family and comrades on home leave (e.g. RE1918-06-25 (ch. 8)) here Richard is trying to organise something to offer comfort to the sister of one of his best friends – which might also end up in the creation of another channel of communication between the men in Egypt and their families in Swansea.

Richard's next letter was begun on 29 October.

RE1918-10-29

Dear Mother,
        Just a few lines to let you know that all is well with
me, hoping that things are alright at home. I have not
received a letter from you for some time now but I expect
one with the next mail. I am not sure whether I sent you my
present address or not, so in case I haven't here it is Pte R. R.
Eustis 368053, R.A.M.C. No 7, P of W Hospital, Egyptian
Expeditionary Force. The old unit (3rd Welsh) has finished,
hence I am here in Egypt, at a prisoners of war hospital. It is
quite a change after being practically in the line three years
to have a job like this, but I don't know how long we shall
be here. Sammy Rees was with me until a few days ago, but
he was called away to join the Royal Engineers to work at
his trade. He is now two stations nearer Cairo than I am, so
perhaps I shall be able to see him now & again for he is not
so very far away. Dd Rees Thomas is still up in the line with
an Indian Fd Ambulance. I have had a letter from him since I
am down here. He is alright. Ivor Lewis is also up there, but I
haven't heard from him at all.
        Oct 30th I received your letter dated Sept 5 yesterday
and I am sorry to hear that letters are slow reaching you.
I saw a bit in the newspapers sent out here about the two
accidents at the colliery there, it must have been a very sad
affair. I heard from Aunt Charlotte about Twm Evans.[6] I am
very glad to hear that Gab has passed Leading Telegraphist.
He sent me one of those photographs taken in a kilt, and
I think he looks very smart, too. He would make a better
soldier than a sailor. Still he is better off there than he would
be in any branch of the Army, at least I would far rather be in
the Navy than the Army. I have no more to tell you this time,
so I close with
                    Love to all from
                            Dick

The Ottoman Empire signed an Armistice on 30 October
that brought the fighting in the Middle Eastern theatre to an
end the following day. Richard's next letter was written from his

prisoner-of-war hospital in Egypt the day before the Armistice with Germany came into force in Europe.

RE1918-11-10

Dear Mother,

I was very pleased to receive your letter dated October 9ᵗʰ and am glad to hear that all are well at home there. So Johnny Phillips has been home on leave from France, eh? I suppose he has a month home, time expired? Well we cannot get it from here anyhow, owing to the submarine danger or something. Yes, the old Unit has been broken up and most of us are together here at Tel-el-Kebir, but I am the only one from the village. First of all Dai and I were sent to another Unit together, after a few days I was recalled, then I came down here, Sammy Rees & I. We had only been here a few days when Sam was called away to join some Royal Engineers, to work at his trade, so now I am left on my own. But don't worry. Having been on this game for four years, I think I can hold my own anywhere. So Ivor has had the Military Medal eh? Well, he is just the sort to get anything like that. Good luck to him, may he live long to wear it. I am very pleased to hear that one of the three of us has attracted attention. I had a letter from Gib the same time as yours. He seems to be as fit and cheerful as ever. From what I can understand he would not like to leave the old tub now after being on it so long. As you say it is about time they gave me leave, but I don't see any signs of it and what is more, I am afraid that if the war was to end tomorrow we should have to remain here until we secured these Turkish prisoners which will take some time yet. We keep about two thousand of them here and bright clean specimens they are too. You can smell them half a mile away. At present I am on night duty and there are only two Britishers looking after the whole issue but we have a few Turkish orderlies, who are no good whatever. There is a great difference between a job like this and a Field Ambulance, but for preference give me a Fd Ambulance. From what I hear, our old Division is at Alexandria, so Dai R.Thomas must be down there ready to

leave the country. But there, I don't think it will be so very long now before the whole lot will be over, and although there is plenty of work here, I cannot grumble for we have plenty of food, and we can buy almost anything we want, so it isn't so bad is it? Well I have no more to say this time so
I close with love to all from
Dick

Richard's belief that 'the whole lot' would be over soon was correct, as also was his supposition that it would take some time for him and his comrades to be repatriated.

Given the delay of at least a month between letters being sent from Wales and arriving with Richard, he was unaware as the war came to a close of Ivor's wounding. There is no indication that he was aware that Thomas J. Cole, one of his acquaintances from home, had been killed on the Western Front on 1 September 1918, nor of the death of the other Treboeth man who fell that month in France, Sidney Phillips. Richard was ignorant of the death from pneumonia of William Davies, formerly a co-worker with him at Mynydd Newydd, on 29 October, and of Thomas Davies on 6 November.[7] Also, there is no way he could have known that two more Treboeth men would die of their wounds within the next eighteen months.

Notes

1. 'Arholiad' (exam) refers to the Sunday school examination organised annually by the Welsh Independents denomination.
2. In colloquial Welsh, 'sbel' means 'rest'.
3. The National Eisteddfod was held at Neath from 6 to 9 August 1918.
4. The Battle of Tel-el-Kebir, fought on 13 September 1882, was a comprehensive victory for the British forces over the Egyptian army.
5. At the time of the 1911 Census George was living in Belle Vue Street, Swansea with his mother and his sister Elleanor.
6. For both of these items of news, cf. GE1918-09-10 (ch. 10).
7. It is possible that Richard had corresponded with this William Davies: see chapter 3 and chapter 15.

12

Ivor Eustis in England and Wales, October–November 1918

The collection contains two postcards and three letters that Ivor sent to his mother in the month after he was wounded on 8 October. The earlier missives are written with the express purpose of reassuring the family that the wound is not serious, and the tone is very light, even joyful. He tells his mother 'I have struck lucky again' after he arrives in hospital in England, and finishes the message with 'Cheer up!' Then he was posted to the RWF Depot in Wrexham, and the two letters from here are again positive in their tone. The letter Ivor wrote three days before the Armistice is overflowing with exultation that the war is coming to an end and the Kaiser is sure to get his comeuppance – this contains the phrase that gives this book its title.

The first postcard has upon it the printed emblem of the Canadian Service Chaplain, next to which Ivor has written 'Canadian Hospital'. It has the censor's stamp and although it was written on 9 October from 'France, (Somewhere behind)', the postmark is 11 October 1918. This means it is quite probable that this postcard was not received at Mynyddbach until after the subsequent one.

IE1918-10-09 Postcard

Dear Mother,

Just a line to let you know that I am all right and having a good time on my way down to hospital, having stopped a lump of shrapnel with my head yesterday morning.

The wound is nothing much, a bit of a cut in the forehead above the left eye, and all I am afraid of is that it will heal too quickly, for, do you know, a bed of blankets is better than a bed of earth and grass. I'll write again as soon as my journey comes to an end. Ivor

The second postcard was written and posted on 12 October. The address is given as 'Blighty'.

IE1918-10-12 Postcard

Dear Mother,

Just another line to let you know that I have struck lucky again, having arrived in England this morning and am now at a hospital at Chatham. I never thought for a moment that I would leave France. Don't worry about me, for I am simply laughing here! and the wound is nothing more than a cut over the eye which is not affected at all though it is as black as charcoal. Letter later

Cheer up! Ivor

The letter from Chatham that has survived in the collection is dated simply 'Sunday', but it is highly likely that it was written the day after the postcard above. Ivor wrote it on YMCA notepaper from 'Ward 4, Fort Pitt Mil. Hosp., Chatham', with a note beside the address saying 'We might leave this place at any time'.

IE1918-10-13

Dear Mother,

I was talking to some of the boys here just now and I was told that when a man is wounded the news is conveyed to his parents and that the card is marked 'Serious'. I don't know whether this is true or not, but in case it is, and something like that lands at Pengwern Road just put it in the fire and think no more about it. What is troubling me most just now is the fact that I am causing an endless amount of worry to you at home, especially as I am in hospital and have come back to England. You know it sounds ten times worse than it really is, and I would be far more comfortable if I knew that you were not worrying about me. Honestly, there is nothing the matter with me except a clean cut in the forehead, about 2 inches long and about $^1/_{16}$ inches deep over the left eye which is not affected in the least bar being blackened a bit. So rest contented that all is well, for candidly if I had my way, I would just put a bit of plaster on it and come home on leave. I enclose a sketch of what it is like, I don't think I can do more.

Well, I have no room to grumble about the way I have been treated since I got hit. Since I reported at the dressing station I got every comfort possible under the circumstances and when I arrived at No 56 General Hosp. at Etaples I got a bed and a suit of 'blues'[1] and that is when I became a patient. We had a great welcome at Dover and also at Chatham there being numerous 'kind ladies' there distributing cigarettes and chocolates.

This place is quite all right – in fact the bed is so comfortable that it takes me some time to make up my mind when to get up. What is also great is the fact that we can go back into it any time we like so you can guess how much time I spend out of it. If you happen to be in bed when meal time arrives the nurse brings it to you, so we are doing well.

I can wish for nothing more or better concerning the treatment I get from the Doctor and staff. They are all extremely kind and considerate, especially the nurses – bless them all! There is plenty to occupy our time here and to keep us merry and bright, including a Y.M.C.A and freedom to the town.

At present the boys are sitting around the fire and an old gramophone is keeping us lively. I'll never forget one night in Etaples – the last day I spent there. I went to bed soon after tea and after a while I woke up to hear a clear voice from a gramophone singing 'There's a ship that's bound for Blighty' and I thought to myself – what a poor chance I stand. But I was away that night, little as I expected it.

No more this time

love to all Ivor

No other communications from Chatham have survived, but it is clear that Ivor did not stay long at the hospital for he was soon on a visit home. On 24 October he was presented with a medal and a treasury note by the Treboeth and District Succour Fund.[2] The next we hear of him, he was writing from 'Sgts Mess, R.W.F. Depot, Wrexham' on (Friday) 1 November.

IE1918-11-01

Dear Mother.

What do you think of the above address? I landed here 'by mistake' on Thursday night and here I have remained since. They said nothing about it, and even spared me an explanation by saying that they were sorry they did not let me know in time, and so, of course I said nothing more about it. Ha! Ha!

It is quite a nice place, & quite different from what I expected. It is situated just on the edge of the town, and consists of the usual Barrack Square in the middle and blocks of buildings all around, and unlike other Barracks I have seen, there is very little 'military' about it except for the cannons which are stuck on the square, polished up to the knocker, and tales of their capture etc etc on brass plates fitted in the muzzle. Except for these and of course the soldiers knocking about, one would not know the place was the headquarters of a famous regiment like the Royal Welch – spelt with a 'c', why, I don't know.

I do not think I shall stay here long – in fact I am practically certain of it, because they only keep unfit men here, with categories of B_2 and under, while mine is B_1 which to all intents and purposes is the same as A_1. Undoubtedly Limerick will be my final destination.

The Mess is an excellent one – as good any day as the one we had at Kinmel. The food is famous, and the parades easy – so I'm laughing again.

I will write again soon
                  with love to all – Ivor

There is a postscript to this letter: 'Had a grand time in Rhyl. If any letters arrive for me enclose them in another envelope and send them along.'

Ivor was still at Wrexham a week later, when he wrote a letter which, despite its acknowledgement of bad news from home, is overflowing with joy and relief in the knowledge that the war is coming to a close.

IE1918-11-08

Dear Mother,

    Just a few lines to let you know that I am quite all right and am enjoying myself here, though I never expected to be here so long. Also, I received your letter all right, with Dick's new address, and so I was able to post him another letter straight away last night.

    It is with deep regret that I hear of the death of poor Dai Thomas of Heol Ddu. Why I was only speaking to him when I was on leave when he was joking about the Flu and all that. It must have been very sudden, and besides it was only a short time ago that his uncle died.

    We have had some more splendid news tonight about the 'Ole Warrrr!' It's coming to an end fast and poor old Kaiser Bill is surely 'yn crynu yn ei 'scydie' [*quaking in his boots*] when he thinks of what is going to happen to his old Fatherland. For myself, I have not much to say about it, except that 'Boys Jack Eustis' have each had a 'go' at him, somewhere or other. I don't wish him and his crew any harm – for they never managed to hurt me – it was our own boys that gave me that Black Eye. Still, I sincerely hope that they will string him up to the nearest lamp-post by the toe-nails with barbed wire, have a dentist to extract one of his teeth every half hour, have him inoculated seven times a day, and put on him one of those inhabited shirts that I was the victim of in France, tying his hands behind him so that he couldn't scratch himself. I would not object to putting two mustard plasters on his chest and another one inside the seat of his

trousers, and I'd have him vaccinated in 50 different places
and after eight days when the scabs had formed, I'd invite all
the kids in the village to come and tickle them with nettles.
I don't suppose all my good wishes come true, still I hope
it won't be a case of 'hen gount – talu byth' [*old debt – pay
forever*] with for [*sic*] he ought to be made to pay for the
damage he's done.

love from – Ivor

Thus the letters sent by the Eustis brothers as the war was being
fought come to an end, with Ivor's mischievous fantasy about what
should be done to the Kaiser for his misdeeds. Jack Eustis's boys
knew that they had done their duty, and believed that their war had
concluded.

Notes

1. 'Hospital Blues': the uniform provided to convalescent soldiers in the
    First World War.
2. *CDL*, 25 October 1918, 1. Note that he is referred to as 'Sergt. Eustace'.

13

November 1918–
January 1919

This chapter is arranged differently to the previous ones as it contains letters from all three brothers, as well as one written by a friend, Dai Harris. They are generally organised chronologically, though the final letter that has survived from Gabriel is included before the letter from Dai Harris to give some more context to its content.

These letters tell of the different experiences and feelings of the three brothers after the Armistice. Their previous letters show that they had been thinking about what they would do with their lives after the war ended, but now that issue was pressing. They were all naturally anxious to go home as soon as possible, and now that the immediate danger of the war had passed, there was much opportunity for frustration and boredom to set in.

The first letter in the collection to have been written post-Armistice was sent by Gabriel from the Royal Naval Barracks in Chatham, where he had been sent after leaving the *Saxon* on 18 November. He wrote on (Friday) 22 November:

GE1918-11-22

Dear Mother,

Just a few lines to let you know how things are going. I suppose you've had my other letter by now, saying I was leaving the old Saxon. I did not like it at all being there over three years & now when all the scrapping is over being fetched in here. I expect I'll have another ship before long for I have no hopes of getting out for good for some time yet. I had a fair journey down, left the old Saxon at 6.0 pm Monday night & arrived here yesterday afternoon about 3.0. I was messing about from one department to another up to 8.30 pm last night; when you can guess I was only too glad to get turned in for a sleep.

Today again it's been the same & and I have not half finished yet even. Probably I won't be allowed to settle down properly until about Monday, when I start at my own game again. I understand I am to take over a class for instruction (some instructor me eh?) but I hope it doesn't last long, I would far rather be at sea than here. All the Ldg Tels here have a class each so I suppose I will have to fall into line. I'll let you know all about it in my next.

Love to All

Gib

P.S. Tell Auntie Charlotte I got her letter of Nov 11th & will write first chance.

Ivor had also been on the move, from the RWF's barracks at Wrexham to its base in Limerick. The letter he sent home on 26 November forms part of a family conversation about plans for the future, and although we only have access to one side of the discussion, it is clear that there was a major disagreement about what was best for Ivor, and for the other siblings.

IE1918-11-26

Dear Mother,

I received your letter last night and I see that the topic of what I am to do when I leave the army is quite the thing at home just now.

I see everyone is anxious to see me stick to the same line but as I told Auntie Charlotte there are some difficulties to be overcome. Bear in mind that I am quite willing to do any thing to please you, and the reason that I wanted to give up the idea of teaching any more was that these difficulties were more than we could manage.

First of all, there's the cost of sending me to College and keeping me there for at least 2 years. Now who is going to bear the brunt of that? You cannot reckon on Dick, poor old boy, I expect he will be thinking of settling down for life as soon as he is free again. Then there is Gib – he does not intend going back to the Duffryn, and quite right too. He thinks of going in for something with more work for the brain than for the muscles, and so perhaps he will be some months before getting a well paid job.

Besides this there is ready money required to keep the girls going, Danny will soon be at it and of course he is too [*sic*] get the very best of what we can give him as soon as our hands are free. Bessie will soon be eligible for College, and Grace and Lottie will have to carry on at Gowerton for some considerable time to come.

So you see, we want money, we want it badly, and we want it quickly; already I have cost the house much more than any of the others.

Again, I have been almost three years in the Army, and you know what that means – I have done no work in my own line since I have been in it, and so it is quite possible that my old head won't work the way it used to.

However, if you can see your way clear, I am quite willing to carry on with it and do my time in College as soon as possible. You have all done too much for me for me to think of going against your wishes. Besides, I am willing to work hard whether at school in the office or in the works. What do you say? Ivor

There is a postscript to this letter, in which Ivor writes 'Stephens has nothing at all to do with it – don't think he is persuading me'. It is certain that this is Elfryn Stephens, Ivor's old schoolmate. He had also landed in Limerick after being wounded on the Western Front (and he too had been awarded the Military Medal).[1] However, we are not privy to what Ivor and Elfryn's conversations entailed.

Two days later (writing from New Barracks, Limerick), Ivor's disillusionment with his treatment is striking as he discusses the matter which was to dominate his next letters. Although he had been doing the duties of a corporal and sergeant for many months, the army authorities were questioning whether his actual rank was any higher than lance-corporal.

IE1918-11-28

Dear Mother,

I received your letter this evening with the news of the arrival of that bronze medal and the letter from the Adjutant. There is one point that strikes me more than usual that is that the letter is signed by a chap named Phillips; when I left them Captain Searl was the Adjutant and he was a great friend of mine, as far as the huge difference in rank permitted. I wrote to him some days ago asking him what my proper rank was and I had a nice reply from him, in which he gave all the information I had asked for.

Well, mother, I am really very discontented in this rotten shop and the longer I stay here the worse I get. Without a word of a lie, I can say I was far more happy in France, tired, hungry, wet through and alive with vermin, as I was many and many a time.

Of course, I have a roof to live under, a bed to sleep on, with blankets to keep me warm, and regular meals – but what are these, when you are watched like a mouse, and as soon as you do the least irregularity, up you come on the mat.

I don't mind answering for a decent sized crime when I know I have done something queer, but to be fetched up time after time for little things, which are nothing at all when you come to think of them – well, things are really getting on my nerves.

They are still after my stripes and as soon as they can they will get them off me. This is the way you are treated after doing your best both in this country and out of it. In France they were glad to get a man to lead the boys over the top – here they stop at nothing in their endeavour to reduce a chap from his well earned rank. I'll welcome the day when I leave them for good.

Cariad cynes [*warm love*] – Iv.

Two days later, news of his official demotion was confirmed.

IE1918-11-30

Dear Mother,

Once more I have to let you know of a change of address, for, after a week's adventures with this, that, and the other, I have managed to come down with a bump from a Sergeant to a lance corporal. Now don't get vexed about this, because I am not; and don't start thinking that I have been running wild all over Limerick, or that I have murdered half a dozen people. I have done nothing of this kind, I have only been fighting the law, which states that I am a lance corporal, whereas I am convinced that my rank according to orders is Sergeant. However, they have won the first few rounds but the fight is not over yet – and when it is, I shall either be a Sergeant or a Private, no half and half for me.

Well I see by Auntie Charlotte's letter that you have decided to get rid of me again for another 2 years, hoping no doubt, that by shutting me up in a College, to keep me out of trouble for that time. Ha! Ha! Well, I'm willing enough, but don't forget that I have warned you all about the greatness of the task you are undertaking.

Can you send me a few things which I am short of in my kit, such as a pair of drawers same as I used to wear before the war, & a towel. You see, I left some things behind at Wrexham because they were in the wash when I left, and I have written to the boys to send these things to you. So if you send me these two articles I can carry on for the time being, till the whole bundle arrives from Wrexham, if ever they do.

One more item. Thanks for sending that letter along to me which came from France but I did not like the fact that it had been opened. I hope you were satisfied, and I hope you will not open any more.

Dim rhagor [*No more*]

Yours affectionately

Ivor

Meanwhile Gabriel had the opportunity to take leave from Chatham. The second letter below (GE1918-12-11) suggests that it was for four days. The letter he sent on 4 December after returning to his barracks mentions that he travelled with two Mynyddbach men.

GE1918-12-04

Dear Mother,

Arrived here at 9-20 AM just nice time. Had a fair journey, no chance of a nap, too crowded, all the way. Left Willie Haydn at Victoria, Iorwerth Evans came with me to Blackfriars Station, where I caught 7-30 train for Chatham.[2] Have not reported yet at school, been having a wash & square up, etc. will re-start with same class this afternoon. Had your letter of Nov 29th, no letters forwarded on from Saxon yet, expect some with every mail now. Lots of talk here about 12 days leave for all hands Xmas & New Year, first lot to go on Dec. 16th. Hope it's true & that I click with the first issue.

Will let you know exactly soon as I know for certain myself.

Love

Gib.

The next letter, just dated 'Wednesday' was almost certainly written a week later, again from the Royal Naval Barracks in Chatham.

GE1918-12-11

Dear Mother,

I'm not sure whether I wrote a letter to you as well as the P.C. when I returned here, but anyhow it's time you had another so here goes for a brief one. I am back on the same job & with the same class as I had before going on those four days. Things are a little better now that I'm getting into the routine of the place but still I don't want to stop here a day after Xmas if I can help it. I want to stop here until the 16th at least as all the signal & W/T [Wireless Telegraphist] ratings

are to have <u>12 days leave</u> commencing on the 16th to return on
the 28th. So I have great hopes of having <u>this</u> Xmas at home
at any rate, it's a practical certainty bar accidents or draft. It
would be rather aggravating & disappointing if I were drafted
to a ship now within a few days wouldn't it? It seems I only
just caught that last leave of mine in time as all such leave was
cancelled the day after I left here. Of course that was only
in view of this Christmas leave & will probably be restarted
in the New Year. I am looking forward to Monday I can
tell you, if only to get out of this place for 12 days, without
having Xmas at home. I am also anticipating a few good feeds
so you had better 'provision ship' in good time.

What does Ivor say about it? I expect he'll get this
12 days also & I hope he gets home same time as me. I am
expecting a letter from him every day now, & also from Dick.
Well I must conclude now Mother, look out for Gaboose any
time after the 16th.

Love to All,
Gib

P.S. Some more parcels being sent for me from the Saxon, <u>be</u>
<u>careful with them</u>, one will be a camera, <u>don't open them</u> &
<u>keep them there till I arrive</u>, if they come before I get home
please.

While Gabriel was at Chatham training new recruits, Ivor
was kicking his heels in Ireland, waiting for the opportunity to be
demobbed. One of the letters in the collection is missing the first
two pages, and thus it is not known to whom it was addressed at
Mynyddbach nor when it was written, but it is a fair guess that it
was written in December 1918, as Ivor was continuing his struggle
to get the army authorities to recognise his rank as sergeant.[3]

IE1918-12-a

Still, I am not worrying about this. I've roughed it before and
so I can still fight my own battles.

Well we had a lecture on Demobilisation today and
the speaker dropped a hint that men like myself whose
courses have been cut short, have a good chance of getting

out of the army early in order to pursue their studies; however he would not answer any questions on the matter, as his subject was Demobilisation and there was another man following in a few days' time with a lecture on this Educational scheme of theirs. This will be the man to answer all my questions and I shall not fail to put them before him. This chap we had today gave us a lecture on the subject first and then invited us to ask any questions we liked, so that he would be able to explain what points we were doubtful about.

They are also very keen on us youngsters signing on for a few years longer. What a hope they've got of getting me to soldier any more after the way they have treated me since I came from France. They are offering a kind of bonus of £50 for a further 4 years service and a month's leave. But they can offer what they like, they won't get me to put my signature there – No! decidedly not, not all the bait in all the army would induce me to remain 2 minutes longer than what is absolutely necessary. Not that I dislike the life, in fact I have taken a liking for it as a whole, especially the active service part of it, but I have had enough of it and now my song is 'Home, Sweet Home.'

Hoping all is well at home and that we shall all be there soon.

Yours affectionately
Ivor

The next dated letter from Ivor in the collection was begun on Sunday, 8 December 1918 – six days before the General Election was held. By this time, he had been moved to Ballyvonare, a convalescent home for recuperating soldiers in a remote part of northern County Cork, 3.5 miles from Buttevant.

IE1918-12-08

Dear Mother,

On my return from 'Kirk' this morning your letter awaited me, having been readdressed from Limerick by Stephens who is still there.

I am afraid that I have been 'grousing' too much
since I have been in the lovely Emerald Isle not that it is
unwarranted but it does seem bad form to grumble, so
I won't do any more of it. Still I have the consolation of
knowing that I am not hiding anything from you. It is rotten
here and quite as bad in another way at Limerick.

Well I was much surprised to hear that Gab had been
home, though of course it is not to be wondered at, seeing
that he is stationed at Chatham. And he seems to be having
a rotten time too! Ha! Ha! We all are in the soup it seems to
me and having roughed it for some years we are all beginning
to grumble when the war is over. I suppose we are all sorry
that we are coming home again soon – Ha! Ha! not half!
Well, there's better times in store, as the old saying goes.

As I have said, I have been to 'Kirk' this morning (as
the Jocks call church) and it was with them that we went.
There are only Scotch troops here besides Royal Welsh and
so they joined the two parades and we marched to the cinema
hall together headed by the Bagpipes. We are very pally
with the Jocks and get on much better with them than with
Patrick and his tribe.

(Monday) Had to leave off suddenly yesterday. Today
I had two letters from Uriel together with the ballot paper
and the best way I can find is to present Dad with my vote
and let him do the best with it. I am no politician anyway.

No more for the present – Ivor

A postscript states 'Complete the address on the enclosed & forward
to Gib'.

Being a 21-year-old male, Ivor had been enfranchised by the
Representation of the People Act of 1918. Thus the first chance
Ivor had to vote, he passed on the opportunity to his father. It is
unlikely that either Gabriel and Richard exercised their constitu-
tional rights for the first time in this election, as amongst the letters
from Gabriel from this period there has been preserved a Ballot
Paper Envelope (obviously unsubmitted), and in the same envelope as one of Richard's letters there is a blank unused 'Form of
Declaration of Identity'.

A week later Ivor wrote again to his mother from Ballyvonare:

IE1918-12-15

Dear Mother,

It is Sunday afternoon and a very wet one at that, and
though this is nothing to be surprised at in Ireland, still one
could do with a bit of dry weather on the Holy Sabbath.

They made a list of the men who are going home with
the first lot for Christmas leave and of course old Eustis was <u>not</u>
among them. This means that I shall not be home for Xmas and
that is definite. The first lot went this morning and they will be
away for 12 days. The next lot will not start until the first has
returned so we shall have to wait and see for the time being.

<u>Monday</u>
The telegram from Gib arrived this evening and makes things
look rather 'wet' for our intended operations for Christmas.
The worst of it is that they have pasted a notice up to the
effect that no applications for leave will be granted except in
the case of death or serious illness in the family, and every
man will get his 12 days leave when his turn comes and no
sooner. But notice or no, I'll have a shot at it tomorrow
morning, trusting to my imagination and my oratorical
abilities to bring me success, so wish me luck. I see Gib will
be home from the 16th to the 28th, just the best period I think.

There is something seriously wrong somewhere or
other, and I really don't know who is to blame for it. In the
first place, that parcel you sent me has not arrived yet and
I am beginning to give up hope of ever seeing it. Besides
this, there are umpteen letters either gone astray or, well,
perhaps they were never written. For instance it is more than
3 weeks since I heard from some people who used to write
to me three and four times a week. I know this for a fact that
the post corporal is exceedingly careless with the mail; he is
a chap who never went out on service and I suppose he is
not particular whether he loses his job or not now that the
scrapping is over.

As regards the other little affair, it has taken a
serious turn to the bad. They have started paying me the
King's Shilling which means that I am in debt, and they are

withholding my pay until I am square again. This is what I
expected, and as I have given them quite a good time to make
the inquiries they said they wanted to make, I intend taking
another plunge into the Orderly Room and try my luck again.

So on the whole, things are delightfully Irish in this
part of the world. Still, though the tail of my shirt is hanging
out I still have a smile on my dial again. I really cannot help
smiling at my bad luck, and I always keep thinking of the old
saying 'After the Lord Mayor comes Twm Evan Y Clâs.'

No more at present hoping you will give Gab a busy
time

with love from Ivor

Ivor wrote to Gabriel himself on Tuesday, in a letter brimming
with anger at his treatment by the authorities. Unfortunately, only
the first three pages of this letter have survived.

IE1918-12-17

Dear Gib,

Your letter addressed from Chatham to Limerick
on the 5th inst, arrived here today and I can assure you it
was quite an event of national importance in this one-eyed
miniature Pentonville. Sorry to hear about your Paddy's rise
especially where the splosh is concerned for it's exactly the
same with me.[4] I don't care a Tinkers Toss-up for the stripes I
dumped but just think of the credit I am done out of.

I was promoted Lance Jack in July 1916 and they
have got that recorded up all right. Next, about October
I was promoted to full Cpl but they never entered this up
in records, nor the subsequent promotion I had both in
England & France. This means that I have been discredited
with the following Items:-

(1.) 1916 Oct to Dec @ 4d per day £0-18-8 (Cpl)
(2.) 1917 Jan to Dec @ 8d per day £12-3-4 (Sergt)
(3.) 1918 Jan to Sept @ 4d " " £3-14-8 (Cpl)
(4.) 1918 Sept to Dec @ 8d " " £2-16-10 (Sergt)

£19-13-0

or approximately speaking they are doing me down by about
£20 for whereas I should have this amount to my credit,
according to them I am just straight. Do you comprè? Well
I am making a bold bid for it anyway and already I have
bothered the life out of the Office blokes about it and they are
saying that they are making inquiries, However, I am going
nap next time and shall take the matter up to the General.[5]
'Watch aur neu coes bren' [*a gold watch or a wooden leg*] is
my motto, and I am going for it neck or nothing.

Do you know I could have come home last Saturday
if I wished, but owing to this matter not being satisfactorily
squared up, I deferred my demob to a later date. All teachers
and students etc went last Saturday, but I loftily declined my
cheque pending this financial deal.

Also, I think it is looking decidedly Irish on my
12 days leave coinciding with yours! I was not among the
first batch otherwise I should be home now. Maybe I shall
just manage to get a squint of you before you return, that is if
my luck is in,

Despite Ivor's pessimism in the letter to his mother about being
able to secure home leave for Christmas, it appears that he did manage it. The above is the final letter from him in the army that has
survived, so details are very sketchy, but in the letter, below, which
Gabriel wrote just after his visit home, he clearly states that Ivor was
there. This conveys only a few details on what he did and whom he
met. However it is very likely that at this visit Gabriel and Ivor were
presented with cards from Mynyddbach chapel, wishing them good
fortune and safety, as well as a merry Christmas and a happy New
Year. (Gabriel's has survived, in the original envelope.) Printed on
the card was a special poem written by Gwyrosydd for those sons
of Mynyddbach who were serving in the armed forces:

> I chwi Nadolig dedwydd iach,
> Medd Calon Eglwys Mynyddbach;
> Llawer gweddi daer o'r lle
> Aeth ar eich rhan at orsedd Ne',
> Tra chwi'n cadw y gelynion
> Draw o'n gwlad a gwaed eich calon.

Mae ein Mawl i'r nef yn esgyn
Am nerth a gawd i goncro'r gelyn,
Pan ddewch adref, yn cystadlu
Fyddwn am eich llaw i'w gwasgu:
Duw Ior wnelo'r byd yn ddoethach,
Ac na foed son am ryfel mwyach.

[*Literal translation:*
To you, a healthy happy Christmas
says the heart of the church at Mynyddbach;
many an earnest prayer from this place
has gone on your behalf to the throne of Heaven,
while you were keeping the enemies
away from our land with the blood of your heart.

Our Praise ascends to heaven
for the strength that was had to defeat the enemy,
when you come home
we will be competing to press your hand;
may the Lord God make the world wiser
and there be no more talk of war.]

The letter from Gabriel which he wrote to Aunt Charlotte from the barracks in Chatham on the evening of 28 December is buzzing with optimism, although he apologises for failing to visit her while he was home. It ends with a rhyme that was traditionally sung to friends and neighbours at the New Year.

GE1918-12-28

Dear Auntie & All,
　　　Just a line to let you know I'm back in the workhouse again feeling umpteen times better after my lovely holiday. Leaving Landore about 7.55 this morning the train only stopped at Cardiff, Newport & Reading & arrived at Paddington at 12.10 pm, about the fastest return trip I've made. I had just time for a bit of chaff before catching the 1-32 pm from London Bridge & arrived here about 3-15p.m. When I gave in my liberty ticket at the guard house the

'crusher' (Naval police) kindly informed me that I was late,
I said 'looks like it' & the only reply I got was 'Op it', so
we're A1 at Lloyds again. It isn't absolutely exhilarating to
be back here again after a fortnight's enjoyment & especially
to return to the scrumptious bill of fare obtaining in this
man's establishment. I had a thin slice of Bread & butter
for tea & a dry Bread and cheese sandwich for supper &
that after the good spreads I've been tucking into this last
fortnight or so! Oh my ----- ! Never mind it's Sunday
tomorrow, so we may get a sausage or some 'burgoo' or
some other substantial feed like that for breakfast. I've
done absolutely nothing in the way of work yet & outside
divisions & church parade tomorrow morning I won't do
anything until Monday. Plenty of time to worry about work
when it comes.

Well now I'm really very sorry that I neglected you
all this time, but time seemed to fly so, it seemed as if I
had hardly been home a day when it was time to return.
Of course, the fact that Ivor and so many other chums of
mine were also home is responsible, but then I should have
managed a few trips to Laurel Cottage withal. I intended
making up a bit of lee way on Friday morning but Davy
Harris came up as I was dressing & then it was almost
impossible to get away. Now I can only apologise again
& promise to 'do better next time,' which I hope won't be
so long as I imagined. There's a lot of talk here just now
about an early demob but I can't see how they can very well
manage it. Anyhow early or late, I can 'grin and bear it' as
before I suppose.

Well you'll have to excuse brevity this time – this is
only the fourth letter for me to write tonight & it's getting
nigh 'lights out.'

> Blwyddyn Newydd Dda i Chwi i Gŷd
> Pob un trwy'r ti; Tra-la-la-la-la -
> Dyn bach (ag) yn y blaen.
> [*A Happy New Year to you All*
> *Every one through the house Tra-la-la-la-la -*
> *The little Man (and) so on*]

Wishing you one & all a very Happy & Prosperous
New Year,

Gib

The 'Davy Harris' mentioned in Gabriel's letter is undoubtedly
Dai Harris. He was in the navy, had corresponded with Richard
whilst he was stationed in the East and is mentioned in a number
of the letters of Gabriel and Richard in 1918.[6] The following letter
was sent by Dai from his home in Roger Street on 17 December
1918. No envelope has survived, but it is likely that the letter was
sent to Egypt and then returned to Wales after missing Richard.
Dai's letter reveals a lot about the kind of subjects that the soldiers discussed in their private communications: plenty of local
news and gossip (not all of which can be interpreted at this distance), grumbling at bureaucracy, disparaging comments about
the (former) enemy and looking forward to being reunited at
home.

DH1918-12-17

Dear Old Dick,

I was very pleased to receive your letter tonight, and
pleased to learn that you were in good condition same as yer'
'umble. So you have left Palestine at last, well I suppose it's
the first step for home, the sooner you get here the better
you will like it no doubt. Ha, Ha, so you've lost your stripes,
what capers have you been up to, eh, could be worse eh!
Hard lines on you chaps getting separated at the last go off
like that, they might as well have kept you all together now
till you are demobilized, Red tape again.

I'm glad that I am not amongst your Turks then, ships
are lousy enough, but they are not so bad as those guys are,
why not dump them in the sea somewhere. Where the devil
do they get all the money from, especially gold, pinched it or
what. I suppose there is no chance of getting a revolver out
there, I'd like to get hold of one, that is the worst of the navy,
you can't get things like that for souvenirs.

Bryn Thomas the vicarage has been home, he was
in Hosp. at Brighton not far from where I was, but I did

not know in time about it.[7] Do you know who is going to get married day before Xmas, Ivor Griffiths, Dai Griffiths' brother, some husband for someone, I'll be sorry for her. It's needless to tell you of the carryon with Dai Evans and Alice by your home there, some lively times I assure you. Yes your Ivor is the lad, the proper stuff, I daresay I shall meet him this time, I expect he will get Xmas leave, I hope so anyhow, I haven't seen him since he is in the Army, I've heard that Bryn Harris (Caersalem, Emlyn Harris's brother) has had the M.M. too, some decorations in the district.[8] I believe there are more medals than deaths from the district, I mean death in action. Gib has had a rise too he has had the Hook, and on the instructional staff in Barracks. So you've got proper disgusted with Palestine and Egypt, well I don't blame you. Well old son I must say you have a devil of a good memory, you say in your letter that you will not forget the photo this time, but I'm damned if you haven't gone and forgotten it again. I'll have to come out there and tie something about your fingers, anyhow I'm still looking forward to getting it sometime or other.

Well I'm home now since Saturday on demobilizing leave home until recalled, when that will be I don't know, so hurry up old son and let's see your dial at this place once again. News is very scarce with me this time, though I'm never an interesting letter writer. I will close trusting you will get this letter alright.

Best of Luck & good wishes.
I also wish you as Merry a Xmas as possible and a bright New Year.

From your old Pal
Dai Harris

There was of course a time lag of over three weeks between letters being sent from Wales and arriving in Egypt, and so it is likely that Dai Harris's letter arrived in the country at around the time that Richard was leaving. In the letter below, which Richard wrote on 20 December 1918, he was still responding to the news from home of October and November. It also helps to give the context to Dai's comments about the prisoners' gold.

RE1918-12-20

Dear Mother,

Just a few lines to let you know that I received your letter the other day, and I am pleased to hear that all are well at home there. I have nothing to complain about here, for I am more comfortable than I have been since I came out here, being only two of us in a tent with a bed each and a table, a Turk to bring us a cup of tea, before we get up in the morning, to look after our things, do our washing , &c, &c. So you can just imagine how things are, I am living in a state just like a two thousand a week lord. Ha! Ha! Ha! You'd laugh to see how we carry on here, Turkish and German prisoners do everything & all we do is to see that they do it.

I am hoping for a few days leave to Cairo from here soon when I hope to have a good time. Dai Thomas is still in Alexandria as far as I know, but I haven't heard from him for about a week. I haven't heard from Sammy Rees for some time, although he is only a few stations away from where I am still, he & I were not as thick as Dai & I. Glad to hear that Ivor has been home on leave, but am sorry to hear that he has had a clout over the eye. I suppose that before Ivor could get back to France the second time, it was all over. It was a good job too, for I did not fancy his being there at all. In fact, I would sooner be there myself than him. Still all's well that ends well.

I sent a letter to Gib a few days ago. According to his letters, he's having a very good time of it up in Scotland, what with submarines to chase. He shouldn't be so long before coming home altogether now, but I'm afraid I shall be stuck here for sometime at least till we clear all the Turks back to Constantinople. I have heard that Ivor Lewis is now on a ship as orderly running between Alexandria and Constantinople but I don't know whether it is true or not. The first batch of Turks are being sent from our hospital tomorrow to Constantinople, but I am afraid that a half of them will be dead before they reach there, for they are in a very poor condition. But although they don't look as if they have had any food for weeks & their clothes comprise mostly

of sacking, they have plenty of money on them and the funny
part about it is that it is mostly gold; Egyptian, English,
French, Italian & Turkish sovereigns having been found
on them. Needless to say I have one or two of them, but
whether I shall be able to keep them, I do not know. I had a
letter from Ivor today from Wrexham, he seems to be having
a decent time there. I have no more to tell you this time, will
write again in a day or two,

from

Dick

The next surviving letter was written three days later, and
responded to the reaction to the end of the war in Wales.

RE1918-12-23

Dear Aunt Charlotte,
        I was very pleased to receive your letter the other day,
dated 19th Nov. and am glad to hear that all are well there.
As you say, there must have been great rejoicing at home
there, when they learnt that the fighting had finished. Of
course, we couldn't realize it here, because we were out of
the fighting altogether the last few weeks. I am not surprised
to hear that the people had processions & thanksgiving
meetings all over the place. We have been very fortunate
as a family, considering that two of us have been in it since
the very beginning, and then Ivor comes in to go through
the thickest of the whole fighting. Yes, I heard that he was
slightly wounded, but he was fortunate to get back to Blighty
with it. I am sorry to hear that Uriel is in hospital with
dysentery, but perhaps it is better that he had it there, than if
he came out here or to India, for there is so much about here
and I have seen it absolutely ruining great big healthy men.
Stephens, Loughor, suffers terribly from it at times and he
has to be very careful what he eats for the slightest thing will
bring it on for him.[9] The Influenza is just as bad out here as it
is home there; for a few of our boys have succumbed to it or
rather to the septic pneumonia that sets in after it, unless one
is very careful.

To change the subject, a Captain of ours came on to me yesterday saying 'I have very good news for you Eustis.' 'Have you, sir?' 'Yes, you are going home very, very soon, but you will have to stop over Christmas, to help us to win this football match.' What do you think of that eh? I have been waiting for that for a long time, but it happens to be at an awkward time of the year. Still I am prepared to take the risk to get home, but I'm afraid I shall have to be very careful. Well, I think it is pretty certain about it, so I want you to tell all concerned not to write to me any more, because they will only go astray. Barring accidents I hope to be home before the end of January. Now that is good news isn't it? I don't think I shall be able to write to tell everybody not to write to me, or send me any parcels, so tell all concerned

I am too delighted to think of writing any more so I close with love to all

from

Dick

Richard's optimism about the swiftness of his repatriation was misplaced, for he was still in Egypt when he wrote from 'Demobilisation Camp' on 14 January 1919.

RE1919-01-14

Dear Mother,

Just a few lines to let you know that all is well with me, etc, and that I am only waiting here for a boat to bring me home. I daresay that you have received my last letter telling you not to write me any more letters as I was expecting to come home. I sent that a few days before Xmas and about 2 days after Xmas I was sent on here along with a few more from the same unit. There are thousands of us here altogether, and I have never been in such a camp. The food is terrible and what money we had coming here has gone to buy food. Sammy Rees came into this camp a day or two after me, and he was lucky for he was put on a draft at once, and he has already sailed. D.R.Thomas, Ivor Lewis & I are still here, but we expect to go with the next lot. Dai has been in here since Dec 27th, I came on the 29th, Sam came on the 31st & still he has gone before any of us, so you see, they have no system at all about sending drafts home. But now they have arranged us according to the dates we arrived in the camp, so I am living in hopes of being on the next boat that leaves here.

Ivor is lucky, being in England at present and I daresay that he will be home before you receive this letter, for his group are being called in here from all over the place here. Now the next you will hear from me will be a telegram from Devonport, or Southampton, or wherever I land to say that I have arrived in England. When you get that wire, I want you to wire to Gib (& Ivor if he won't be there before me) telling him that I expect to be home in about two days so that he can apply for leave to come home, if only for a day or two. Then I will wire again from Paddington to say what time I shall be in High St Station. There will not be any misunderstanding at all, and you needn't listen to any rumours that we are coming, that will cause you to go back and fore to the stations to meet us. I will let you know everything so don't listen to any tales about the village there. I don't think I can do anything plainer than that.

I told our post-orderly at the unit (No 7 P of W) to send any letters that might come for me, home, so perhaps you have already received one or two of them. Parcels, I told him to give to a pal of mine that I left behind there, so if you sent anything, you needn't worry, although I shall not get them, my mate will, so it will be alright.

I have no more to tell you this time so I close with Love to all, hoping to be with you very soon.

Yours,

Dick

There is also a postscript scribbled by Richard's signature: 'I have just heard that my draft is sailing Thursday night, Dick.' If so, then he departed Egypt on 16 January. He wrote a postcard home on a postcard of the American Red Cross in Italy on 1 February, although it is postmarked six days later.

RE1919-02-01 Postcard

Dear Mother,

      Am on the way home. At present I am travelling up by rail through Italy. We are already feeling the cold, after being in Egypt for so long, but it will take more than cold weather to kill one on the way home. As far as I can understand I & D. R. Thomas should be home about Feb 15th. We are together on the same train.

      Yours, Dick

Thus the family's collection of material generated by the servicemen-brothers comes to a close. However, that is not the end of the story of the First World War's impact upon the family, and the wider community.

Notes

1. 'Fforestfach', *HoW*, 5 April 1919, 5.
2. See Appendix 2. 'Bill Hayden' was also mentioned in the very first letter in the collection: see ch. 2.
3. Whether this could be the second part of the letter from Ivor to Gabriel, IE1918-12-17, has been considered. However, this is unlikely as the size of the paper is different, and the first surviving page of this letter is numbered '3', whereas the first three pages of the latter letter are extant.
4. Paddy's rise: a demotion.
5. Go nap: to risk everything on one attempt.
6. A diary entry of 14 August 1917 notes that Richard received a letter from Dai; he wrote back three days later. He also wrote to Dai on 3 December 1917.
7. See Appendix 3.
8. See Appendix 2.
9. This is most probably Thomas Grongar Stephens, brother of Ivor's friend Elfryn. See ch. 6 and appendix 3.

14

Aftermath

At some point in early 1919, all three brothers were back home in Mynyddbach and the family was reunited. One consequence of this is that the family collection dries up: clearly there was no need for correspondence to pass on news, and there is no further information in this family archive on the activities of Richard nor Gabriel. Thus the evidence that is used in this chapter is sometimes sketchy, with dependence upon family memory.

Mary Eustis, the mother, died in 1927 aged sixty-one. John Eustis, the father, died in 1947 aged eighty-three. Both are buried in the graveyard of Mynyddbach chapel.

14.1: Richard's daughter Betty Jenkins and her daughter Rhian; Richard Eustis; John Eustis (photograph dating from approximately early 1945)

14.2: Family photograph from August 1964, taken at Mynyddbach chapel on the wedding day of Grace's daughter Pamela. In the photograph are Daniel Eustis and his wife Rose; Hannah; Lottie; Mary Lizzie and Richard; Elizabeth Ann; Gabriel and Theodosia

Richard married Mary Lizzie Morgan early in 1919. It appears that he stuck to his resolution not to return to work underground. When his cousin Uriel Rees opened a shop locally, Richard went to work for him as a delivery driver. Uriel made quite a success of the business, acquiring a larger shop in Morriston. Richard and Mary Lizzie had two children; he died in 1975.

Gabriel married Theodosia Jones in 1924. He took on a variety of jobs and spent many years as a local agent for Pearl Assurance. In the latter part of the war Theodosia had worked in the munitions factory at Pembrey as a secretary, but she later trained as a midwife, and is well remembered to this day by the older generation in the Treboeth area, many of whom were brought into the world by her. Gabriel and Theodosia had three children; he died in 1970 and is buried in Mynyddbach.

14.3: Gabriel and Theodosia Eustis on their wedding day: in the photograph are Elizabeth Ann; Ivor Humphreys (best man); Gabriel and Theodosia; Joseph Jones (father of the bride); May (Theosodia's cousin) and the Rev. James Davies

There is, however, in the collection a fair amount of information related to Ivor, although there are still some gaps. It is not known exactly when he was demobbed, but it seems that he had a temporary position at a local school for some months in 1919. In the autumn he took up a place at Bristol University. He wrote a letter from his digs in Clifton to his little brother on 18 December 1919:

Dear Dan,

I received your letter last week but I did not have time to answer it till now. It was a very good letter, Dan, I did not know you could write so well.

Our holidays will start next Saturday, and I shall be coming home Friday night. I will be coming by train because it is too far to walk, and I have not enough money to buy an aeroplane yet. Ask Lottie for a map of England, and try to find Bristol on it.

How are you getting on with your sums? I expect you have finished all the sums in the book I gave you.

How fat is the clecwydd [*gander*]? I was reading the newspaper yesterday, and it said that the clecwydd could not go down to Granny now, because it was too fat to go through the gate.

from Ivor

Ivor celebrated his twenty-third birthday on 4 March 1920. Two of the cards he received from friends are in the collection.

Then, in May 1920, the fragment of shrapnel moved. He underwent a procedure in Bristol hospital to try to remove it from his temple but he died on the operating table on Sunday, 16 May. His brother Gabriel had to travel to Bristol to recover the body and take it back to Mynyddbach.

Among the letters in the collection is one to Hannah from Ellen Cranfield, Ivor's sweetheart, written the day after Ivor's death. Inconsolable in her grief, she wrote a few lines, ending 'no one knows or understands how much he meant to me. Can't write anymore.' – the 't' at the end of 'meant' has been superimposed over an 's'. Those familiar with the wealth of the Welsh poetic tradition may be reminded of the seventh-century lament, 'Ystafell Cynddylan' (reputed to be the oldest recorded literary work by a woman in northern Europe): 'I shall weep awhile; then I shall fall silent.'[1]

Another letter of condolence, written in impeccable Welsh with a great depth of feeling by T. James from the South Wales Training College, Carmarthen, has the ink smudged, where tears have fallen.

The funeral was reported in a local newspaper under the headline 'Heroic Student | Mynyddbach Sergeant dies of wounds.'

> Poignant scenes were witnessed at the funeral at Mynyddbach on Thursday of the late Mr Thomas Ivor Eustis, a young student at Bristol University, who died earlier in the week following an operation at a Bristol Hospital for the removal of shrapnel from the temple.

The report continues, calling Ivor 'One of the best known boys in the Mynyddbach and Morriston districts' and although it muddles some of the details of his military service, it states that he was awarded the Military Medal for 'making an heroic attempt to save one of his officers'.

> All who had come into contact with Eustis knew him as a boy of lovable disposition, ready at all times to help in a good cause, possessed with ability both in the realms of sport and a scholar, and withal modest almost to a fault.
>
> At Bristol he was very popular, and the grief of his colleagues there was shown by the presence of a number of them at the funeral, six acting as bearers.
>
> The Rev. James Davies, Mynyddbach officiated at the last obsequies, a feature being the remarkable attendance, the cortege reaching the whole length of the road from the deceased's parents' home to the cemetery … There was a large number of wreaths, including beautiful tributes from the students of Bristol University and the staff of Llangyfelach Council Schools.[2]

A further obituary can be found in the Bristol students' magazine, *Nonesuch*:

> We deeply regret to record the death on May 16th of Thomas Ivor Eustice. Like so many others he took up his work here

after going through the vicarious experience of warfare; his loss now is, therefore, the greater. We in Bristol University can ill afford the passing away of so versatile a student.[3]

Another letter in the collection, quite breathtaking in its heartlessness and pomposity, was written to 'Relatives of the late Thomas Ivor Eustis' by J. Victor Evans, executive officer of Swansea Borough's Local Food Control Committee. On 2 June (six days after the funeral) he demanded the return of Ivor's ration card. 'Please note that unless same is returned to me immediately proceedings will be taken against the responsible person for unlawfully retaining the card after the death of the rightful holder thereof.'

Ivor's death was recognised by the authorities as being war related, and thus his grave was furnished with a headstone supplied by the Imperial War Graves Commission.[4] This gives his rank as 'Serjeant'.

Ivor's name is among the 2,274 dead of the First World War commemorated on the Swansea Cenotaph. His name is not however in the Welsh National Book of Remembrance, kept at the Temple of Peace in Cardiff, which lists 35,000 servicemen with Welsh connections who died in the war. Another omission, not easy to explain, is that Ivor's name is not included on the war memorial at Gowerton School which commemorates thirty-five old boys who fell. Nor is Ivor's name on the memorial to those from Bristol University who were killed in the war.

As noted in chapter 1, there are two Rolls of Honour at Mynyddbach chapel. On the longer list, created in June 1921, the names of the three who died – Thomas J. Cole, Edgar Williams and Ivor – are surrounded by a black box. There is also a more ornate marble memorial in the chapel to these three who died.

There is one more item in the family collection, which dates from four years after Ivor's death. This is an invitation to Mr and Mrs Eustis to be present at the unveiling of the Treboeth War Memorial. The memorial, located outside Treboeth Public Hall, is in the form of a Celtic cross. Twenty names were listed on a bronze plaque, which was duly unveiled on 2 August 1924.[5]

The programme for the ceremony shows that it was primarily religious in tone. There were speeches by a brigadier-general and a local dignitary, three hymns (one in English and two in Welsh) and contributions from the vicar of Swansea and four local ministers (including the Rev. James Davies who gave the closing benediction). Both 'Hen Wlad fy Nhadau' (the Welsh national anthem) and 'God save the King' were sung.

The programme contains a poem written by Enoch Richards from Clydach (under the bardic name 'Ap Perllannog'). This shows that many of the aspects of 'the language of 1914', such as references to sacrifice, courage and freedom, could still be current ten years later.

> Dreboeth! fro ferth, am aberth ei meibion,
> Yn llif rhed hiraeth yr holl frodorion;
> Drwy wae, O Walia! gwaed dy wrolion,
> Yn donnau roddwyd i'n cadw'n rhyddion.
> Maen milwyr – arwyr yw hwn, – saif ei sail
> Yma'n Gofadail am hen gyfoedion

> [*O Treboeth, the pleasant neighbourhood, for the sacrifice*
>   *of its sons*
> *Longing flows through all its inhabitants*
> *Through adversity, O Wales, the blood of your brave ones*
> *Was given in waves to keep us free*
> *This stone is the stone of soldiers – heroes – its foundation*
>   *stands here*
> *As a memorial to former contemporaries*]

Ivor's name was memorialised also within the family. When Richard and Mary Lizzie had a son in 1923, he was named Thomas Ivor Eustis, but was known as Ivor. In the Second World War he was conscripted into the army and hated it, but at the war's end was posted to Germany where he met a woman who became his wife.

Both of Gabriel's sons were called up: John served in the Royal Air Force and Rowland was conscripted into the Army. Also, the youngest of the Eustis brothers, Daniel, had his twenty-eighth birthday on 3 September 1939, and so another one of 'bechgyn John ni' was called upon to do his bit. He served with the RAF, but as he had a perforated eardrum he was unable to fly and so served as ground crew.

There is only sketchy evidence to say very much more about how the Eustis family regarded the Great War as it receded into the past. For some branches of the family the memory faded, so that the details

14.4: Ivor Eustis in his sergeant's uniform

of the brothers' involvement was forgotten. For others, elements of the story remained vivid. The two sisters, Bess Ann and Lottie, who lived in the family home in Pengwern Road after the parents' death, kept the letters and also a large photograph of Ivor in uniform. Gabriel did not pass on many of the details of his war service to his children, but the story of how he had to travel to Bristol to collect his younger brother's body was a painful memory that he shared with them, so that ninety-seven years later his daughter can recount the details.

Notes

1. Aled Llion Jones, *Darogan: Prophecy, lament and absent heroes in medieval Welsh literature* (Cardiff: University of Wales Press, 2013), p. 93.
2. *HoW*, 29 May 1920, 5.
3. 'In Memoriam', *Nonesuch*, June 1920, 75.
4. Since 1960 the organisation has been known as the Commonwealth War Graves Commission.
5. The plaque was stolen in 2012 and has been replaced by a marble tablet with the same text as the original.

15

Patterns and perspectives

A much quoted dictum by Linda Colley is that 'Identities are not like hats. Human beings can and do put on several at a time.'[1] Extending this analogy, one could say that the Eustis brothers carried with them an assortment of hats as they served, in addition to the regimental cap, rating cap or helmet which they were issued as military personnel. The brothers went into the armed forces with a set of loyalties (familial, community and national) and beliefs about who they were and where they fitted in. To people they knew they could variously be sons, brothers, relations, workmates, classmates, teammates, fellow chapel-goers, fellow townspeople or fellow countrymen. There were three who, by the end of the war, saw one of the brothers as a sweetheart and potential spouse.

Most of the evidence that has come down to us in the collection of letters is concerned with Richard, Gabriel and Ivor as close family members – sons or brothers. It is within this familial framework that the conversations revealed in these letters took place, and yet the content is so rich that it allows us to examine a range of different issues related to the way the brothers saw themselves. The first part of this chapter explores the collection as a whole through different lenses, in order to gauge which elements of the brothers' identities are revealed in the letters, and to see what conclusions can be reached about what elements of their 'civilian' selves persisted even though they donned a military uniform.

The aim of the military training undergone by infantrymen such as Ivor was to break down their individuality and mould them anew as units in the military structure. The training regimes that had developed in the nineteenth century were 'rigorous and intentionally disruptive' and designed to 'create soldiers that were replaceable and interchangeable'.[2] Private soldiers were there to receive and obey orders without question: the NCO (whether a lance-corporal, a corporal or a sergeant) was there to obey orders from above and relay them to those below. Given their more specialised roles, the training of Richard and Gabriel perhaps allowed a little more room for individual action and decision-making but still, in the broader scheme of things, they were but small cogs in an enormous military machine.

The Eustis brothers did indeed make efficient and valuable servicemen. Richard gave precious medical assistance to those who needed it on the field of battle, and fulfilled his role conscientiously in the field hospitals. Gabriel was clearly effective enough in his job to deserve his promotion to leading telegraphist. In addition to the evidence that Ivor was an effective trainer and a valuable NCO, his Military Medal can speak for itself as proof of his courage and contribution. Yet the three of them never abandoned their civilian identities, despite their years of training and service. The letters, as a corpus, show how the connections with the family back in Mynyddbach were so strong, so lively, so intrinsic to their being, that the physical distance between them was bridged, and any attempts to wipe away their 'civilian' perspectives were doomed. The family conversations revealed in these letters kept the brothers anchored in the world they knew before they donned uniform. They kept up the channels of communication with the whole family, knowing that the letters sent to one family member would be read by another: as Gabriel put it in a letter to his mother 'I thought it was all the same whether I wrote to you or Aunty Charlotte.'[3] The connections with home were nourished and sustained. One strategy of communication which could perhaps begin to fill the physical gap left in the home by the absence of the brothers was to arrange a visit to Pengwern Road by a comrade on home leave.[4] Similarly, Richard sought to foster a connection between his sister Hannah and Nellie, the sister of his comrade George Morris Williams.[5]

Politics, class and *y werin*
On the face of it, there is almost nothing that is explicitly political in these letters. There is one joking reference to Lloyd George coming to Pengwern Road for tea, but otherwise we can take Ivor's bestowing of his vote to his father with the declaration 'I am no politician' as being representative of the lack of party political engagement displayed in the letters.[6]

Scratching beneath the surface there are hints of some attitudes on political matters. Gabriel's comment on the fact that the firemen have gone on strike in his father's colliery is 'it's a pity they have nothing better to do'.[7] Richard's comment on the 'combing out' of the mines (a vigorously contested move to conscript young colliers) is so nonchalant that it implies he had no objections to this intrusion of the power of the state into his former co-workers' lives.[8] Do these statements display such a lack of working-class solidarity that it makes it problematic to characterise the brothers as 'working class' at all?

One question which arises is why did Ivor not put himself forward for a commission? This pathway was open to him. Early on in the war the *Gowertonian* magazine celebrated the fact that several old boys had received promotions: assuming that the correct Gabriel Williams has been identified in the records, he ended the war as a second lieutenant. However, there is no evidence that Ivor sought promotion beyond the rank of sergeant. Despite his talent and intellect, was there a sense of inferiority that came from his working-class background? Referring to Captain Searl, his commanding officer in France, Ivor called him 'a great friend of mine, as far as the huge difference in rank permitted'.[9] Is it the case that Ivor could not envisage bridging that 'huge difference' to become an officer himself, and so he was better off staying with his own sort amongst the other ranks?

There is however a possibility that using the lens of the British class system to analyse the identity of the Eustis brothers is not helpful. For those brought up in Victorian Wales, there was an alternative to seeing themselves as 'working class' or 'middle class', and that was to subscribe to the idea of *y werin*: the notion that Wales was a classless, or one-class, society. The principal promulgator of this vision (or myth) was Owen M. Edwards, a tireless educationalist and journal editor who has been described as 'perhaps the most powerful single personal influence upon the generation up to 1914'.[10] The word *gwerin* translates as 'folk' or 'common people', but in Edwards's conception, fuelled by a selective reading of Welsh history, the *gwerin* were the mass of the population linked by birth and circumstance to a traditional Welsh-speaking culture that embodied qualities such as a love for singing, poetry, Liberalism, Nonconformity and a Welsh patriotism that accepted its place within the Imperial British framework. One aspect that was central to this vision was the passion showed by ordinary Welsh people for education (and which is remarked upon even by those who prefer a hard class-based analysis to the woolliness of the *gwerin*).[11] The Eustis family collection provides ample evidence that this was the case in this household. The family as a whole clearly had a passion for education. Ivor, the most academically talented of the three, made plain his delight at his sister Lottie's decision to try for the scholarship at Gowerton, his old school. All three brothers enthusiastically congratulated her on her success. They knew that education provided a pathway to rewarding employment: after all, their beloved Aunt Charlotte was a teacher.

Attitudes to religion

One element of their civilian identity that was challenged by their experiences during the war was their Welsh Nonconformist faith. The community in which the Eustis brothers grew up was greatly concerned about religion, and Christian ideas and ideals permeated through many different aspects of their lives. All the evidence suggests that the older members of the family took their faith seriously, and that attending the services at Mynyddbach congregational chapel was not a mere weekly ritual but an integral part of their identity.

Leaving such an environment for the very different mores of a military training camp must surely have come as a culture shock. However in the sole surviving letter written by Gabriel in 1914 there is a reference to going to see an evangelist preacher, and Ivor's letters contain various references to chapel activities at Kinmel Park. One has to bear in mind that the 'audience' for these letters was in most cases the staunchly chapel-going mother or aunt, and so some of the references to attending services may have been included to please them, but still there is no evidence here of a turning away from the religious practices of their youth.

Similarly, one needs to read with caution the references the brothers make to temperance and avoiding alcohol. In his first letter to his mother from France, Ivor made disparaging comments about one of his comrades who was a 'boozer'.[12] Writing to Aunt Charlotte shortly afterwards, Gabriel declared he was glad that Ivor was 'sticking to his blue ribbon' – the mark of an abstainer – and went on to decry the influence of alcohol upon those involved in the war.[13] The only source we have to judge whether the brothers' private practices kept to these public pronouncements comes in Richard's diaries. These show that at various times Richard drank heavily – sometimes beer, sometimes whisky – but that he was aware that it was not good for him and at various junctures he tried to stop. Thus on 8 October 1917 he wrote 'There is beer in the camp pretty often, but I don't touch it.'

Having been steeped in this religious atmosphere (and remember that being a miner at Mynydd Newydd, he would have also encountered the prayer meetings before starting work on Mondays), there is evidence that Richard had adopted more of a sceptical attitude. As his unit approached Jerusalem, he confided to Ivor that he was '[n]ot ... interested in the Biblical side of it'; he also told his mother that he was less interested in Sunday school matters than his sisters.[14] On the other hand, in his diary evidence can be found that he had not totally turned his back upon the religious tradition of his upbringing. In the early months of 1916 the diary entries for many Sundays note that he attended the Welsh Nonconformist service. He went to hear the Rev. Hughes, a chaplain attached to the RWF, on 14 May 1916 (describing the service as 'fine') and six days later had a conversation with him in his tent (calling him a 'very good sort'). In 1917 he sought out the Rev. Abraham Rees Morgan, whom he knew from Treboeth. Even though he saw for himself that Jerusalem did not live up to expectations, being 'as dirty as any other town or village out in these parts' Richard knew that a Bible from the city would greatly please his aunt, and so he sent her one.[15]

Family matters: health, food and money

Martha Hanna has noted that when men in uniform engaged in a conversation about domestic matters, 'they simultaneously affirmed their civilian identity, as fathers, husbands, and sons, and engaged their parents, wives, and children in domestic conversations that helped efface the distance that separated them'.[16] Thus even the most mundane discussions in the letters regarding ailments, food or money served the purpose of bridging the physical gap that existed between the brothers and Mynyddbach – and the letters contain plenty of references to all three subjects.

At various points in the collection there are worries about the health of most of the family members: ailments which afflicted the brothers' grandmothers, father and sisters are all mentioned. It is

clear from the letters that the family considered the health of some
of the siblings to be robust, and others to be susceptible to illness.
Richard and Gabriel were in the former category, together with
Lottie. When Ivor wrote home with an enquiry about the health of
Grace, Daniel and Bess Anne, he wrote that he need not ask after
Lottie for she would 'be all right no matter what would happen'.[17]
However, Ivor was one of those considered to be vulnerable to ill-
ness – and perhaps he fretted about his health more than his elder
brothers, so his letters contain much more detail about his ailments.

Food is a constant topic of discussion. One gets the impression
that the letters from mother Mary and Aunt Charlotte must have
regularly contained enquiries about the brothers' diets, as such a
high proportion of their letters home discuss the issue. As might
be expected, the general tone of the brothers' replies is that there is
nothing to worry about as they are getting enough to eat – even if
one suspects that was not always the truth. There was also a dependence upon the family to supply food for the brothers, either as a
treat to break the monotony of camp food (as in Ivor's request for
gooseberry tart) or to make up for real deficiencies in the diet. The
latter was certainly the case for the men of the EEF for long periods
of their service, where their supplies were quite inadequate and real
hunger was only staved off by obtaining extras. The fact that the
food parcels that were received were shared out with their peers
also assisted in strengthening the bonds of comradeship. As Roper
puts it, the food in these parcels 'was not only appreciated for the
personal comfort it provided, but because it could be offered to
others'.[18]

It can also be argued that the donations of gifts by the women-
folk back home made them feel that they were making a tangible
contribution to the men's well-being. The brothers were conscientious in acknowledging the receipt of the parcels and thanking the
sender for the contents. Looking at Richard's letters it is also clear
that he wrote to acknowledge parcels that were not received, in
order to stave off any potential disharmony at Mynyddbach.[19] The
brothers also expected any items they sent home to be acknowledged, as is seen in Richard's fretting over whether the Bible from
Jerusalem has been received by Aunt Charlotte.[20] When a family
member consistently failed to send a line of acknowledgement, it
caused hurt. Sam Eustis was clearly a favourite uncle, and although

the brothers were aware that he was 'not fond of writing', the failure of anyone else back home to send a word of thanks on his behalf was disappointing.[21]

It is clear that the financial situation of the family was often precarious. Without the safety net of a welfare state, a period out of work for the father, John Eustis, meant a real struggle. Even having Gabriel home on leave for a period of five weeks meant that 'the exchequer ran very low'.[22] Thus all three brothers sent money home, both intermittently according to need and by regular arrangement. When the father was out of work due to a wrist injury, Ivor sent as much as he could spare 'to keep things going'.[23] He also emphasised (written large and underlined) 'I'll pay the postage' in the letter requesting gooseberry tart.[24] The money that Richard sent home was however not just to plug a gap in the family's current financial situation but also part of his planning for the future. In August 1918, being vexed by his separation from Mary Lizzie and clearly dreaming of matrimony, he told his mother that he was relying on her 'to put some of that money by for me, to give me a start'.[25]

In the two surviving letters from one serviceman brother to another, there are frank discussions about money matters.[26] In Ivor's letter to Gabriel written a month after the Armistice in a mood of utter disillusionment with the army, one gripe examined in detail is the financial implication of his de facto demotion.[27]

Dreaming, making plans and expectations for the future

The word 'dream' only appears in the collection of letters in one written by Ivor from Kinmel Park in which he is going 'to the same old bed, to dream the same old dreams'.[28] However, the word does appear more regularly in the most personal items to which we have access: Richard's diaries for 1916 and 1917. For example, on 13 August 1917 he recorded that he had had 'a vivid dream of home'. Sometimes his dreams spurred him to action: on 5 February 1916, the day after dreaming of Cambridge, he wrote a letter to his landlady there.

As they fought, the brothers were imagining the future and making plans for it. In February 1917 Richard Eustis and three of his comrades pledged to meet up in a London pub exactly two years later. One of them was dead two months after the promise was made; Richard would have just arrived back in Britain, but there is no evidence as to whether he kept the tryst. Richard's letters also show that he imagined his return home on many occasions during his long service in Egypt and Palestine. When he was still over six months away from leaving the East, he envisaged himself returning home without any fuss via the back roads.[29]

One pivotal concern that would always be in the background, even when it was not voiced openly, was how long would the war continue. In a letter written towards the end of the war, Gabriel states that when he joined the navy, he expected that the war would be over within eight months.[30] This optimism was shared, even if it was misplaced. In a letter of January 1915, Richard could write to Ivor 'let's hope that it will soon be over' and in August 1917 he wrote to Aunt Charlotte 'I'm hoping that the war will soon be over now'.[31] Later on, in May 1918, his optimism turned out to be accurate when he replied to his mother, who feared that the war would not be over until 1919, that he was confident it would be concluded in 1918.[32]

The brothers' experiences in the war clearly gave them food for thought as they considered their futures. Richard had been a collier before the war: having seen the wonders of Ancient Egypt and experienced some of the 'exotic' aspects of life in contemporary Egypt and Palestine, he had cause to reconsider his options for his future after returning home. He wrote from Palestine in May 1918 that having come to enjoy 'life on the surface', he was unlikely to return to work underground.[33] Ivor reported at the end of the war that Gabriel also would be looking for a job more challenging than his pre-war employment at the tinplate works.[34] Ivor himself had begun to consider his options even before he had experienced the front. In early 1917 he declared that he did not know what he was going to do after the war: 'I shall certainly have to begin all over again'.[35] As he convalesced in Ireland after the Armistice his disillusionment shines through, as he considered turning his back upon the clear pathway to academic success that had always been his ambition.[36]

One aspect that appears to have been prominent in their thoughts as they imagined the future was the dream of finding a wife and settling down. Here one is obliged to follow circumstantial evidence for almost nothing has survived of the brothers' communications with their sweethearts during the war years. The two postcards that have survived which Richard sent to Mary Lizzie from Egypt are rather bland – although perhaps that should come as no surprise for as he was sending her a letter or postcard most weeks, often there would not be much new to say. Gabriel's letters to Theodosia have been destroyed and all we have to show of Ivor's courtship with Ellen Cranfield is her distraught letter on hearing of his death.

However, it is beyond any doubt that there were hopes and expectations of marriage as the brothers' correspondence with their girlfriends blossomed. Was it perhaps some kind of hint when Mary Lizzie sent Richard a piece of her cousin's wedding cake in 1917?[37] Matrimony is very much in the air in the letters of 1918. Writing from Palestine in 1918 (having been away from home for almost three years), Richard wrote 'It seems to me that all the boys at home there are getting married one by one.'[38] He returned to this thought a few months later, as he imagined returning home to see so many old friends married, and noted 'They are all going one by one.'[39] In March 1918 he wrote to his mother how she was 'not likely to keep either Ivor, Gabe or myself long, after we come home again, for there are three already claiming us'.[40] The three sweethearts were also mentioned in his letter the same day to Hannah, in which he envisaged the three brothers returning to 'square up matters, and settle down once more to home life'.[41] The word 'home' appears five times in the former letter and six times in the latter. Yet there was a gnawing worry as Richard remained so far away from Mynyddbach and Morriston (Mary Lizzie's home) that circumstances might be changing without him knowing about it, and helpless to do anything. In this same letter to Hannah he noted 'I have not heard from Morriston for about a fortnight, what's wrong I don't know.'

Thus the available evidence points to the resilience of the brothers' civilian and familial identities. The letters were a bridge, connecting the men with home: their dreams and aspirations were clearly anchored in their home community. Their sojourn in uniform was always understood as a transient phase.

The second part of this concluding chapter attempts to analyse the collection of letters in terms of broader, more abstract concepts. To what extent do the brothers' ideas of masculinity make themselves known in these letters – what expectations were put upon them as young *men*? How did their national identity as Welshmen affect their responses to the situations that they faced, and to what extent was their Welshness superseded or trumped by feelings of Britishness?

The Eustis brothers fought *for* various ideas and structures as well as fighting *against* a variety of foes and evils. The physical, bodily 'enemy' was, variously, German or Turkish, a soldier, a sailor or an airman, but on a philosophical level there were also enemies: the elements of thought that made up 'militarism'. A non-exhaustive list of these elements (as they would have been understood by a Welsh person reading the newspapers of 1914) would include arrogance, authoritarianism, a tendency to use violence as the first resort, including violence against civilian targets, a hierarchy based upon martial attributes, intolerance and a lack of empathy for others. On the other hand, what we might call the 'language of 1914', as deployed to encourage young men to enlist, highlighted a range of virtues and ideals that provided a stark contrast to 'Prussian Militarism': *dyletswydd*/duty, *anrhydedd*/honour, *cyfiawnder*/justice and righteousness. Thus the volunteers of 1914 were not only fighting *against* militarism but *for* these virtues and ideals.[42]

The war of 1914 was also understood as a defensive war. The volunteers were defending their families and communities against the kind of violence that had struck families in German-occupied Belgium and northern France. They were also defending their culture against German aggression – and that was explicitly understood as defending the national culture, language and traditions of Wales, as well as defending British culture and institutions. The evidence for the Welsh dimension to the understanding of the conflict is explicit in the recruiting speeches of Welsh politicians, Nonconformist ministers and other community leaders, and in the work of the poets.[43]

This idea of a defensive war was also promulgated by local newspapers and dignitaries with its spotlight tightly focused upon the local level. When poets portrayed nightmare visions of how the Germans might come to lay waste Welsh homes and families, the implication was that those who volunteered to serve were defending their own homes and families from such a fate. These young men thus instantly became 'local heroes' (the title given to the column of photographs of dead or wounded servicemen in the *Cambria Daily Leader*). When the men returned home on leave to Treboeth/ Tirdeunaw/Mynyddbach they were the subject of veneration by the community in public ceremonies (organised both at the level of the local community and by the chapels). Their names were on display in Rolls of Honour in the chapels that were the cornerstone of public life in this community: Mynyddbach's contemporary Roll of Honour urged its members to pray for the men who had volunteered. These ideas persisted, so that when Treboeth's war memorial was unveiled ten years after the conflict began, a local poet could declare that the blood of the men 'yn donnau roddwyd i'n cadw'n rhyddion' [*was given in waves to keep us free*].

The home community also provided a very lively information network. Richard's diary notes a very wide range of correspondents, including a number of old acquaintances from home who were serving in the army or navy. As he served with a number of friends from his home patch, Richard, in particular, could also glean information from their correspondence with home. It seems as though almost wherever they went, the Eustis brothers would come across men they knew. It is possible that Gabriel may have had the chance to pick up news from home via Dai Harris, for they were sometimes stationed in the same port. It is also likely that there was a line of communication between Ivor and Richard via the Stephens brothers, with Elfryn Stephens based at Kinmel Park with the former and Grongar Stephens serving in Egypt/Palestine with the latter. All this would serve to re-inforce the brothers' links with their home community and to strengthen the notion that the servicemen and their loved ones were at one, fighting the enemy together.

The enemy

The brothers faced a variety of different enemy personnel in their war service. The majority of enemy troops that Richard saw were Turks, though the Ottoman forces were reinforced by German units. He also faced danger from enemy aircraft, most of which would have been piloted by Germans. Gabriel's ship, and those that the *Saxon* protected, were principally menaced by German U-boats. On the Western Front, Ivor was under fire from German infantry and artillery. Did this lead to the brothers hating their enemies, or showing contempt for them?

In the case of Richard, there are signs that, like so many British soldiers in the eastern theatre, he regarded the Turkish soldiers with a degree of condescension, as inferior to the British troops.[44] When he writes to Ivor that they have given 'Johnny Turk the damnest

hiding he ever had in his life' that is both a statement of the super-
iority of the attackers of the 53rd (Welsh) Division and the weakness
of the defending Turks.[45] When he came into close contact with
defeated Turkish soldiers in the prisoner-of-war hospital, he was
dismissive towards them in his letters home, with a highly ironic
reference to them as 'bright clean specimens', whose smell could be
detected half a mile away.[46] Further indications of statements deni-
grating the Turks come in Dai Harris's letter to Richard, in which
Dai echoes some comments that were written in Richard's letters
about Turks being 'lousy' and worthless.

For Gabriel, there are only a few references to the Germans he
was fighting against. In his letter to little brother Daniel he described
the job he and the two brothers was doing as 'wado'r hen Germans'
(*smacking the old Germans*).[47] Referring to the food shortages that
both he and the family at home were suffering he states that 'the
Germans are a sight worse off than us'.[48] In one of Ivor's first letters
home from Kinmel Park, to a sister, the issue is dealt with jocularly:
'I'm sorry for the Germans I'll meet out across the water.'[49] There
is a much darker humour in his letter home at the end of the war in
which he imagines visiting indignities upon the Kaiser, but here he
says that he bears no malice towards the Germans per se: 'they never
managed to hurt me'.[50] Indeed, in terms of characterising a nation
in a negative fashion, Ivor's comments about the short-changers he
had encountered shortly after arriving in France show that he had
developed a prejudice against the French.[51]

For all three brothers, there were other enemies to be faced, such
as foul conditions, disease and climate. As in so many other aspects,
self-censorship is at work here, and it is clear that the brothers often
make light of their circumstances so as not to cause anxiety back
home. There are more details in Richard's diary for 1916 and 1917 of
his pains, sores, illnesses, thirst and dreadful living conditions than
there are in the letters he sent home. One can compare the bland
statement to his mother from that 'we have been so busy here for
the past few weeks' with the hardships he laconically details in his
diary from late December 1917.[52]

Language and Welsh identity

Although the brothers came from a Welsh-speaking family, most of
the letters were written in English: the exceptions to this rule tell us

something of the Welsh language's place in an unequal bilingual situation. Note that the letters of Dewi David (reproduced in David, *Tell Mum not to Worry*) and the Roberts brothers (reproduced in Roberts, *Witness these letters*) were almost entirely in English even though in both cases the family language was Welsh.[53] The Welsh words that are dropped into the English-language letters are often words that would predominantly be encountered in a family conversation. There are multiple references to food, such as Ivor's reference to 'crustyn' and 'paste goosberris', and Richard's reminiscences about 'Bara-lawr', 'Paste Gig' and 'Cawl Pen'. Mention is made of some minor ailments, such as Ivor's reference to a 'fellwm' (properly spelt 'ffelwm': whitlow) and 'cornwyd' (abscess). Others are familiar Welsh phrases, such as Richard's reference to 'ar lan y môr' or Ivor's to 'crynu yn ei 'scydie'. There are also some family terms, such as Richard's quoting of their Uncle Sam Eustis's phrase 'bechgyn John ni'.

One wonders whether it is significant that Ivor's only sentences written in Welsh in this collection come at the end of the final letter which he wrote before he embarked upon the campaign in which he was wounded. This letter contains, at its beginning, Ivor's clearest declaration of his belief and faith in Britain's cause, and closes with a sentence in Welsh declaring his love for everyone at home. Ivor was surely aware that this might prove to be the final letter his family received from him.

The two substantial pieces written in Welsh come in the letters written by Gabriel and Richard to their youngest brother, Daniel (b.1911). Bearing in mind what Richard says on a few occasions about the schooling he had, it seems fair to say that Daniel had not yet had English caned into him by Mr Higgs.[54] Yet, despite this smattering of Welsh, as a whole the corpus is utterly dominated by the English language.

The First World War did not create the linguistic conditions in Wales whereby one language had centrality and power and the other was marginalised. This situation had developed over centuries and the dominance of the English language in all official matters had become part of the accepted order, very rarely challenged. Welsh had space in the home and the chapel but in other spheres English dominated.

Nor did the First World War create the conditions whereby English became a language of communication for Eustis family members. As noted, letters from relatives in Canada were written in English from the 1890s onwards. The first letters in the collection, from England in 1914, were written in English when there was no question of compulsion by censors. This shows that English had an important place as a language of intra-family communication before the impact of a long and arduous war was felt. However, the separation of the brothers from the family meant that English became, for a time, the principal language for their communication.

Although two of the three brothers served with 'Welsh' units, the language of their military service was English. Richard served in a unit raised in the Swansea area with a large number of bilingual acquaintances, and there were some opportunities for him to use the language in religious services and in his performances with the choir. Yet as he did his duty in England, Gallipoli, Egypt and Palestine, it is clear that the Welsh language had a marginal place in his consciousness. His diaries for 1916 and 1917 are written entirely in English. Many of his new friends in the 1/3rd WFA were English speakers. When he notes that Captain Richards told him some long-anticipated news in Welsh, one can take it that on other occasions they spoke in English.[55] Similarly, Richard's diaries note that he wrote three letters to William Davies in Welsh, but we have no evidence to suggest that he wrote in his family language to any other correspondents, save his little brother Dan.[56]

Although he did have several periods of home leave in 1914–18, Gabriel's opportunities for speaking Welsh were more limited as he served on board a small ship: he makes no mention of Welshmen among the crew of the *Saxon*. Ivor spent the longest time in Wales during the war years, and during his time at the training camp the Welsh language did have its space: in particular, with regard to the provision of religious services. However, the language of instruction and duty in Kinmel Park was of course English.

Thus the three brothers were, for the first time in their lives, thrust into an environment that was remote to Wales and the expectations of Welsh culture. Of course, this could be positive, and even liberating, as in Richard's opportunities to visit the ancient colleges of Cambridge, the pyramids of Egypt and the sights of the Holy Land. It also gave Richard the freedom to get up to mischief in the bars of Cairo and Alexandria. The obverse of this is that being in a 'non-Welsh' environment for the first time in their lives, it gave the brothers occasion to consider what it was that gave them a Welsh identity. Ivor addresses this issue in the letter he wrote in September 1918, stationed in France but out of the trenches, as he reflects upon the qualities of Morris, the near-monoglot Welshman who floundered in the alien environment of the army. He was 'not much of an Englishman, though he was a decent little Welshman'.[57] Ivor clearly knew that he himself was 'Welsh' rather than 'Welch', and regarded with bemusement the archaic spelling used in the RWF's barracks at Wrexham.[58] Richard found that the stereotype of the Welsh as a musical nation meant that he had the opportunity to perform in his unit's choir at a variety of events. Another stereotype, of the Welsh as a rugby-playing nation, was also apt in his case: one could ponder to what Richard's unit's matches against English, Australian or New Zealand units were understood as 'international' contests, with the 1/3rd WFA representing Wales?

It is possible, however, that their war experiences had little long-term impact upon the surviving brothers' use of language. A nephew states that Richard and Gabriel always spoke Welsh together (this would be in the years after the Second World War) and that Richard and Mary Lizzie always spoke Welsh to one another. Gabriel's daughter confirms that the language of their home was emphatically Welsh. Thus the fact that their communication was in the English language for four years and more did not permanently change their family language.

British patriotism

Only occasionally do we see explicit statements of British patriotism in the letters. In the entire collection of Richard's surviving writings there is no explicit 'flag-waving' for Britain, England nor Wales. He does show pride in his division, the 53rd, but he does not stress that they are a Welsh unit. Richard's extant letters do not in fact name 'Wales' at all. There are seven references to 'England', including twice when he writes of his hope of 'leave to England'.

Gabriel's letters contain one phrase that smacks of British stoicism and fortitude. Within the context of pondering when and how the war will come to an end, Gabriel shows his faith that Britain's victory is inevitable: 'What does it matter anyhow as long as we win the war & that we will do, if it takes us ever so long.'[59] In another letter he tempers his report that he is avoiding some work with the statement 'Not that I'm doing nothing for "Uncle George" or the old country': this jocular reference to the king is the only reference to him in the collection.[60]

There are two more explicit declarations of patriotic British pride in Ivor's letters. Writing to his sister Lottie (and urging her to try her best in the forthcoming exams) he declared 'Now I want you to remember that Britain is fighting against her enemies for fair play to little nations such as Belgium who did her duty in trying to drive the enemy back.'[61] Then in Ivor's final letter from the trenches which, as previously noted, bears the shadow of the possibility of his death in action, he states he is 'ready for a bit more good work for our dear old country', and writes 'the more I look around me the more consolation I find in the knowledge that what we are about to endure is for the sake of our country – "Blighty" as we call it'.[62]

However, the use of the word 'Blighty' in this affirmation of Ivor's willingness to sacrifice himself for his family's country does highlight the ambiguity over the question of which country he had in mind. Ivor was a subject of the United Kingdom of Great Britain and Ireland, but nowhere in his letters do the terms 'UK' or 'United Kingdom' appear, nor are they to be found in the other two brothers' letters.

This word, 'Blighty' appears eight times in the collection, with the first appearance being in Richard's letter to Ivor: 'I am glad to hear that all's well with you & that you are still in that land called Blighty.'[63] He used the word again after the end of the war when he had heard that Ivor's wound had led to his return to Britain. Gabriel used the word twice in 1918, both times in relation to hoping that Ivor would be in Blighty rather than France. Ivor used the word twice in his letters from France, first referring to 'this mysterious illness in Blighty' and then in the sentence quoted above. Then, the postcard he sent home on the day of his arrival in an English hospital was addressed simply 'Blighty'. The following day his letter recalled the gramophone in Étaples playing the highly sentimental song 'There's a ship that's bound for Blighty.'[64]

In contrast the word 'Britain' only appears twice, both times in the letter from Ivor to Lottie (quoted above) in which he urges her to do her duty. This letter has the collection's most explicit consideration of 'duty', as Ivor exhorts Lottie to do her best in the scholarship exam, as her 'duty to Britain and to Mother and Father', just as her big brothers are doing *their* duty on the fighting fronts, and just as Belgium did its duty in resisting the enemy.

So what is this 'Blighty' that the brothers referred to, dreamed about and fought for? Gerard DeGroot declares that 'Blighty was a place, an idea and a set of warm-heated, cozy emotions'.[65] The notion of 'Blighty' bypasses any considerations of who is in power at Westminster or any divisions that might exist in terms of class or status; it does not evoke any thoughts of king or empire, but rather conjures up images of 'home', wherever that might be. It was a bespoke concept that varied according to the social class and the geographical provenance of the individual. It was also a convenient fudge for the avoidance of stating exactly which country the British soldiers were fighting for. That is, the Welshman, the Scotsman and the Englishman could agree that they were defending 'Blighty' without having to specify what they were seeking to safeguard.

Masculinity

The concept of gender has invigorated much historical writing over the past few decades, as researchers have incorporated the idea that ideas such as 'masculinity' and 'femininity' are not fixed nor determined by biological differences, but are constructs that can and do shift with time and circumstance.[66] As John Tosh and Michael Roper put it, 'masculinity (like femininity) is a *relational* construct, incomprehensible apart from the totality of gender relations'.[67]

Tosh, Roper and others have analysed the ideas about 'imperial manliness' that were predominant amongst the boys and young men of middle-class Edwardian England, which stressed stoic endurance, physical and mental toughness and self-control.[68] It is argued that by the time of the First World War these ideas had seeped down to the lower middle classes and sections of the working class.[69] Studies within a Welsh context confirm that many of these concepts of manliness crossed the linguistic and cultural barriers to become accepted by young Welsh men.[70] It was from the external qualities that a man's internal character was judged, and so it was important to be seen to be have the appropriate manly qualities.[71]

Thus there were expectations put upon Richard, Gabriel and Ivor Eustis as men – and, of course, this was particularly so in the febrile atmosphere engendered by the crises of the war. The use of language heightened the pressure upon young men to 'do their bit':

the 'language of 1914' emphasised words such as 'duty', 'honour' and 'sacrifice'. This was as true in Swansea's bilingual periphery as it was in any metropolitan core.[72] Rivalry between nations, regions, towns, localities and villages fuelled the recruitment drive, as no self-respecting man wanted to belong to a place that could be scorned as disloyal. Rivalry between institutions was also a driver of volunteering, and again there are many examples from the Swansea district. For many weeks in the early months of the war, the *Cambria Daily Leader* printed lists of the volunteers from different workplaces, with the underlying message that those companies not represented with a long list were not loyal to king and country. The rivalry between the Church and the Nonconformist denominations facilitated recruitment drives within chapels that had formerly been wedded to a message of peace. Rugby clubs boasted about how many of their team had volunteered – and all the better in those cases such as Mansel RFC (for whom the brothers' cousin, Thomas Henry Matthews, played) where the club could brag that the entire first XV had joined the colours.

The first of the brothers to join up was the eldest, Richard, and in his case the fact that he was part of a peer group that was already attached to a territorial unit made it certain that he would be embodied and, along with every one of his comrades, agree to serve overseas. Gabriel volunteered three months after Britain's declaration of war: in the only letter to have survived from the early period, is there a hint of boasting in the fact that 'some very big chaps' have been rejected by the Royal Navy, while Gabriel has made the grade?[73]

There is a hint of paternalism in the two surviving letters sent by Richard to Ivor in 1914 and 1915 – he addresses his younger brother as 'Dear Kid'. Interestingly, this is the same term used by Ivor in his letter to his younger sister Hannah just after he had become a soldier. In this letter Ivor makes the point that Hannah now has 'three big brothers' fighting for her: he has graduated to the same level as his two elder brothers.[74]

One of the ideas that follows from the notion that gender is a relational concept is, in a nutshell, that a principal characteristic of being masculine is *not* being feminine, and conversely femininity is defined in large part by *not* being masculine. One aspect that can follow from this is that men who want to bolster their own image as masculine might point out the 'feminine' characteristics of other males. We have this exemplified in Ivor's letter to Hannah regarding Gabe Williams. Whereas in the letter written the same day to their mother, Ivor just notes that Williams has been to see him; in the letter to his sister he denigrates Williams's masculinity: 'he looks slightly diminutive when compared with myself ... sometimes you make a mistake and forget that you're talking to a man'.[75]

Ideas regarding gender roles are not fixed but contingent upon attitudes within society which can change according to circumstance. Given the challenging conditions of 1914–18, it is no surprise to find that researchers have identified a variety of changes in attitude, and despite the limited advances that women made in some areas, it is DeGroot's contention that 'War imposed masculine virtues upon society, thus reinvigorating notions of separate spheres.'[76] Certainly, whenever the issue of who should be serving in the armed forces comes up in the letters, together with the related questions of who should not be serving and who should be forced to join up, the brothers demonstrate firmly their idea that it is man's work, and men's duty. Ivor's first letter from France makes it crystal clear that he does not believe that sister Hannah should be volunteering to serve in uniform: it is her brothers' job to do that.[77] Some individual men that had not joined up are the subject of scathing comments, such as Richard's remarks about Harry Watkins and Dai Evans.[78] It is clear that the brothers regarded those men who were fit and healthy as shirking their duty if they avoided war service, especially (as evidenced in numerous letters of 1918) when youths were being conscripted. In a letter to sister Hannah, Gabriel referred to those who sought exemption as 'white-livered, chicken hearted, windy, white feathered, cold footed young cubs'.[79] Despite the light-hearted tone of the rest of this letter, this description can be taken at face value: the fact that Gabriel refers to these as 'young "<u>men</u>"' who should be grovelling for pardon strongly implies that he regards them as lacking in masculine virtues. After Richard voices pity for young Thomas Cole as he was sent to France, he broaches the subject of conscientious objectors, and although he refuses to express his opinion, the indications are that he was satisfied that they had been 'pinched' by the authorities.[80]

Those men whose bravery on the battlefield led to their being decorated are singled out for praise. There is a hint of boasting as

Richard tells Ivor that his unit has had two more Military Medals, and there is certainly local pride in the comments from late 1918 that three Mynyddbach men (including of course Ivor himself) have been thus honoured.[81]

Stoicism; dealing with death; fatalism and paying the price of war

Having been in the army for some eight months, Ivor had come to the conclusion that it was best to be content like his brother Richard, and not to trouble about events, 'for once you start looking for complaints and start grumbling at your luck, you'll never finish'.[82] A year later, he wrote in a similar vein: 'after a while you all come to laugh at your misfortunes, instead of worrying over them'.[83] The word 'grumble' appears five times in Richard's surviving letters, with him saying each time that he has nothing to complain about. Gabriel's letters home, also, are characterised by cheery optimism. The word 'glad' appears fifteen times in the sixteen surviving letters he wrote while attached to the *Saxon*.

Given that one of the reasons for writing home was to allay the anxiety felt by the loved ones at home, one common thread running through these letters is to play down the dangers they are facing. The words 'worry' or 'worrying' appear over thirty times in the letters, most often in phrases such as 'there is nothing to worry in the least about' or 'don't worry, you know that I am well able to look after myself wherever I go'.[84] These attempts to alleviate the anxiety back home lead to situations where one brother deflects concerns regarding his own circumstances by showing concern for another's situation. Thus Richard declared his hope 'that it will all be over before Ivor will have to go out to France', and later worried that Ivor's enthusiasm would lead him to 'push himself abroad'.[85] On the other hand, Ivor states his opinion that Richard and his comrades were having 'a rougher time of it' in Palestine that he was in France.[86]

This comparison of the conditions faced by servicemen in different theatres occurs on numerous occasions. Richard wrote from Egypt to Aunt Charlotte 'surely things are not half as bad with me here as they are in France'.[87] Regarding his cousin Uriel Rees he wrote 'I would much rather see him go to India or Italy than France'.[88] With perhaps a touch of envy, Richard declared that Gabriel was better off in the navy than he would be in the army.[89]

There are other levels of comparison within the letters. Gabriel compares his separation from his best friend Bunty with Richard's separation from Dai R. Thomas when their unit was broken up.[90]

When he had been stationed in Egypt for a year, Richard gave his thoughts on Ivor's situation in a letter home: 'Well, I hope he won't be too eager to go abroad. No doubt there is a great deal to be seen in foreign countries, but he will find that he would have to pay dearly for what he saw, the same as I've had to.'[91] Over the next two years and more, Richard continued to pay for the decision to go to war, in terms of his health and well-being, suffering a variety of minor ailments and one that hospitalised him for a week. He was persistently in a state of anxiety regarding his ignorance of what was going on at home, and his inability to act to rectify any situations that might arise there. Yet he was also clearly proud of what he was doing, and the role of his unit in giving Johnny Turk a hiding. The bond he formed with his comrades was strong – perhaps it is not going too far to say that he acquired some additional brothers. One of the most remarkable comments in the diaries is Richard's declaration after arriving back in the front line on the Egypt/Palestine frontier, having had a week's leave, that he is 'glad to be home'.[92] Perhaps in a similar vein is Ivor's suggestion when writing with dissatisfaction from Ireland, that in his time in the front line 'hungry, wet through and alive with vermin' he was happier than in his present situation.[93]

Richard, during his service in Gallipoli and Egypt/Palestine, was the brother who had to witness death most frequently. It is clear that he managed to compose himself and continue to do his duty – as he wrote following the slaughter of the First Battle of Gaza, 'Sight of blood & dead don't affect me at all'.[94] The stoical frame of mind could harden to become a fatalist attitude at a time of imminent danger. This coping mechanism is seen most clearly in Ivor's final letter before the attack that was to leave him wounded: 'I know it is really very sad, still what's got to be – got to be, as the boys put it, and we are powerless to alter it.'[95]

Loss
Many historians have noted the long-term impact on soldiers who were unable to settle down into the routine of their previous lives after experiencing total war. Even those who were not physically disfigured by the war could carry their mental scars.[96] The evidence

suggests that Richard and Gabriel managed to shake off most of the traces of the war. The war years proved to be pivotal points of change in their lives, leading to marriage and a change in careers, but it seems that they did not indulge in nostalgic reminiscing and they did not seek to pass stories about their war activities down through the generations. Can we accept this as an act of forgetting rather than a strategy of repression?

Yet there is one long-term impact of the war upon the family which trumped all the others, and remained a constant, painful, reminder of the tragedy of 1914–18. Ivor's death was perhaps all the more cruel and devastating to the family because it occurred eighteen months after the Armistice. Re-reading Richard's confident words of 23 December 1918 –

> We have been very fortunate as a family, considering that two of us have been in it since the very beginning, and then Ivor comes in to go through the thickest of the whole fighting. Yes, I heard that he was slightly wounded, but he was fortunate to get back to Blighty with it.

– one is reminded of Paul Fussell's dictum that 'every war is ironic … but the Great War was more ironic than any before or since'.[97]

Some historians have taken Fussell to task for his insistence upon the futility of the war, arguing that the First World War did achieve some positive results, though it is rarely argued that it was worth anything like the cost. Prior and Wilson, for example, point out that the war did 'halt the march of expansionist militarism'.[98] However much the newspapers of 1914 exaggerated the details, the atrocities committed by the German army in Belgium and France were real. The argument that this was indeed a defensive war for the British state is not bogus: it was not possible for a state that depended upon the power of the Royal Navy to countenance seeing the ports on the continental side of the Channel fall into hostile hands. Consequently one should not begin a study of the First World War with the preconception that it was entirely futile, nor should one end with a blanket statement that it was so. Just like beauty, futility is in the eye of the beholder.

Thus one who gazes at the territorial gains made by the British Empire in the post-war settlement might see some recompense for the million-plus dead of that empire: some kind of payback for their sacrifice. The United Kingdom (or at least, the 78 per cent of the territory that remained united after the secession of twenty-six Irish counties) could look at its place in the pecking order of the 'Great Powers' with pride in the after-glow of the Armistice. In the months thereafter Wales was proud of its part – the word 'victory' was used with abandon. One who profited from the wave of jubilation and relief was Lloyd George, who was cast (or who cast himself) as 'the man who won the war'. The Welsh press put him on a pedestal and entrusted him with the job of bringing the spoils of war home to Wales.[99] One reward that came to Swansea as a direct consequence of the war was its university college. The powers-that-be were minded to increase the provision of tertiary-level education in Wales and the promoters of Swansea's claim used 'Swansea's great part in the war' as they sought to 'reap the fruits of the untold sacrifices' by establishing a college.[100] At the time of the laying of the foundation stone of the Swansea cenotaph, by Field Marshall Earl Haig on 1 July 1922, the notion of a noble sacrifice leading to a victory for right and justice was still strong. The memorial's wording is 'Pro Deo Rege et Patria' (For God, King and Country).

The memorial in Treboeth, commemorating twenty local men who died as a result of the war, was unveiled in 1924. The biblical verse chosen as an inscription, 'Mur oeddent hwy i ni nos a dydd' (They were a wall unto us both by night and day) indicates that idea of the 'defensive' war was still current.[101] Similarly, the verse penned for the unveiling ceremony fits into the view of the war as something necessary and indeed noble, which was the dominant standpoint throughout the war years.

The memorial to the three dead in Mynyddbach chapel contains two lines that are very common inscriptions on memorials to the war dead. At the bottom is the line 'Cariad mwy na hwn nid oes gan neb; sef, bod i un roi ei einioes dros ei gyfeillion' (Greater love hath no man than this, that a man lay down his life for his friends).[102] At the top the memorial declares 'Mewn angof ni chânt fod' (They shall not be forgotten).[103]

As long as the brothers and sisters were alive, there was no way that Ivor was to be forgotten. But as the years passed he, like the other two men on this memorial and like all of the other dead from the First World War, became an unknown soldier – just another name on a memorial. What exactly did his death achieve? What did his nation, his community, his family gain from (to use the contemporary term) his sacrifice? Those who knew and loved him lost an inestimable amount. They wept awhile but now they are silent.

Notes

1. Linda Colley, *Britons: Forging the nation, 1707–1837* (London: Pimlico, 1992), p. 6.
2. Michael S. Neiberg, *Soldiers' lives through history: the Nineteenth Century* (Westport, CT: Greenwood, 2006), p. 46.
3. GE1918-08-29 (ch. 10).
4. IE1916-09-20 (ch. 4); IE1916-09-24 (ch. 4); RE1918-06-25 (ch. 8).
5. RE1918-10-20 (ch. 11).
6. GE1918-09-13 (ch. 10); IE1918-12-08 (ch. 13).
7. GE1917-11-20 (ch. 10).
8. RE1918-05-12 (ch. 8).
9. IE1918-11-28 (ch. 13).
10. Kenneth O. Morgan, *Rebirth of a Nation: Wales 1880–1980* (Cardiff: University of Wales Press; Oxford: Oxford University Press, 1982), pp. 103–4. The literature on O. M. Edwards is extensive, but an excellent English-language introduction can be found in Lowri Angharad Hughes Ahronson, '"A refreshingly new and challenging voice": O. M. Edwards's Interpretation of the Welsh Past', in Neil Evans and Huw Pryce (eds), *Writing a Small Nation's Past: Wales in Comparative Perspective, 1850–1950* (London and New York: Routledge, 2013), pp. 127–40.
11. Gwyn A. Williams, 'Mother Wales get off me back', *Marxism Today* (December 1981), 14–20.
12. IE1917-12-12 (ch. 9).
13. GE1918-01-19 (ch. 10).
14. RE1917-11-20 (ch. 6); RE1918-08-22 (ch. 8).
15. RE1918-01-a (ch. 6). Note that Ivor also sent home a 'souvenir testament' from France: IE1918-09-09 (ch. 9).
16. Hanna, 'War Letters: Communication between Front and Home Front', p. 13.
17. IE1916-06-15 (ch. 4).
18. Michael Roper, *The secret battle: emotional survival in the Great War* (Manchester and New York: Manchester University Press, 2009), p. 127.
19. RE1918-05-05 (ch. 8) and RE1918-06-03a (ch. 8); there is also an indication that Richard acknowledged a parcel that had not arrived in a section that has been excised from RE1917-02-26 (ch. 3).

20. RE1918-03-20a (ch. 8); RE1918-03-20b (ch. 8); RE1918-04-14 (ch. 8); RE1918-06-03b (ch. 8).
21. RE1918-05-05 (ch. 8).
22. RE1917-11-20 (ch. 6).
23. IE1917-02-25 (ch. 7).
24. IE1916-07-a (ch. 4).
25. RE1918-08-24 (ch. 8).
26. Richard's letter to Ivor, RE1917-11-20 (ch. 6), includes the comment quoted above about 'the exchequer'.
27. IE1918-12-17 (ch. 13).
28. IE1916-10-28 (ch. 4).
29. RE1918-06-25 (ch. 8).
30. GE1918-09-10 (ch. 10).
31. RE1915-01-13 (ch. 2); RE1917-08-26b (ch. 6).
32. RE1918-05-05 (ch. 8).
33. RE1918-05-12 (ch. 8).
34. IE1918-11-26 (ch. 13).
35. IE1917-01-27 (ch. 7).
36. IE1918-11-26 (ch. 13).
37. Diary entry for 3 May 1917.
38. RE1918-02-20 (ch. 8).
39. RE1918-05-05 (ch. 8); RE1918-05-12 (ch. 8).
40. RE1918-03-20a (ch. 8).
41. RE1918-03-20b (ch. 8).
42. See Stéphane Audoin-Rouzeau and Annette Becker, *14–18: Understanding the Great War* (New York: Hill and Wang, 2002), pp. 94–112.
43. Robin Barlow, *Wales and World War One* (Llandysul: Gomer, 2014), pp. 30–2; Clive Hughes, *'Arm to save your native land': Army recruiting in North-West Wales, 1914–1916* (Llanrwst: Gwasg Carreg Gwalch, 2015), esp chs 1, 7 and 8.
44. See, for example, Edward C. Woodfin, *Camp and combat on the Sinai and Palestine front: the experience of the British Empire soldier, 1916–18* (Houndmills: Palgrave Macmillan, 2012), p. 99.
45. RE1917-11-20 (ch. 6).
46. RE1918-11-10 (ch. 11).
47. GE1917-02-02b (ch. 5).
48. GE1918-02-01 (ch. 10).
49. IE1916-06-10b (ch. 4).
50. IE1918-11-08 (ch. 12).
51. IE1917-12-12 (ch. 9).
52. RE1918-01-09a (ch. 6); for diary entries see ch. 6.
53. David, *Tell Mum Not to Worry*; Roberts, *Witness these letters*.

54. References to hidings or caning at school to be found in RE1918-06-03b (ch. 8); RE1918-06-25 (ch. 8); RE1918-09-30b (ch. 11).

55. Diary entry for 20 July 1917: see ch. 6.

56. Diary entries of 1 April, 8 July and 18 July 1917. Although there were other local men named William Davies, this could be William Davies of Roger Street, whose brother David John Davies had signed up for the 3rd WFA at the same time as Richard. William died on 29 October 1918: see 'Scroll of Fame', *CDL*, 20 November 1918, 1.

57. IE1918-09-19 (ch. 9).

58. IE1918-11-01 (ch. 12).

59. GE1918-02-01 (ch. 10).

60. GE1918-04-24 (ch. 10).

61. IE1918-02-06 (ch. 9).

62. IE1918-09-27 (ch. 9).

63. RE1917-11-20 (ch. 6).

64. For the music and lyrics, see *https://yorkspace.library.yorku.ca/xmlui/ bitstream/handle/10315/14545/JACoo1162.pdf* (accessed September 2017).

65. Gerard J. DeGroot, *Blighty: British Society in the era of the Great War* (London and New York: Longman, 1996), p. xiii.

66. Paul O'Leary, 'Masculine Histories: Gender and Social History', *Welsh History Review*, 22.2 (December 2004), 252–77.

67. Michael Roper and John Tosh, *Manful Assertions: Masculinities in Britain Since 1800* (London: Routledge, 1991), p. 2.

68. John Tosh, 'Imperial Masculinity and the Flight from Domesticity in Britain 1880–1914', in Timothy P. Foley, Lionel Pilkington, Sean Ryder and Elizabeth Tilley (eds), *Gender and Colonialism* (Galway: Galway University Press, 1995); Michael Roper, 'Maternal Relations: Moral Manliness and Emotional Survival in Letters Home During the First World War', in Stefan Dudink, Karen Hagemann and John Tosh (eds), *Masculinities in Politics and War: gendering modern history* (Manchester: Manchester University Press, 2004), pp. 295–315.

69. John Springhall, 'Building Character in the British Boy: The Attempt to Extend Christian Manliness to Working-Class Adolescents, 1880–1914', in J. A. Mangan and James Walvin (eds), *Manliness and Morality: Middle-Class Masculinity in Britain and America* (Manchester: Manchester University Press, 1987), pp. 52–75.

70. Manon Jones, 'Yr "Hen Dri Ohonom": Gwrywdod, y Personol a'r Cyhoeddus yn y Cyfeillgarwch Rhwng D. R. Daniel, Tom Ellis ac O. M. Edwards' (unpublished PhD thesis, Cardiff University, 2015).

71. Michael Roper, 'Between Manliness and Masculinity: The "War Generation" and the Psychology of Fear in Britain, 1914–1950', *Journal of British Studies*, 44.2 (April 2005), 343–62,347–8.

72. Gethin Matthews, 'For Freedom and Justice": The Responses of Chapels in the Swansea Area to the First World War', *Welsh History Review*, 28.4 (December 2017), 678–9.

73. GE1914-11-13 (ch. 2).

74. IE1916-06-10b (ch. 4).

75. IE1916-06-10a (ch. 4); IE1916-06-10b (ch. 4).

76. DeGroot, *Blighty*, p. 304.

77. IE1917-12-12 (ch. 9).

78. RE1916-10-12 (ch. 3), RE1918-06-03a (ch. 8); RE1917-08-26a (ch. 6), RE1918-08-22 (ch. 8).

79. GE1918-09-13 (ch. 10).

80. RE1917-11-14 (ch. 6).

81. RE1917-11-20 (ch. 6); IE1918-09-19 (ch. 9).

82. IE1917-02-18 (ch. 7).

83. IE1918-02-12 (ch. 9).

84. IE1916-10-a (ch. 4); RE1918-09-30a (ch. 11).

85. RE1916-10-12 (ch. 3); RE1917-11-14 (ch. 6).

86. IE1918-08-03 (ch. 9).

87. RE1917-02-26 (ch. 3).

88. RE1918-05-12 (ch. 8).

89. RE1918-10-29 (ch. 11).

90. GE1918-10-30 (ch. 10).

91. RE1916-12-20 (ch. 3).

92. Diary entry for 28 July 1917: see ch. 6.

93. IE1918-11-28 (ch. 13).

94. See ch. 6.

95. IE1918-09-27 (ch. 9).

96. Perhaps the Eustis brothers' cousin Thomas Henry Matthews was one in this category: see Gethin Matthews, '"Buddugoliaeth" / Dadrithio / Creithiau', in *idem* (ed.), Creithiau: *Dylanwad y Rhyfel Mawr ar Gymdeithas a Diwylliant yng Nghymru* (Cardiff: University of Wales Press, 2016), pp. 258–69.

97. Paul Fussell, *The Great War and Modern Memory* (London: Oxford University Press, 1975), pp. 7–8.

98. Robin Prior and Trevor Wilson, 'Paul Fussell at War', *War in History*, 1.1 (1994), 63–80, 74.

99. On this point see 'Buddugoliaeth Lloyd George', *Y Cymro*, 1 January 1919, 4, which declares that Lloyd George is the only politician capable of 'ddwyn adref yr ysbail' (bringing the spoils home).

100. '"Second to none"' and 'Mr F. W. Gilbertson', *SWWP*, 1 February 1919, 2; 'Industry after peace', *HoW*, 1 October 1918, 3.

101. Samuel 25:16.

102. John 13:15.
103. The line appears in 'Yn Nyffryn Clwyd', a poem by Ceiriog.

Appendix 1

List of all the extant letters and postcards sent by the Eustis brothers

GE = Gabriel Eustis; IE = Ivor Eustis; RE = Richard Eustis

Reference	Addressee	From
RE1914-09-19	Ivor	Northampton
GE1914-11-13	Mother	Bristol
RE1915-01-13	Ivor	Cambridge
RE1915-03-13	Ivor	Cambridge
IE1916-05-26 Postcard	Mother	Kinmel Park
IE1916-06-03	Mother	Kinmel Park
IE1916-06-04	Mother	Kinmel Park
IE1916-06-08	Aunt Charlotte	Kinmel Park
IE1916-06-10a	Mother	Kinmel Park
IE1916-06-10b	Hannah	Kinmel Park
IE1916-06-13	Mother	Kinmel Park
IE1916-06-15	Mother	Kinmel Park
IE1916-06-27	Mother	Kinmel Park
IE1916-07-a	Mother	Kinmel Park
IE1916-08-27	Mother	Kinmel Park
IE1916-09-20	Mother	Kinmel Park
IE1916-09-24	Mother	Kinmel Park
IE1916-09-25	Mother	Kinmel Park
RE1916-10-12	Mother	Egypt
IE1916-10-a	Aunt Charlotte	Kinmel Park
IE1916-10-28	Mother	Kinmel Park
GE1916-11-01	Mother	Aberdeen Sailors' Home
IE1916-11-02	Mother	Kinmel Park
IE1916-11-05	Mother	Kinmel Park
IE1916-11-06	Mother	Kinmel Park
IE1916-11-15	Mother	Altcar
RE1916-12-20	Mother	Egypt
IE1917-01-05	Mother	Kinmel Park

Reference	Addressee	From
IE1917-01-14	Mother	Kinmel Park
IE1917-01-27	Aunt Charlotte	Kinmel Park
IE1917-01-30	Mother	Kinmel Park
IE1917-01-31	Aunt Charlotte	Kinmel Park
GE1917-02-02a	Mother	HMT Saxon, Oban
GE1917-02-02b	Dan (brother)	Y Box Sepon, Ar y Mor
IE1917-02-11	Mother	Kinmel Park
IE1917-02-18	Mother	Kinmel Park
IE1917-02-25	Mother	Kinmel Park
RE1917-02-26	Aunt Charlotte	Egypt
IE1917-03-31	Aunt Charlotte	Kinmel Park
IE1917-07-30	Mother	Kinmel Park
RE1917-08-26a	Mother	Palestine
RE1917-08-26b	Aunt Charlotte	Palestine
IE1917-09-09	Mother	Kinmel Park
IE1917-09-30	Mother	Kinmel Park
IE1917-10-a Postcard	???	Kinmel Park
RE1917-11-14	Aunt Charlotte	Beersheba, Palestine
GE1917-11-20	Mother	Saxon
RE1917-11-20	Ivor	Palestine
IE1917-12-06 Postcard	Mother	Southampton
IE1917-12-12	Mother	No. 5 I.B.D [Infantry Base Depot], Rouen, France
RE1917-12-14	Mother	Palestine
GE1918-01-01	Mother	H.M.Trawler Saxon, Inverness
IE1918-01-01	Mother	'A' Company, 17th R.W.F., B.E.F., France
RE1918-01-a	Mother	Jerusalem
RE1918-01-09a	Mother	[Jerusalem]
RE1918-01-09b	Aunt Charlotte	[Jerusalem]
GE1918-01-19	Aunt Charlotte	H.M.T. Saxon, Inverness
GE1918-02-01	Mother	Saxon, Inverness
IE1918-02-06	Lottie	'Somewhere', France
IE1918-02-12	Mother	France
GE1918-02-15	Lottie	H.M.T. Saxon, Inverness

Reference	Addressee	From
RE1918-02-20	Mother	Palestine
GE1918-02-23	Mother	Saxon
IE1918-03-07	Mother	B.E.F., France
RE1918-03-20a	Mother	Egypt
RE1918-03-20b	Hannah	Egypt
RE1918-04-14	Mother	Egypt
GE1918-04-24	Aunt Charlotte	Saxon
RE1918-05-05	Mother	Palestine
RE1918-05-12	Aunt Charlotte	Palestine
IE1918-05-28	Mother	France
IE1918-06-02	Aunt (Charlotte)	France
RE1918-06-03a	Mother	Palestine
RE1918-06-03b	Aunt Charlotte	Palestine
RE1918-06-25	Mother	Palestine
IE1918-07-01	Hannah	France
IE1918-07-04	Mother	France
IE1918-07-15	Mother	France
RE1918-07-18 Postcard	Mother	Alexandria
RE1918-07-26 Postcard	Mother	Alexandria
GE1918-07-27	Mother	Saxon, Inverness
IE1918-07-27a	Mother	France
IE1918-07-27b	Lottie	France
IE1918-08-03	Mother	France
RE1918-08-22	Mother	Palestine
RE1918-08-24	Mother	Palestine
GE1918-08-29	Mother	H.M.T. Saxon, Inverness
IE1918-09-09	Mother	France
GE1918-09-10	Mother	'Same old show'
GE1918-09-13	Hannah	H.M.Super-Super-Dreadnought Saxon, Inverness
IE1918-09-19	Mother	France
GE1918-09-a	Mother	Saxon
IE1918-09-27	Mother	France

Reference	Addressee	From
RE1918-09-30a	Mother	Egypt
RE1918-09-30b	Dan	Egypt
IE1918-10-09 Postcard	Mother	France (somewhere behind)
IE1918-10-12 Postcard	Mother	Blighty
IE1918-10-13	Mother	Ward 4, Fort Pitt Mil. Hosp., Chatham
RE1918-10-20	Hannah	Egypt
RE1918-10-29	Mother	Egypt
GE1918-10-30	Mother	Saxon, Inverness
IE1918-11-01	Mother	Sgts Mess, R.W.F. Depot, Wrexham
IE1918-11-08	Mother	The Barracks, Wrexham
RE1918-11-10	Mother	No 7 Prince of Wales Hospital, Egypt
GE1918-11-22	Mother	123 Hut, North Camp, R N Bks, Chatham
IE1918-11-26	Mother	Limerick
IE1918-11-28	Mother	New Barracks, Limerick
IE1918-11-30	Mother	Limerick
GE1918-12-04	Mother	123 Hut, North Camp, R N Barracks, Chatham
GE1918-12-11	Mother	123 Hut, North Camp, R N Barracks, Chatham
IE1918-12-a	???	???
IE1918-12-08	Mother	Ballyvonare
IE1918-12-15	Mother	Ballyvonare
IE1918-12-17	Gabriel	Ballyvonare
RE1918-12-20	Mother	Egypt
RE1918-12-23	Aunt Charlotte	Egypt
GE1918-12-28	Aunt Charlotte	123 Four Five Six Seven, North Camp, R N Barracks, Chatham
RE1919-01-14	Mother	Demobilisation Camp [Egypt]
RE1919-02-01 Postcard	Mother	Italy
DH1918-12-17 (letter from Dai Harris)	Richard	Roger Street

Appendix 2

Servicemen from Mynyddbach/Tirdeunaw/ Treboeth mentioned in the text

INFORMATION FROM LOCAL ROLLS OF HONOUR, FROM THE 1911 CENSUS AND FROM OTHER SOURCES

	Mynyddbach chapel contemporary Roll of Honour	Mynyddbach chapel (post-war) Roll of Honour	Caersalem Newydd Roll of Honour	Bethel (Llangyfelach) Roll of Honour		List of volunteers from 'Tirdonkin colliery'*	List of volunteers from Mynydd Newydd colliery*	Report of receiving medal from the 'Mynyddbach, Treboeth and District Succour Fund' in the Cambria Daily Leader
Gabriel Eustis	X	X						1918-06-25
Ivor Eustis		X						1918-10-28
Richard Eustis	X	X					X	
Thomas John Cole		X						
(David) Iorwerth Evans	X	X						
Thomas Evans	X	X						
(Thomas) Idris Evans			X					1918-02-02
Walter Evans			X					
Willie R. Evans	X	X						1917-12-10
David N. Griffiths	X	X						1918-06-25
David (Dai) Harris	X	X						1918-02-16
Bryn Harris			X					1918-02-16
Willie Haydn	X	X						1917-12-10
Ivor Humphreys		X						
Trevor James				X				
William (Simon) John		X						
(Edward) Ivor Lewis			X				X	
Thomas J. Mathews	X	X						1918-02-16
Thomas Henry Matthews			X				X	
(D.) Edward Morgan	X	X						1918-02-26
David Thomas Morris			X					1918-06-18

(continued)

	Mynyddbach chapel contemporary Roll of Honour	Mynyddbach chapel (post-war) Roll of Honour	Caersalem Newydd Roll of Honour	Bethel (Llangyfelach) Roll of Honour	List of volunteers from 'Tirdonkin colliery'*	List of volunteers from Mynydd Newydd colliery*	Report of receiving medal from the 'Mynyddbach, Treboeth and District Succour Fund' in the *Cambria Daily Leader*
(J.) Clement Mort				X			
Johnny Phillips			X				1918-09-25
Dai Phillips			X				
Evan Samuel Rees			X		X		
Uriel Rees		X					
Stanley Richards		X					1918-05-08
Brinley Thomas	X	X				X	
David Rees Thomas				X		X	

*Information on men from Tirdonkin colliery in 'Roll of Honour', *CDL*, 19 September 1914, 6; on men from Mynydd Newydd colliery in 'Roll of Honour', *CDL*, 22 September 1914, 3.

Thomas John Cole

1911 Census: 13, schoolboy, living in Caersalem Row, Treboeth
73244, 2nd RWF
Photograph in *CDL*, 20 September 1918, 3.

(David) Iorwerth Evans

1911 Census: 12, Schoolboy, living in Tirdeunaw

Thomas Evans

1911 Census: 16, steel smelter, living in Brython Cottage, Tirdeunaw
1667, RAMC (1/3rd WFA)
Report of marriage in *HoW*, 14 September 1918, 2

(Thomas) Idris Evans

1911 Census: 24, coal merchant, living in Knoyle Street

Walter Evans

1911 Census: 15, coal miner helper (hewer), living in Roger Street
1666, RAMC (3rd WFA)
Report of wounding in *CDL*, 13 September 1915, 3

William (Robert) Evans
1901 Census: 4, living in Bryntywod
Joined Royal Navy 22 January 1915 (K23950)
Report of him home on leave in *CDL*, 22 June 1916, 4

David N. Griffiths
1911 Census: 18, drapery assistant, living in Tirdeunaw
Report of gassing in *CDL*, 8 August 1917, 3

Bryn (Brynley or Brinley) Harris
1911 Census: 13, Schoolboy, living in Caersalem Row, Treboeth. He was
awarded the MM while serving with the West Riding Regt: see *London
Gazette*, 11 March 1919 (Supplement, 3421).

David (Dai) Harris
1911 Census: 17, house joiner, living in Caersalem Row, Treboeth
Joined Royal Navy 18 January 1916 (Wales Z/2873)

Willie Haydn
1911 Census: 17, mason labourer, living in Upper Terrace, Treboeth

Ivor Humphreys
1911 Census: 15, apprentice fitter, living in Garnllwyd
Joined Royal Navy 10 September 1917 (M27641)
(Later the best man at Gabriel Eustis's wedding: see photograph on p. 259)

(Edward) Ivor Lewis
1911 Census: 18, horse handler, underground
1671, RAMC (1/3rd WFA)

Trevor James
1911 Census: 15, schoolboy, living in Pen-y-Banc, Mynyddbach

William (Simon) John
1911 Census: 12, at school, living in Fox Lodge, Cwmgelly

Thomas John Mathews (Tommy Mathews)
1911 Census: 14, tin works labourer, living in Cwm Terrace, Tirdeunaw

Thomas Henry Matthews
1911 Census: 21, labourer at a copperworks, living in Penlan Road, Treboeth
(A cousin of the Eustis brothers, son of John Eustis's sister Margaret)
Worked at Mynydd Newydd colliery when he joined the Hussars on
2 September 1914; served with the South Wales Borderers at Suvla Bay;

reported invalided *CDL*, 10 December 1915, 7. He was discharged from the army on 25 July 1917, suffering from dysentery.

Eddie Morgan
Report of winning MM, *CDL*, 11 January 1918, 3.

David Thomas Morris
1911 Census: 17, auctioneer's clerk, living in Mynyddbach
1670, RAMC (1/3rd WFA)

Clement Mort
1911 Census: 13, schoolboy, living in Pen-y-Banc, Mynyddbach

David Owen (Dai) Phillips
1911 Census: 29, boiler fireman, tinplate works, living in Heol Gerrig, Treboeth
Brother of Johnny, below

John Ivor (Johnny) Phillips
1911 Census: 20, boiler fireman, colliery, living in Garnlwyd, Treboeth
1673, RAMC (1/3rd WFA)

Evan Samuel Rees
1911 Census: 17, house carpenter, living in Knoyle Terrace, Treboeth
1669, RAMC (1/3rd WFA)
Joined on 5 August 1914 – occupation: collier

Uriel Rees
1911 Census: 11, schoolboy, living in Penybryn, Mynyddbach
(A cousin of the Eustis brothers, son of Mary Eustis's brother Thomas)
According to the surviving army paperwork, he enlisted on 10 April 1917 and was then medically examined on 12 July 1917 (aged 17 years and 11 months). He was discharged from the army on 17 July 1919, suffering from dysentery.

Stanley Richards
1911 Census: 19, Teacher at Elementary School, living in Lisbon, Treboeth

Brinley/Brynley Thomas
1911 Census: 17, colliery labourer, living at Mynydd Cadle
1677 RAMC (2/3rd WFA)

David Rees Thomas
1911 Census: 20, coal haulier, living in Roger Street, Treboeth
RAMC (1/3rd WFA)

Appendix 3

Information on servicemen from other parts of
Swansea and West Glamorgan mentioned in the text

Sgt William Bowen is very probably:
T4/174013, Army Service Corps
Resident of Pentregethin Road, Cwmbwrla (see 'Scroll of Fame', *CDL*,
13 December 1916, 4); report of him winning the Military Medal, 'Honours
for local soldiers', *SWWP*, 30 March 1918, 2.

Aubrey Harris
1911 Census: 22-year-old assistant in business, living with his family at
91a Woodfield Street, Morriston (English-speaking). Conscripted into the
Army Service Corps, M2/222263, September 1916; transferred to Tank
Corps, 302172.

(John) Elfryn Stephens and (Thomas) Grongar Stephens
1911 Census: both living with their parents and two sisters at Stonyland,
Loughor. Grongar was fifteen and a draper; Elfryn was thirteen and at
school. The family was recorded as bilingual.
   Grongar Stephens's medal card (1818 RAMC) states that he first served in
the Gallipoli campaign on 11 August 1915. Elfryn Stephens (46143 RWF) was
wounded in the thigh in 1918 ('Scroll of Fame', *CDL*, 17 September 1918, 3).

Bryn Thomas
Richard refers to meeting Bryn Thomas of Vicarage Road, Gabriel names 'Bryn
Thomas, Clyndu' and Dai Harris mentions 'Bryn Thomas the Vicarage' who
was in hospital in Brighton. These are the same individual: 'Scroll of Fame',
CDL, 31 August 1918, 3, states that Pte Brin Thomas of 83 Vicarage Road,
Morriston 'has been wounded in France and is now in hospital at Brighton …
He has seen three years' active service in Egypt and a few months in France.'

Gabriel Williams
In three letters, Ivor refers to Gabriel Williams from Cwmbwrla: it is possible that he is the 16-year-old schoolboy living at 78 Pentregethin Road at
the time of the 1911 Census. It is very probable that the soldier referred to
is 29585 RWF. This Gabriel Williams landed in France on 24 June 1916, was
wounded on 28 August 1916 (gunshot wound left hand) and evacuated back
to Britain. He was then attached to the 62nd Training Reserve Battalion as
TR/4/22330, before receiving a commission as 2nd lieut. in the Cheshire
Regiment in late November 1917.

Select bibliography

Treboeth and the surrounding area

Matthews, Gethin, *Gwrol Ryfelwyr Caersalem Newydd* (Treboeth: Treboeth History Society, 2014).

Treboeth Historical & Pictorial Record (Treboeth: Treboeth History Society, 2013).

Wales and the First World War

Barlow, Robin, *Wales and World War One* (Llandysul: Gomer, 2014).

Cragoe, Matthew and Chris Williams (eds), *Wales and War: Society, Politics and Religion in the Nineteenth and Twentieth Centuries* (Cardiff: University of Wales Press, 2007).

Hughes, Clive, *'Arm to save your native land': Army recruiting in North-West Wales, 1914–1916* (Llanrwst: Gwasg Carreg Gwalch, 2015).

Jones, Ieuan Elfryn, 'A Welsh perspective on army chaplaincy during the First World War: the letters of Abraham Rees Morgan MC', in Michael Snape and Edward Madigan (eds), *The Clergy in Khaki: New Perspectives on British Army Chaplaincy in the First World War* (Burlington, VT: Ashgate, 2013), pp. 57–73.

Llwyd, Alan, *Colli'r Hogiau: Cymru a'r Rhyfel Mawr 1914–1918* (Llandysul: Gomer, 2018).

Matthews, Gethin (ed.), *Creithiau: Dylanwad y Rhyfel Mawr ar Gymdeithas a Diwylliant yng Nghymru* (Cardiff: University of Wales Press, 2016).

Matthews, Gethin, '"For Freedom and Justice": The Responses of Chapels in the Swansea Area to the First World War', *Welsh History Review*, 28.4 (December 2017), 676–710.

O'Leary, Paul, 'Wales and the First World War: Themes and Debates', *Welsh History Review*, 28.4 (December 2017), 591–617.

Powel, Meilyr, 'The Welsh press and the July Crisis of 1914', *First World War Studies*, 8 (2017), *http://doi.org/10.1080/19475020.2017. 1385408* (accessed December 2017).

Britain and the First World War (general)

Audoin-Rouzeau, Stéphane and Annette Becker, *14–18: Understanding the Great War* (New York: Hill and Wang, 2002).

DeGroot, Gerard J., *Blighty: British Society in the era of the Great War* (London and New York: Longman, 1996).

Holmes, Richard, *Tommy: The British soldier on the Western Front 1914–1918* (London: Harper Perennial, 2005).

Pennell, Catriona, *A Kingdom United: Popular Responses to the Outbreak of the First World War in Britain and Ireland* (Oxford: Oxford University Press, 2012).

The EEF's campaign in Egypt and Palestine

David, Rhys, *Tell Mum Not to Worry: A Welsh Soldier's World War One in the Near East* (Cardiff: Deffro, 2014).

Dudley Ward, C. H., *History of the 53rd (Welsh) Division (T.F.) 1914–1918* (Cardiff: Western Mail, 1927).

Woodfin, Edward C., *Camp and combat on the Sinai and Palestine front: the experience of the British Empire soldier, 1916–18* (Houndmills: Palgrave Macmillan, 2012).

Woodward, David R., *Forgotten Soldiers of the First World War: Lost Voices from the Middle Eastern Front* (Stroud: Tempus, 2006).

The naval campaign in the north Atlantic

Chatterton, E. Keble, *The Big Blockade* (London: Hurst & Blackett, 1932).

Fisher, John, 'Neither fish nor fowl: Mercantile seamen on armed merchant cruisers in the Great War', *International Journal of Maritime History*, 28.3 (2016), 496–512.

Thompson, Julian, *Imperial War Museum Book of the War at Sea 1914–18* (London: Sidgwick & Jackson, 2005).

Family communications at a time of war

ap Glyn, Ifor, '"Dear Mother, I am very sorry I cannot write to you in Welsh …": Censorship and the Welsh Language in the First World War', in Julian Walker and Christophe Declercq (eds), *Languages and the First World War: Communicating in a Transnational War* (London: Palgrave Macmillan, 2016), pp. 128–41.

Blight, David W. (ed.), *When this cruel war is over: The Civil War letters of Charles Harvey Brewster* (Amherst: University of Massachusetts Press, 1992).

Hanna, Martha, 'A Republic of Letters: The Epistolary Tradition in World War I France', *American Historical Review*, 108.5 (December 2003), 1338–61.

Hanna, Martha, 'War Letters: Communication between Front and Home Front', in Ute Daniel, Peter Gatrell, Oliver Janz, Heather Jones, Jennifer Keene, Alan Kramer and Bill Nasson (eds), *International Encyclopedia of the First World War* (2014), http://encyclopedia.1914-1918-online.net/article/war_letters_ communication_between_front_and_home_front (accessed June 2017).

Lyons, Martyn, *The writing culture of ordinary people in Europe, 1860–1920* (Cambridge and New York: Cambridge University Press, 2013).

Roberts, G. D., *Witness these letters: Letters from the Western Front 1915–18* (Denbigh: Gee, 1983).

Roper, Michael, 'Maternal Relations: Moral Manliness and Emotional Survival in Letters Home during the First World War', in Stefan Dudink, Karen Hagemann and John Tosh (eds), *Masculinities in Politics and War: gendering modern history* (Manchester: Manchester University Press, 2004), pp. 295–315.

Masculinity and war

O'Leary, Paul, 'Masculine Histories: Gender and Social History', *Welsh History Review*, 22.2 (December 2004), 252–77.

Roper, Michael, 'Between Manliness and Masculinity: The "War Generation" and the Psychology of Fear in Britain, 1914–1950', *Journal of British Studies*, 44.2 (April 2005), 343–62.

Roper, Michael, *The secret battle: emotional survival in the Great War* (Manchester and New York: Manchester University Press, 2009).

Tosh, John, 'Imperial Masculinity and the Flight from Domesticity in Britain 1880–1914', in Timothy P. Foley, Lionel Pilkington, Sean Ryder and Elizabeth Tilley (eds), *Gender and Colonialism* (Galway: Galway University Press, 1995).

Index